Profitably Buying and Selling Broadcast Stations

by

Erwin G. Krasnow

John M. Pelkey

and

John Wells King

of

Garvey Schubert Barer

iUniverse, Inc.
New York   Bloomington

iUniverse books may be ordered through booksellers or by contacting:

iUniverse
1663 Liberty Drive
Bloomington, IN 47403
www.iuniverse.com
1-800-Authors (1-800-288-4677)

Because of the dynamic nature of the Internet, any Web addresses or links contained in this book may have changed since publication and may no longer be valid. The views expressed in this work are solely those of the author and do not necessarily reflect the views of the publisher, and the publisher hereby disclaims any responsibility for them.

ISBN: 978-1-4401-6951-9 (sc)
ISBN: 978-1-4401-6952-6 (ebook)

This publication is designed to provide accurate and authoritative information about the subject matter covered. It is sold with the understanding that it does not constitute legal or other professional advice. If legal advice or other expert assistance is required, the services of a competent professional should be sought. Moreover, any tax advice contained in this publication is not intended to be used, and cannot be used, for the purpose of avoiding tax penalties. Readers are prohibited from using the information contained herein to market or promote any particular transaction or form of transaction.

The analysis and materials contained herein are the opinions of the authors and in no way should be construed as being the official or unofficial policy of any governmental body or the publisher.

Printed in the United States of America

iUniverse rev. date: 10/29/2009

TABLE OF CONTENTS

CHAPTER FOUR 77

CHAPTER FIVE...97

BREAKING THE CODE: HOW TO USE THIS BOOK

If you are interested in buying, selling or investing in a broadcast station, this book is for you. It is designed to decode the mysteries of broadcast station purchase and sale contracts and present the most innovative contract strategies in today's marketplace.

Profitably Buying and Selling Broadcast Stations guides you step-by-step over that long, often rocky, road from the initial letter of intent to the closing, helping you to avoid the potholes and pitfalls in between. With proper planning, you can prevent many costly mistakes and sleepless nights by avoiding problems that could surface after the closing due to inadequate due diligence or incomplete document preparation. Some of the helpful information contained in this book includes:

Letters of Intent

➢ Provides guidelines on whether you should rely only on a "handshake deal," enter into a letter of intent, or, instead, immediately proceed to the preparation of the definitive documents.

➢ Provides a detailed checklist of points to consider treating in a letter of intent.

➢ Identifies the factors that a court will consider when deciding upon the enforceability of a letter of intent.

Anatomy of a Purchase and Sale Agreement

➢ Discusses the considerations involved in deciding whether to do a stock deal or an asset transaction.

➢ Outlines the provisions of a comprehensive asset purchase agreement.

➢ Describes the representations and warranties, as well as the affirmative and negative covenants, for which a prudent buyer should negotiate.

➢ Provides a handy checklist of closing documents, prorations and adjustments, and special conditions essential to the closing.

➢ Includes a short course covering topics like indemnification, risk of loss and breach of contract, and discusses bulk sales laws, liquidated damages and other legal esoterica.

The Legal, Financial and Engineering Due Diligence Process

➢ Explains what due diligence is and why it is important.

➢ Outlines the due diligence process involved in the sale and purchase of a radio station and provides guidelines on the breadth and depth of the process.

➢ Identifies some typical due diligence "land mines" for buyers.

➢ Provides tips on assembling your "due diligence team" to achieve a thorough, effective review while avoiding costly duplication of efforts.

➢ Includes a comprehensive checklist of the issues that might be included in the legal due diligence process.

➢ Provides a detailed checklist of four aspects of a due diligence engineering review: determining the upgrade potential of the targeted radio station, assessing potential competition, determining whether a station is operating in accordance with the FCC rules and its authorizations, and inspecting the equipment of a station.

Satisfying the FCC

➢ Provides a short course on FCC rules and polices governing radio station transactions.

➢ Offers sample clauses designed to avoid FCC pitfalls that can kill the deal.

➢ Advises on such topics as avoiding an unauthorized transfer of control and expediting the FCC application process.

➢ Explains in straightforward terms the FCC's "rule against reversion" and the

Commission's policies on hypothecation and security provisions.

A Seller's Perspective

➤ Suggests practical methods for developing an effective strategy for selling a radio station.

➤ Provides a checklist of activities that the seller should engage in before and after signing the contract … and before and after the closing.

➤ Discusses a range of contract provisions designed to protects the Seller's interests.

A Buyer's Perspective

➤ Describes ways to avoid surprises concerning the condition of the equipment, the status of the real property, the accuracy of the financial statements, and the seller's handling of the accounts payable.

➤ Suggests ways to structure environmental and engineering audits and assessments to eliminate the risk of multimillion dollar liabilities.

➤ Presents some positive as well as punitive approaches to address the potential of a "material adverse change" in the operation of the station between the signing of the contract and the closing.

➤ Illustrates some creative uses of accounts receivable.

Closing the Transaction

➤ Details the tasks that must be accomplished at the closing.

➤ Identifies the "closing documents" – the various agreements, schedules, certificates, and other documents that the parties to a transaction typically exchange.

➤ Highlights those closing documents that usually require more time and effort to prepare.

The Appendices

This book also includes appendices containing additional practical information and illustrative samples of agreements and documents that expand on the points covered in the text. Most readers regard appendices as "after-thoughts." However, the appendices in this book are an integral part of the text. They provide "concrete" examples to enhance your understanding and should be explored and used extensively. The following is a brief description of each of the appendices:

Appendix A contains a sample Confidentiality Agreement, which we recommend that the seller and potential purchaser sign prior to negotiating a letter of intent, or if no letter is contemplated.

Appendix B includes four illustrative letters of intent that might be regarded as a starting point to be tailored to your individual objectives and concerns.

Appendix C contains a sample Consulting Agreement whereby a principal of the buyer serves as a consultant to the seller until the transaction closes.

Appendix D provides a short course on FCC policies governing Time Brokerage Agreements, also known as Local Marketing Agreements (LMAs), titled "ABCs of LMAs," and a suggested checklist to be used by the licensee-seller to assure compliance with FCC rules and policies and the terms of the LMA.

Appendix E contains two illustrative Time Brokerage or Local Marketing Agreements, including one which is drafted to enable the buyer to air programs and sell advertising during the period between the execution of the definitive acquisition agreement and the closing.

Appendix F contains a table listing the license expiration dates and renewal application filing deadlines for radio stations in each of the states, the District of Columbia and U.S. territories and possessions.

Appendix G contains three sample "due diligence" requests for information; one is based on a request prepared by a financial institution while the other two were prepared by prospective buyers.

Appendix H contains a sample Rescission or Unwind Agreement used by sellers and buyers who close the transaction prior to the time that the FCC grant of the assignment or transfer application becomes a final order no longer subject to appeal.

* * * * * * *

In a nutshell, this book contains virtually everything you want – and need – to know about selling or acquiring a broadcast station. The more informed you are, the better able you will be to make sure that any document you sign provides assurance that you will get what you bargained for. As you read this book, we caution you to keep in mind that the many rules, regulations, and laws cited in this text may change. And, while this book presents a "snapshot" of these interactive elements at the time we go to press, you should carefully check the status of these elements as they bear on your decision to buy, sell or invest in a broadcast station and, if you'll pardon the commercial, we recommend that you consult with experienced legal counsel.

Good luck!

A FEW MORE WORDS FROM THE AUTHORS

We want to thank Jim Carnegie, the publisher of Radio Business Report (RBR) for spawning the idea for this book. In large part, this book builds upon and updates concepts and principles previously set forth in *Radio Deals: A Step by Step Guide* (Radio Business Report, 2002). We would also like to thank and acknowledge Eric Werner, a Senior Advisor with the National Telecommunications and Information Administration at the U.S. Department of Commerce, who with Erwin Krasnow, co-authored *Radio Deals*. His contribution to that work provided a significant foundation for our own efforts here.

Countless people have influenced this book, including virtually everyone we have dealt with in the broadcast sale and acquisition process. However, we wish to single out the following individuals for their special willingness to provide their insights and expertise: Larry Brant and Lowell Turnbull, Partners, Garvey Schubert Barer; Jay Williams, Jr., President, Broadcasting Unlimited, Inc.; John S. Sanders, Principal, Bond & Pecaro, Inc.; H. Taft Snowdon, Senior Supervisory Attorney, Media Bureau, Federal Communications Commission; Garrison C. Cavell, President, Cavell Mertz and Associates, Inc.; and Gary Shorman, President, Eagle Communications, Inc.

Some portions of this book have previously appeared in the following publications:

- Erwin Krasnow, Geoffrey Bentley and Robin Martin, *Buying or Building a Broadcast Station in the Nineties* (Washington, DC: NATIONAL ASSOCIATION OF BROADCASTERS, 1991)

- Robin Martin and Erwin Krasnow, *Radio Financing: A Guide for Lenders and Investors* (Washington, DC: NATIONAL ASSOCIATION OF BROADCASTERS, 1990)

- Erwin Krasnow, Robin Martin and Kevin Reymond, *Buying a Broadcast Station: A Guide to Due Diligence* (Carmel, CA: PAUL KAGAN ASSOCIATES, INC., 1993)

- Erwin Krasnow, Robin Martin and Dean Brenner, *The Business Aspects of Selling a Broadcast Station*, BROADCAST FINANCIAL JOURNAL, July/August, 1988

- Erwin Krasnow, *Buying a Broadcast Station: The Legal Due Diligence Process*, BROADCAST CABLE

FINANCIAL JOURNAL, September/October, 1991; revised version reprinted in BROADCAST LAW REPORT, October, 2000

- Erwin Krasnow, *Broadcast Station Acquisitions: FCC Considerations*, BROADCAST CABLE FINANCIAL JOURNAL, November/December, 1991; revised version reprinted in BROADCAST LAW REPORT, October 2000

- Erwin Krasnow, *Anatomy of an Asset Purchase Agreement*, BROADCAST CABLE FINANCIAL JOURNAL, January/February, 1992

- Erwin Krasnow, *Broadcast Acquisition Contracts: A Buyer's Perspective*, BROADCAST CABLE FINANCIAL JOURNAL, July/August, 1992

- Erwin Krasnow and William Crispin, *Letters of Intent: Renegotiation Insurance or Recipe for Disaster?*, BROADCAST CABLE FINANCIAL JOURNAL, May/June, 1993; reprinted in CABLE T.V. AND NEW MEDIA LAW & FINANCE, June, 1992

- Erwin Krasnow, *Buying a Broadcast Station: The*

Due Diligence Process, BROADCAST CABLE FINANCIAL JOURNAL, December/January, 1994; reprinted in CABLE T.V. AND NEW MEDIA LAW & FINANCE, January, 1994

- Erwin Krasnow and Frederick McConville, *How to Make Sure Your Closing Isn't Too Close for Comfort*, BROADCAST LAW REPORT, November 2000; reprinted in THE FINANCIAL MANAGER, February–March 2001

- Erwin Krasnow, *Art of the (Media) Deal: Tips and Techniques for Effective Negotiating in the Broadcast Business*, THE FINANCIAL MANAGER, November/December 2004.

- Erwin Krasnow and Melodie Virtue, *How to Squeeze Maximum Value from Your FCC License*, RADIO INK, May 2005.

- Erwin Krasnow, *The ABCs of LMAs: A Short Course on FCC Policies*, SMALL MARKET RADIO NEWSLETTER, May 2006.

- Erwin Krasnow and James Pfau, *Borrower Beware: Few Industries Challenge Lenders like Broadcasting. Here's*

How to Make the Most of a Tricky Relationship, THE FINANCIAL MANAGER, May/June 2006.

- Erwin Krasnow, *Clearing the Air: Deconstructing the Myths and Misconceptions About Buying Broadcast Stations*, MEDIA LAW & POLICY, Fall 2006.

- Erwin Krasnow, *Eleven Costly Myths and Misconceptions About Buying Broadcast Stations*, THE FINANCIAL MANAGER, November/December 2006.

- Erwin Krasnow and John Knab, *Friends and Family, In Tough Times, Loans from Friends and Family Can Help More than Hurt --- If Done Right*, SMALL MARKET RADIO NEWSLETTER, May 2008.

- Erwin Krasnow and John Wells King, *Financing a Station in Difficult Times*, RADIO WORLD, March 2009.

Don't hesitate to send us an email with questions or comments. Your ideas will help us strengthen the book in future editions.

Erwin G. Krasnow
ekrasnow@gsblaw.com

John M. Pelkey
jpelkey@gsblaw.com

John Wells King
jking@gsblaw.com

CHAPTER ONE

TO WRITE OR NOT TO WRITE: THE TORTUOUS LETTER OF INTENT

After the buyer and seller have worked out the basic terms of their deal, a letter of intent serves to memorialize those terms in anticipation of the formal agreement. While generally intended to be non-binding, a letter of intent states the parties' intention to enter into a transaction and recites the basic business points (*e.g.*, purchase price, timetable, form of consideration), thereby helping to move the deal along. Unfortunately, too often parties enter into letters of intent without a great deal of thought. Indeed, in some radio transactions, the letter of intent — also referred to as a "memorandum of understanding" or "agreement in principle" — is drafted by the broker using a fill-in-the-blanks boilerplate letter. By contrast, in other situations, the letter of intent is drafted — and redrafted — by multiple lawyers and can become the subject of seemingly endless negotiations between the parties. One of the benefits of a well-drafted and negotiated letter of intent is that it can make the negotiation of the definitive agreement speedier and easier.

Inattention to the consequences of a letter of intent can be costly. In one dramatic case for example – the proposed acquisition of Getty Oil by Pennzoil – the letter of intent formed the basis of a jury award of $11.2 billion. Now that we have your attention, we will give you some suggestions on the do's and don'ts of letters of intent.

The Letter of Intent: Renegotiation Insurance or Recipe for Disaster

Let's assume that you and a prospective buyer have arrived at a price for the sale of a radio station, or have at least determined a formula for setting the price. Should you be content with just a "handshake deal" until a definitive agreement is executed at some later date?

Ask a lawyer any question and you invariably get the same answer: "It depends." There is no absolute rule as to whether there should be a letter of intent in a transaction — it depends on the facts involved. Certain factors may lead to a decision to put an agreement in

1

principle in writing. One reason may be that the parties will feel bound to a greater degree if the agreement is corroborated by a signed document than if it is not. Also, the longer the parties wait to place their oral understanding in writing, the greater the chance for misunderstanding. This is especially true when the terms of the deal are relatively complicated and a written letter will serve to assure that there has been no miscommunication on the essential terms of the transaction. Another good reason for a letter of intent is to convince a third party (such as a bank, if financing is required) that the transaction is viable. Another benefit of a letter of intent is that it can keep the seller from using the buyer as a stalking horse to negotiate a deal with a third party if the letter of intent contains a "no shop" clause.

One legal scholar has commented, in only slightly irreverent terms, that a letter of intent is a form of "anti-renegotiation insurance." Such letters represent an explicit moral obligation of the parties, which reasonably principled business executives seem to take quite seriously. Also, a letter of intent can provide a structure for the transaction from which the definitive agreement can be drafted and might allow the parties to make announcements to customers, suppliers, and employees, which

is often desirable. From a buyer's perspective, a letter of intent containing a "no shop" clause provides a definite period of time in which the seller is prohibited from marketing the station to other parties. This provision usually has the effect of making the seller take the letter of intent more seriously and encourages both parties and their lawyers to complete the definitive agreement before the "no shop" deadline expires.

The well constructed letter of intent serves five main purposes. First, it sets forth the details and structure of the transaction, thus saving time for the buyer and the seller in briefing and rebriefing their respective lawyers as to what was intended. Second, it helps to keep the parties and the lawyers from renegotiating the essential terms of the deal. Third, it helps to insure that the seller stops marketing or entertaining offers while the definitive agreement is being drafted. Fourth, the deadline in the "no shop" provision helps to keep both sides focused on getting the deal done. Fifth, signing a letter of intent early on facilitates compliance with regulatory requirements. A pre- merger notification report can be filed under the Hart-Scott-Rodino Antitrust Improvements Act of 1976 upon executing a letter of intent, thereby starting the clock on the application waiting period (see Chapter Three).

Also, as discussed in Chapter Four, one way to expedite the processing of an assignment or transfer application is to file the letter of intent with the FCC and advise the Commission that the definitive agreement will be filed shortly.

Where a letter of intent is entered into by the parties, we recommend against a public announcement or notification of the proposed sale to vendors and employees. There is too much risk of personnel distraction or loss due to the time lag between signing the letter of intent and the definitive agreement, during which time it is very difficult to assure the seller's employees as to the new owner's intentions. There is also the potential embarrassment for both parties if the announced deal does not materialize.

In some situations, a letter of intent may be unnecessary or undesirable. In deals involving small amounts of money, it may be preferable to move ahead directly to the ultimate agreement rather than waste time, money and energy in negotiating a detailed letter of intent. Often the key factor is the length of time expected to elapse between the letter of intent and completion of the definitive agreement. The shorter the period, the less desirable it is to enter into a letter of intent. Also, the parties may not be ready to sign a letter of intent because an agreement has not been reached on important details, or one or both of the parties is not ready to issue a public announcement. Of course, to a seller that is quietly negotiating with more than one party, the signing of a letter of intent is not desirable until those negotiations are complete.

Prior to obtaining a letter of intent or if there is no letter of intent, we recommend that both sides to the transaction sign a confidentiality agreement. The seller should insist that the buyer sign a confidentiality agreement so that word of the impending sale does not leak out to advertisers, employees and competitors. It is also in the interest of the buyer to insist that the seller sign a confidentiality agreement to prevent the seller from using the letter to shop for a better deal. Appendix A contains a sample confidentiality agreement.

Points to be Covered

Typically, a letter of intent takes the form of a letter addressed to the seller, signed by the buyer, and then countersigned and dated by the seller or, in the case of a sale of stock, by the selling shareholders. When there are large numbers of shareholders, it is desirable to have the letter of intent countersigned by the principal shareholders. If any trouble is anticipated from minority shareholders, the buyer would be well advised to obtain their signatures as well.

Although letters of intent vary, the following checklist identifies several points that might be covered:

- [ ] a statement of the nature of the transaction (*e.g.*, acquisition of stock, purchase of assets, merger, etc.).

- [ ] in the case of an asset deal, a description of (a) the assets being acquired (*e.g.*, whether or not the accounts receivable are being purchased, whether the assets are being acquired free of liens and encumbrances and with or without the assumption of liabilities) and (b) the excluded assets; or, in the case of a stock deal, a description of the stock to be purchased.

- [ ] a description of the purchase price or the formula for determining the purchase price.

- [ ] the payment terms (*i.e.*, the consideration to be paid or exchanged at the closing and, if applicable, the amount and timing of any deferred payments).

- [ ] if deferred payments are involved, the type of any security to be provided to the seller (*e.g.*, security agreement, personal and/ or corporate guarantees, stock pledges, etc.).

- [ ] any special arrangements the buyer will require relative to any of the seller's officers, directors or employees (*e.g.*, covenants not to compete, consulting agreements, stock options, employment agreements, etc.).

- [ ] responsibility for the drafting of the purchase and sale agreement (normally it is the buyer's counsel who drafts the agreement).

- [ ] a statement of conditions precedent to consummation of the transaction (*e.g.*, subject to the prior approval of the Federal Communications Commission, and where a filing is required under the Hart-Scott-Rodino Antitrust Improvements Act of 1976, the Department of Justice and the Federal Trade Commission; approval by the Board of Directors and in some cases, the shareholders of the parties; the execution of a definitive asset or stock purchase agreement; no material adverse change between execution of the definitive agreement and the closing; a financing contingency, etc.).

- [ ] any necessary disclaimers (the letter of intent should clearly state whether or not it is intended to constitute a binding agreement — a topic discussed later in this chapter).

- [ ] a provision giving the buyer access to those agreements, books and records necessary to permit the buyer to complete its due diligence and to flesh out the provisions of the purchase agreement.

- [ ] escrow arrangements (*e.g.*, provision for placement of funds in escrow upon the execution of the letter of intent and/or the definitive agreement; whether the escrow will be the agreed-upon amount of liquidated damages; whether there

will be a post-closing indemnification escrow).

- [ ] responsibility for payment of brokerage or finder's fees, recording fees, transfer taxes and other transactional costs.

- [ ] maintenance of the confidentiality of information.

- [ ] public announcements (*e.g.*, no party will issue any public announcement concerning the transaction without the prior approval of the other party).

- [ ] the deadline (if any) for the execution of a definitive agreement and/ or the period of exclusive dealing (*i.e.*, the length of time the seller is obligated to refrain from soliciting, encouraging or considering other offers for the sale of the assets or stock).

Many letters of intent state that the definitive agreement will contain such representations, warranties, covenants and indemnification provisions as are customary and appropriate to transactions of similar size and nature. Some letters include specific representations and warranties about such matters as the condition of equipment and compliance with FCC rules. Other letters deal with such subjects as the allocation of the purchase price for tax and accounting purposes, responsibility for payment of fees, expenses and taxes, covenants concerning the conduct of business before the closing, and the need for a "final order" issued by the FCC consenting to the sale. The more points covered, the more a letter of intent begins to look like a blueprint for a formal agreement. Such a comprehensive letter of intent could save time, or it could serve as a red flag to all parties if it appears that fundamental issues cannot be resolved — a clear signal that more time will be needed to reach a definitive agreement.

Appendix B contains examples of four different forms of letters of intent. These letters should be regarded as a starting point to be tailored to meet your individual objectives and concerns. There is no such thing as a standard letter of intent applicable to all proposed transactions.

To Bind or Not to Bind

Lawyers burned by letters of intent have characterized the document as "an invention of the devil" to be avoided at all costs. This hostility stems from one of the principal problems with letters of

intent: the unpredictability of their enforceability in litigation.

Predicting the enforceability of letters of intent has baffled sophisticated business executives and legal experts alike. Generally speaking, most business executives assume that a letter of intent is simply an unenforceable "agreement to agree." Probably the most famous, and most costly, expression of this point of view was made in the midst of the battle between Texaco and Pennzoil for the Getty Oil Company. There, the Chairman of Getty Oil, Sidney Peterson, responded to a question from the Chairman of Texaco, John McKinley, concerning whether Getty was still available notwithstanding an "agreement in principle" that Getty had signed with Pennzoil. Peterson's response — "the fat lady has not yet sung" — has become a permanent fixture of American corporate folklore. Texaco acquired Getty and Pennzoil sued. Texaco later disclosed to the Securities and Exchange Commission that its "liability from the [Pennzoil] suit [was] not expected to be materially important." An $11.2 billion error in judgment by experienced corporate executives and high-priced Wall Street lawyers is a sobering reminder to anyone who contemplates entering into a letter of intent but wants to leave some wiggle room. The "fat lady" sings softly at times.

The reported cases are not particularly reassuring to a party who does not wish to be bound by a letter of intent. Judicial decisions analyzing the enforceability of letters of intent have come down all over the board. The reason for this is twofold. First, whether a letter of intent is binding is a factual question, not a legal issue. Second, some courts have decided to imply from the letter of intent a duty to negotiate in good faith for a final agreement. Anyone considering a letter of intent should be familiar with both of these considerations.

The factual issue in letter of intent litigation focuses on whether the parties intended to be bound before the execution of a definitive purchase agreement. The factual rather than legal nature of this question carries some very practical consequences. First, factual questions are to be decided by the trier of fact. This means that summary judgment may not be available to the station owner who decided to accept a higher offer after entering into a letter of intent, because the material question of the parties' intent remains in dispute and will be decided by a judge or jury only after a potentially long and expensive trial. Because this issue is factual rather than legal, "forum shopping" (*i.e.*, choosing a state whose law is thought to be

more favorable) may not always guarantee a favorable result. The jury or the judge (in the event of a bench trial) looks at all of the facts concerning a particular case to determine what the parties intended. Since the facts in any two cases are rarely, if ever, identical, the jury or the judge has wide latitude in reaching a decision.

Even more troublesome is the application in letter of intent cases of a "duty to negotiate in good faith." For example, in one case, the parties entered into a letter of intent that expressly stated that they would be under no further obligation to each other if they failed to agree upon and execute a definitive sales contract. The seller attempted to back out of the letter of intent when a second suitor came along with a better offer. Notwithstanding the clear language of the letter of intent, the court imposed on the seller a duty to negotiate in good faith. The practical result is that the seller had the burden of demonstrating that it acted in good faith when it did not follow through on the letter of intent.

The Yellow Brick Road to Practicality

An all too familiar scenario involves a buyer and seller who have a "handshake" deal and, in their eagerness to memorialize their understanding, rush through the drafting of a letter of intent. Both parties are relaxed about the wording of such a letter of intent because they believe it is non-binding and they save their energies for the drafting of a definitive agreement.

We suggest that you think twice before deciding on the next step following a handshake. Decide whether and to what extent you want to sign a letter of intent which is binding. You need to be aware that a court may decide that a letter of intent is binding even though one or both parties did not sign with such an intention. Make sure that your intent, for example, not to be bound, is stated explicitly in the letter of intent, if this is your wish. Also, be aware that a letter of intent may give rise to implied covenants such as a covenant to negotiate in good faith even where the intent not to be bound is clear. (Some buyers include a provision in the letter of intent specifically obligating the seller to negotiate during the "no shop" period.) A fundamental issue is whether a letter of intent is necessary or appropriate for the particular transaction or whether proceeding directly with the drafting of a definitive agreement provides a more practical course.

If you decide on entering into a letter of intent, draft the document carefully with a full appreciation of all of the pitfalls that can result. If your goal is to preserve some "wiggle room," but the circumstances seem to justify a letter of intent, then the following steps should be taken:

First, the letter of intent should contain a clear and unequivocal statement that the parties do not intend to be bound until a definitive contract is executed. All subsequent communications should uniformly be consistent with this approach. Most of the litigation concerning the enforceability of letters of intent arises from letters that do not clearly reflect the intent of the parties on enforceability. Two of the illustrative letters of intent in Appendix B explicitly identify the terms that are binding (*e.g.*, confidentiality, no shop, access, publicity, etc.) and those that are not (*e.g.*, the purchase price, the amount of the escrow, excluded assets, etc.).

Second, the letter of intent should set forth the basic terms of the deal without great specificity — leave open some real substantive issues for the final negotiations.

Third, if your lawyer cannot assure you that your letter of intent will be unenforceable, consider adding a modest "liquidated damages" provision. While this may, practically speaking, result in a determination that the letter of intent is binding, it may also serve as a basis for limiting your liability. Obviously, if you want the letter of intent to be binding, insist on the insertion of a liquidated damages provision with a healthy but realistic amount of damages.

A letter of intent should never be entered into casually. Since we know that the fat lady is capable of singing softly, listen very carefully before entering into a letter of intent.

CHAPTER TWO

TWO SIDES TO THE PUZZLE:
THE PURCHASE AND SALE AGREEMENT

Samuel Goldwyn once quipped that an oral contract isn't worth the paper on which it is written. He might have said that a written contract has similar value if its provisions do not accurately reflect the understandings of the parties so as to avoid disputes and litigation. This chapter provides a general outline of the contents of a purchase and sale agreement that affords protection to both the seller and the buyer. The chapters that follow discuss issues of special relevance to the buyer, the seller, the FCC, and certain closing matters.

As with any acquisition, a radio station purchase can be structured in one of two ways: (1) the buyer can acquire the assets of the seller's business; or (2) the buyer can acquire the stock (or other equity investment) of the seller's business. Which structure the parties select will often depend on the tax consequences of one structure versus the other. Tax implications (*e.g.*, available net operating losses, recapture of depreciation, investment credits) can have a significant impact on the costs and value of the transaction to each of the parties. For this reason, it is advisable that both the seller and the buyer obtain tax advice very early in the process. Tax consequences aside, the distinction between a stock transaction and an asset deal can be important for other reasons as well.

In a stock transaction, the purchaser acquires an ownership interest in the existing corporate owner of the radio station from one or more of its shareholders and, accordingly, acquires an interest in <u>all</u> of the liabilities of the corporation (whether or not disclosed) as well as all of the assets. Although the references in this book are to stock purchase agreements involving the purchase of the stock of a corporation, similar considerations may apply if the acquired entity is a partnership or a limited liability company taxed as a partnership. Stock acquisitions can be advantageous from an operations standpoint because they preserve some continuity with a station's existing vendors, lease arrangements, and the like. In a stock deal, however, the seller customarily has a tax liability on the difference between its adjusted basis in the stock and the stock price paid by the buyer. Sellers generally prefer a Stock Purchase Agreement because it (a) avoids "double taxation" (*i.e.*, taxes on the corporation and on the shareholder(s)), (b) potentially reduces the amount of taxes because the transaction generally is taxed at capital gains rates which are lower than ordinary income tax rates, and (c) allows the shareholders to step away completely from the business.

In an asset deal, the buyer acquires only those assets, including contracts, specifically negotiated to be sold and specified in the purchase agreement. The buyer generally does not acquire assets other than the assumed contracts or any of the liabilities of the seller. Although accounts receivable are not usually retained by the seller, the buyer will try to negotiate to acquire the receivables at the expense of a higher purchase price or the assumption of trade liability, to establish an immediate cash flow. Typically, asset purchases have more favorable tax implications for the buyer, particularly if the seller's station is a relatively new one that was built, rather than purchased, by the seller. The vast majority of radio station transactions are asset sales rather than stock deals. Accordingly, this book focuses primarily on the instrument used to memorialize such transactions: the asset purchase agreement. While each asset purchase agreement

must be tailored to meet the needs of the parties to the transaction, the provisions discussed in this chapter are typical of those contained in an agreement for the sale and purchase of the assets of a radio station.

The asset and stock transactions described above assume that the acquisition will be a taxable transaction. It is possible to structure the transaction as tax-free, in whole or in part, to the seller either through a tax-free reorganization in the case of using buyer's stock as consideration or a simultaneous or deferred exchange of radio stations. The liberalization of the FCC's multiple ownership rules in the 1990s and the significant appreciation in value of some stations prompted many sellers to defer their income tax liability by conducting exchanges under Section 1031 of the Internal Revenue Code. The use of buyer's stock in a tax-deferred exchange raises multiple federal securities issues, in particular the need to register the stock under the Securities Act of 1933 or to come within an exemption from the registration requirement.

TAX-DEFERRED EXCHANGES OR STATION SWAPS: AN OVERLY SIMPLIFIED EXPLANATION OF A COMPLICATED SUBJECT

With respect to station swaps or tax-deferred exchanges, the assets of one or more radio stations are exchanged for the assets of one or more other stations pursuant to Section 1031 of the Internal Revenue Code. In a typical tax "deferred" exchange, prior to a conveyance of assets (the "relinquished property"), the seller (the Taxpayer) executes a "Deferred Exchange Agreement" with a "Qualified Intermediary," assigns to such Intermediary the Taxpayer's rights under the asset purchase agreement, and gives written notice of such assignment to all parties to the asset purchase agreement. At the closing for the sale of the relinquished property, the Taxpayer conveys the relinquished property directly to the buyer and the buyer delivers the net sale proceeds to the Intermediary. Within 45 days following the sale, the Taxpayer must identify "replacement property" in a written communication signed by the Taxpayer and delivered to the Intermediary. Within 180 days following the sale or the due date (with extensions) of the taxpayer's return for the year of the exchange, whichever is lesser, the Taxpayer assigns to the Intermediary the Taxpayer's rights under the asset purchase agreement for the replacement property, delivers written notice of assignment to all parties to such asset purchase agreement, directs the Intermediary to pay the purchase price directly to the seller of the replacement property, and acquires the replacement property directly from the seller in completion of the exchange.

Alternatively, the replacement property may be acquired prior to the Taxpayer's conveyance of relinquished property. In the typical "reverse" exchange, pursuant to Revenue Procedure 2000-37, the Taxpayer executes a "Qualified Exchange Accommodation Agreement" with an "Exchange Accommodation Titleholder" (the Titleholder), and assigns to the Titleholder the Taxpayer's rights under the asset purchase agreement. The seller then conveys the replacement property to the Titleholder at the closing. Within 180 days thereafter, the Taxpayer must execute an asset purchase agreement and convey the relinquished property in exchange for the replacement property.

Regardless of the type of exchange being conducted (simultaneous, deferred or reverse), a conveyance of multiple assets is broken down into exchange groups, and the sales proceeds allocated among the exchange groups based on value. For example, the proceeds allocated to "realty" could be exchanged for other "realty" and the proceeds allocated to "equipment" could be exchanged for equipment of like kind. To the extent the proceeds of any exchange group are not reinvested in other property of like kind to the assets in that exchange group, gain may be recognized.

Agreements come in all shapes and sizes. More is not necessarily better - a lengthy contract, no matter how bulky, provides no assurance that it will protect the parties or minimize the chances of litigation. Agreements also differ stylistically - for example, some contracts contain a special section devoted to "definitions" (*i.e.*, defining the major terms used in the agreement), while others include "definitions" within the pertinent sections. In any form, a well-drafted agreement satisfies the expectations of both parties.

Purchase agreements do not make exciting reading; however, they play an important, indeed central, role in effectuating the purchase and sale of a station. Signatories should know and understand all of their provisions. Here is a section-by-section overview of some of the most common provisions in purchase agreements.

Inside: The Assets to be Purchased

An experienced buyer of radio properties knows the importance of identifying in the contract all of the assets of the station that will be necessary or useful to the continued successful operation of the facilities. Customarily, this is achieved by a general recitation that the buyer is acquiring "all of the tangible and intangible assets owned by Seller and used or useful in connection with the operation of the station," with the exception of any excluded assets separately identified elsewhere in the agreement. This general recitation is often accompanied by an enumeration of some of the specific assets being purchased (which is included "without limitation" of the general statement that "all" assets are being acquired).

A list of assets typically includes a description of the physical assets (tangible personal property) associated with the station (*e.g.*, towers, transmitters, studio equipment, furnishings, vehicles, spare parts, etc.); contracts, leases and other agreements to be assigned (often with a special provision for trade or barter agreements); a description of any real property to be transferred; and any intellectual property (*e.g.*, copyrights, trademarks, trade names, call letters, telephone numbers, domain names and registrations, logos, slogans, rights to the content of websites and all good will associated with such intellectual property, etc.). The detailed description of the specific assets to be sold is usually contained in schedules attached to and made a part of the agreement. Most schedules describe the real property, the inventory (and/or tangible personal property), the FCC licenses, intangible personal property (such as copyrights and trademarks), and the contracts, leases and other agreements which the buyer agrees to assume.

Customarily, the purchase agreement will provide that seller assign to the buyer all station contracts that deal with the operation of the station. In some instances, however, those agreements may not have been reduced to writing or may be in the process of being renegotiated while the buyer and seller are negotiating the purchase agreement. Under those circumstances, the buyer may not be able to accurately assess either the potential benefits or the potential liabilities of those agreements that the buyer would be assuming as a result of those agreements. One solution to this problem is to permit the seller to conclude its negotiations after the execution of the purchase agreement but to adjust the purchase price at closing based upon the results of those negotiations. For example, the parties to one purchase agreement agreed that if the new tower lease into which the seller was entering resulted in net rental income that was less than a certain predetermined amount set forth in the asset purchase agreement, the purchase price would be decreased by the present value of the difference between that predetermined amount and the net rental income that would be realized during the term of the renewed lease.

In addition to the foregoing considerations, the growth of the Internet has necessitated further expansion of the asset list. Most radio stations in the U.S. maintain a presence on the World Wide Web, and many of these are also using the Internet as a medium for their broadcast content. In this environment, a prudent buyer cannot ignore the need to include the "*e*"-assets of the station when drafting the contract for the purchase of a radio station.

At a minimum, website assets that need to be considered include web hosting agreements; domain name registrations; service provider agreements for website components, including audio streaming and third-party video content (e.g., news, weather, traffic) and related e-commerce agreements. Although copyright licenses for streaming are not assignable (a buyer must obtain its own), the records of seller's performance royalty payments to SoundExchange should be included assets, to enable the buyer to respond to a claim of copyright infringement for any period prior to closing.

Two contrasting approaches to this issue can be found in two agreements. In the first agreement, the buyer obtained a broad clause in the recitation of assets to be acquired that encompassed:

> All Domain leases and Domain names of the Station, the unrestricted right to use of HTML content located and publicly accessible from those Domain names, and the "visitor" email data base for those sites.

This type of provision would appear to afford the buyer solid general protection for the most desirable e-commerce assets of the station. It is not tailored, however, to address any particular concerns that the buyer or the seller may possess with respect to the assets, such as any limits restricting the seller's ability to convey its interest or any collateral obligations or commitments related to the assets

that may have to be assigned and assumed in connection with the transfer. Nor does the general language above protect the seller from possibly giving away too much. By contrast, a similar provision in another agreement does address such issues. In that deal, the parties provided specifically that assets encompassed by the purchase and sale would include:

> all of the Seller's rights in and to, to the extent assignable and to the extent relating primarily to the Stations, any Internet Domain Name, any Internet Web page, the content accessible therefrom and the visitor data collected; provided, however, that any contract related thereto constitutes an Assumed Contract.

While neither of these provisions defines the appropriate scope of such an Internet assets provision, they do evidence that the subject is one that warrants careful consideration by both sides, and careful attention to drafting by counsel.

Customarily, the seller will retain the accounts receivable and any amounts to which the station might be entitled as a result of station operations prior to the closing date. Even if the agreement provides that the buyer will collect the accounts receivable, those collections and any receipts for amounts owed to the station as a result of operations prior to the closing usually are turned over to the Seller. This is not always the case, however. For example, in one agreement, the parties provided that, among the assets to be sold to the Buyer were "all accounts receivable and all amounts payable to the station, if any, from the United States Copyright Office or such arbitral panels as may be appointed by the United States Copyright Office that relate to the period" prior to the closing. Although the provision is unusual, its use can make sense in a situation where the seller is trying to wrap up affairs. In return for a fixed increase in the price paid to it at closing and the ability to close out its operations sooner than might otherwise be the case, the seller foregoes the uncertain future income it would have received from the collection of accounts receivable and possible future payments from the Copyright Office.

Outside: The Assets Excluded from the Transaction

The agreement must also describe the assets that are not to be purchased. Assets ordinarily excluded and, therefore, retained by the seller, include:

➤ Cash or cash equivalents (*e.g.*, certificates of deposit or Treasury bills)

➤ Accounts receivable

➤ Any contracts, agreements and leases other than the agreements specifically assumed by the buyer

➤ Any rights to refunds of federal, state or local franchise, income or other taxes or fees arising out of activities occurring prior to the closing date

➤ Life insurance (and its cash surrender value)

➤ Security deposits paid to utility companies or other parties

➤ Seller's corporate records, except records pertaining to or used in the operation of the station

➤ Any pension, profit-sharing or employee benefit plans

➤ Trade deals, in some instances

Some sellers include the call signs of the station as excluded assets. This can be important if the seller has other radio properties that it will continue to operate following the sale and wants to be able to use the call sign on one of them. In such cases, the agreement customarily requires the buyer to submit the proper request to the FCC for authority to change the call letters of the station effective on the closing date.

How Much: How and When

One section of a purchase agreement deals with the consideration to be paid for the acquisition, and usually lists the aggregate amount of the purchase price. The purchase price can be based on a formula (for example, as a multiple of broadcast cash flow). If non-competition and/or consulting agreements are involved, the section may also indicate the amount of money allocated to these agreements. In the past, buyers often preferred to earmark a portion of the purchase price to such agreements in order to take advantage of more favorable tax treatment; payments pursuant to non-competition and consulting agreements can be treated by the buyer as a deductible expense. However, this is no longer the case because non-competition expenses are now deductible over a 15-year period (not the duration of the covenant or the payment period) under Section 197 of the Internal Revenue Code of 1986,

as amended, and thus are, for tax purposes, the same as goodwill.

The section on purchase price usually discusses whether there is an "earnest money" escrow deposit. In most transactions, the escrow fund serves as an assured funding mechanism for the payment of "liquidated damages" to the seller in the event of a breach of contract or default by the buyer. ("Liquidated damages" are the amount of damages that a party who breaches a contract is required to pay without reference to the actual injury suffered by the non-breaching party.) Typically the amount of the escrow deposit is 5% of the purchase price, although the seller may insist on an escrow deposit approaching 10% if the buyer does not have an established track record of closing on its purchases. The escrow payment might be in the form of cash or an irrevocable letter of credit. The cash or letter of credit is deposited with a financial institution, the broker, or counsel pursuant to a negotiated escrow agreement. The escrow agreement usually specifies who pays any fees of the escrow agent (it is typically shared by seller and buyer), who receives any interest on escrowed funds, procedures for third party claims, and the manner in which funds shall be paid. A formal escrow agreement usually is included in the purchase agreement as an exhibit.

The purchase price section also spells out how the buyer is to make payment at the closing. The cash portion of the purchase price is usually paid by wire transfer. If part or all of the purchase price is to be deferred, or financed by the seller, a brief description of the terms of the "seller paper" is typically included, accompanied by a promissory note attached as an exhibit to be executed by the buyer at the closing. In most transactions involving seller financing, a prudent seller will also request that the buyer execute one or more financing instruments (e.g., a security agreement, stock pledge agreement, and guaranty agreement(s)). Most buyers will negotiate for a provision which makes seller financing subordinate to bank debt. The seller often obtains a "security interest" in the assets of the station (most often junior in position to a similar right given to the buyer's senior lender). A security interest is a legal interest in property that secures the payment of a debt or other obligation by giving the creditor the right to sell the property to satisfy the debt, and establishes certain priorities to the property among creditors. The FCC prohibits any provision which provides for a security interest in FCC licenses and permits. For a more complete discussion, see Chapter Four. Like the promissory note, such formal financing instruments are usually included as exhibits.

Getting Specific: Allocation of Purchase Price

For federal tax purposes, the purchase price must be allocated among the various assets of the station. Thus, most asset purchase agreements will also address the allocation of the purchase price among the various assets being sold and purchased. The Internal Revenue Service (IRS) requires the buyer and the seller each to file Form 8594, "Asset Acquisition Statement," concerning the allocation of the purchase price pursuant to Section 1060 of the Internal Revenue Code. Most asset purchase agreements include a provision describing the timing of such an allocation (e.g., whether it will be made prior to or shortly after the closing) and the method of resolving disputes (e.g., based on an appraisal of a designated expert). Some contracts contain a provision (or a separate schedule) which sets forth the allocation of the purchase price agreed-upon by the parties. A common provision requires the seller and the buyer to file federal income tax returns and other tax returns reflecting the agreed upon allocation. Since the seller and the buyer have opposing interests in making the allocation, the IRS has generally been willing to abide by any reasonable allocation agreement between the parties. However, if the allocations contained in Form 8594

(Asset Acquisition Statement under Section 1060) filed by the seller and the buyer are not identical, there is a greater likelihood of an audit. The Treasury Department retains the right to review and challenge the allocation.

The allocation of the purchase price may have significant tax consequences and we recommend that you discuss your allocation with your CPA, tax attorney or other financial advisor who understands the tax consequences. The following analysis prepared by John Sanders of the appraisal firm of Bond and Pecaro, Inc., illustrates the financial impact of recapitalizing acquired fixed assets through the example of a single asset:

Suppose an acquired radio station owns a transmitter which is six years old. Let's further assume that the transmitter is in good working order, has been upgraded as necessary, and has been professionally maintained. Tax regulations permit a taxpayer to reduce taxable income by depreciating the cost of an asset over a period of years. This reflects the expectation that the asset will eventually wear out or become obsolete, requiring replacement (*i.e.*, that its value is expended in the business over the asset's useful life). The seller paid $70,000 for the item and depreciated it for tax purposes over a five year period using the Modified

Accelerated Cost Recovery System ("MACRS") depreciation method that is permitted by the IRS. Based upon this approach, the remaining adjusted tax basis and "book value" for the transmitter is zero.

In the case of the transmitter above, since the seller has no adjusted tax basis in the asset, the buyer would enjoy no depreciation benefit if it simply carried over the adjusted tax basis in the asset from the seller's tax return.

However, if the buyer can demonstrate that the asset still has positive value, usually achieved by retaining an independent appraiser, it is possible to establish a new depreciation schedule. For the purposes of this example, it can be assumed that the value of this item, based upon current replacement costs, condition and obsolescence factors, observed depreciation, and with consideration given to the fact that it is tested and installed as part of an operating radio station, is actually $60,000.

Using the $60,000 appraised value based upon allocation of the purchase price, the buyer could start a new five-year depreciation schedule. Assuming a 40% marginal tax rate, the buyer would enjoy the following tax benefits (ignoring present value):

---

* Based upon assumed tax rate of 40%.

Year	Depreciation Percentage	Depreciation Claimed	Tax Benefit*
1	20.00%	$12,000	$4,800
2	32.00%	19,200	7,680
3	19.20%	11,520	4,608
4	11.52%	6,912	2,765
5	11.52%	6,912	2,765
6	5.76%	3,456	1,382
	Total	$60,000	$24,000

The $24,000 in tax benefits over five years that results from "recapitalizing" the asset indicates the significant financial benefits that a buyer can enjoy from appraising all of the assets of the station. However, this simple example belies a number of complexities associated with the process. Perhaps most importantly, the seller is generally required to pay "recapture" taxes on prior depreciation related to the assets which have been re-appraised, adding an element of tension between the interests of the seller and the buyer. The IRS requires that a Form 8594 be filed by both buyer and seller to ensure that consistent values are reported. There may be a need to defend appraised values at a later time. The prudent course of action is to work through this process in consultation with legal, accounting, and valuation professionals.

It is important to recognize that acquired *intangible* assets are subject to tax treatment similar to that of acquired tangible assets. The valuation of these assets also can have a significant financial impact on the acquisition of a radio property. In fact, radio is a business in which a relatively small fraction of the value of a station has historically been attributed to tangible assets. At some stations, 80% or more of the value is attributable to intangible assets such as FCC licenses, talent contracts, favorable leases, tower income agreements, and the like. As is the case with tangible assets, intangible assets must be appraised in a reasonable and documented manner. The income, market, and cost approaches may be employed individually or in combination to determine the value of identifiable intangible assets.

The 1993 Tax Act simplified the tax treatment of acquired intangible assets and created a class of assets designated as "Section 197 assets." This includes most intangible assets including the following:

1. Goodwill, going concern value, and covenants not to compete entered into as part of the acquisition

2. Workforce in place

3. Information base

4. Patents

5. Any customer-based intangible assets

6. Any copyright, formula, design or similar item

7. Any license, permit, or other right granted by a governmental unit or agency

8. Any franchise, trademark, or trade name

No. 7 above includes acquired FCC licenses, typically the core asset of a radio station, while No. 5 includes items such as advertiser contracts, lists, and relationships.

All Section 197 intangible assets, including goodwill and going concern value, are amortizable for tax purposes over a 15-year life on a straight line basis. For example, if the value of an acquired FCC license were determined to be $15,000,000, the buyer of the station would be eligible to amortize $1,000,000 per year (i.e., $15,000,000 divided by the statutory 15-year life).

There are other complexities and limitations related to self-created assets and certain other intangible assets. Certain assets are excluded from Section 197, such as existing leases for tangible property. These are typically amortized over their remaining useful lives rather than the 15-year statutory period.

While the mechanics of Section 197 do not eliminate the need for intangible asset valuation, they do simplify the tax treatment of intangible assets relative to the requirements that prevailed prior to 1993, when taxpayers had to document both a value and a determinable life for each asset that was to be amortized. The "lifing analysis" is no longer necessary in many cases.

In some cases, radio station acquisitions are structured as like-kind exchanges, typically involving a swap of radio stations. These transactions require rigorous financial analysis because the IRS requires that exchanged assets be grouped into specific categories and that a tax be calculated on the gain in those categories. See the discussion concerning like-kind exchanges which appears earlier in this chapter. Goodwill and going concern value are not considered to be exchangeable assets.

In summary, the provisions of the tax code will typically provide a benefit to broadcasters in that most intangible assets acquired in a radio station acquisition can be written off over 15 years. However, there are certain exclusions. Additionally, while opportunities exist to enjoy the benefits of a "tax-free" like-kind exchange, these transactions do require considerable valuation analysis and documentation. It should also be borne in mind that the accounting conventions that govern financial reporting for acquisitions vary in many respects from the tax treatment.

Prorations and Adjustments

The "adjustments process" is an integral part of the closing of a radio station sale transaction. Most acquisition agreements provide that the adjustment time will be 12:01 a.m. or 11:59 p.m., local time on the day of the closing. Typically, adjustments to the purchase price are made in order to offset for the seller's unrealized revenues for services provided prior to the closing or to offset for the buyer any accounts payable attributable to the seller's operation of the station that remain unsatisfied as of the closing. This section of the purchase agreement describes the items of income and expense to be prorated and adjusted at the closing (*e.g.*, prepaid expenses, accrued vacation leave, deposits, trade deals, etc.). It also describes the manner in which the prorations and adjustments will be made. Most acquisition agreements provide for a post-closing adjustment at a date certain (usually 30 to 60 days and less frequently at the end date for the collection of seller's accounts receivable by the buyer) because the exact amount of the adjustment might not be known at the closing or because certain items might be paid after their use (such as utility payments and telephone bills).

For example, one asset sale agreement provided that all accounts receivable would be assigned to the buyer at the closing. However, in the event that the buyer were to collect in excess of $225,000 from the accounts, the excess was to be remitted to the seller on a monthly basis. However, to protect the buyer, the agreement further provided that if the buyer was unable to collect a total of $225,000 from the accounts assigned, any shortfall would be offset from the next payments due under the non-competition agreement.

One particularly challenging issue in the adjustment process can be adjusting for the value of <u>non-cash</u> assets or liabilities. In an agreement for the sale and purchase of a radio station, the parties provided that an adjustment to the purchase price would be made at the time of closing to reflect the difference between (a) the value as of the closing date of all advertising time required to be broadcast by the Station after the closing date according to the terms and conditions of the trade agreements into which the seller had entered, and (b) the value of all property or services to be received by the station after the closing date pursuant to those trade agreements. To the extent that the amount described in the foregoing clause (a) exceeded the amount described in the foregoing clause (b) by an amount greater than Ten

Thousand Dollars, the purchase price was to be adjusted downward by the amount in excess of Ten Thousand Dollars; to the extent that the amount described in clause (a) exceeded the amount described in clause (b) by an amount equal to or less than Ten Thousand Dollars ($10,000), or such amounts were equal or if the amount described in clause (a) was less than clause (b), there was to be no adjustment in the purchase price.

Such an arrangement helps to ensure that the respective interests of the buyer and the seller in the value of the non-cash assets are adequately protected. The buyer's exposure is limited by the use of a fixed benchmark of $10,000. At the same time, the seller is protected inasmuch as the buyer is assuming seller's contractual obligation to air advertisements in accordance with its trade and barter agreements. On rare occasion, agreements are drafted to provide that the purchase price will be increased if the buyer is to enjoy goods or services arising from trade and barter agreements that have a value in excess of the advertising to be aired by the buyer in accordance with those trade and barter agreements. Generally a buyer finds this type of arrangement unacceptable because it depletes the buyer's inventory of commercial time while providing the buyer with goods or services that are of little use or value.

Assumption by the Buyer of Specified Liabilities and Obligations

This section makes provisions for the assumption of liabilities and obligations by the buyer and the seller. Principally, the buyer assumes contracts, leases, and agreements, which are customarily listed separately in a schedule to the agreement. Some contracts are designated as material contracts for which consent to assignment must be obtained from the contracting party as a condition to closing. The seller usually remains liable for all liabilities and obligations accruing or occurring prior to the closing (including obligations arising under assumed contracts, leases and agreements), as well as for any contract, lease or agreement not included in the schedule of contracts to be assumed by the buyer.

It is not uncommon for some of the more important agreements being assumed by the buyer to require the consent of a third party. Customarily, the purchase agreement will require the seller to use "all commercially reasonable efforts to obtain any and all such third party consents." To avoid the situation where the third party seeks a monetary payment in return for granting such consent, the parties to one agreement inserted a clause that "the Seller shall use all commercially reasonable efforts to obtain any and all such third party consents… <u>provided</u>, however, that the Seller shall not be required to pay or incur any cost or expense, other than routine and reasonable administrative costs, to obtain any third party consent that the Seller is not otherwise required to pay or incur in accordance with the terms of the applicable Business Contract or Business License." The parties to that agreement also sought to deal with a situation wherein the third party might refuse to grant its consent, by providing that "if any such third party consent is not obtained before the Closing, the Seller shall, at the Purchaser's request, cooperate with the Purchaser in any reasonable arrangement designed to provide to the Purchaser after the Closing the benefits under the applicable Business Contract or Business License."

Closing

This section specifies the date, time and place of the closing and sets forth the conditions for the closing, including the need for FCC approval and other governmental or third party consents.

Representations and Warranties of the Parties

The "reps and warranties" portion of the agreement consists of promises or statements about the parties' respective status and their authority to perform the obligations under the agreement, as well as the nature or quality of what the seller is selling and the buyer is buying. The section describing the representations and warranties of the seller usually comprises the most extensive portion of the agreement since it is designed to protect the buyer from unpleasant surprises at (and after) the closing. Often a purchase agreement will provide that a breach of a representation or warranty will trigger the non-breaching party's right to indemnification (*i.e.*, to be made whole) for any damages that result from the breach.

The <u>seller</u> typically makes the following warranties, subject to specified exceptions disclosed to the buyer and usually reflected in the schedules to the acquisition agreement:

> ➢ Seller's corporation, partnership or limited liability company is properly organized, in good standing with the relevant state agency that regulates business entities (*e.g.*, the Secretary of State) and is authorized to transact business.

> ➢ Officers, general partners, or members have the authority to enter into and perform

the agreement (the sale of substantially all of a corporation's assets usually necessitates obtaining shareholder approval – under state law, there may be certain time periods for notice; if the seller is a public company, it may be necessary for seller to file and clear a proxy statement with the Securities and Exchange Commission).

- No other consents and approvals are required except those disclosed to the buyer.

- Agreement does not conflict with any law or any other agreement.

- Title to and condition of real property.

- Good and marketable title to and description of the condition of tangible personal property and sufficiency of the tangible personal property for operation of the station in the manner in which it has been operated.

- Contracts and leases constitute valid and

binding obligations of the seller and will be legally enforceable in accordance with their terms.

- Seller owns all patents, copyrights, domain names, trademarks, trade names and similar intangible property rights.

- FCC licenses and other governmental authorizations are in full force and effect.

- Operation of the station is in accordance with all laws and FCC rules.

- No litigation or administrative proceedings are pending or threatened which would adversely affect the station or the transaction.

- Taxes have been paid and tax reports and returns have been filed.

- Insurance on tangible personal property is adequate, is in full force and effect, and is up to date, and no claims have been made.

- All FCC regulatory fees have been paid and all required reports, including biennial ownership reports and Equal Employment Opportunity (EEO) reports, have been filed with the FCC.

- All material contracts, leases and other agreements have been disclosed and are in full force and effect.

- Financial statements have been prepared in accordance with generally accepted accounting principles; they fairly and accurately present the financial condition and operating results of the station; and there has been no material adverse change in the financial condition of the station between the execution of the asset purchase agreement (or the date of the financial statements) and the closing.

- No labor unions or collective bargaining units exist; the seller is in compliance with all laws relating to the employment of labor.

- The closing of the transaction will not impose on buyer any obligation under any of the seller's employee benefit plans.

- Seller has complied with all environmental laws (*e.g.*, no hazardous substances, solychlorinated biphenyls [PCBs], asbestos).

- No insolvency or bankruptcy proceedings are pending.

- Seller has made no untrue statement nor omitted any material fact.

- Seller has not violated the Commission's prohibition against discrimination on the basis of race, color, religion, national origin or sex in the sale of any commercially operated AM, FM, TV, Class A TV or international broadcast station. Seller will be required to make such a representation in the assignment/transfer application and it makes sense for buyer to know well in advance whether seller will be able to make the representation.

The buyer usually makes the following warranties:

> Buyer's corporation, limited partnership, or limited liability company is in good standing with the relevant state's Secretary of State and is authorized to transact business.

> Officers, general partners, or members are authorized to execute and perform the agreement.

> Buyer is legally and financially qualified to be a licensee of the FCC.

> Agreement does not conflict with any law or other agreement.

> Buyer has made no untrue statement nor omitted any material fact.

Although the above representations and warranties are customary in most radio station acquisitions, the scope of the representations and warranties may be severely limited if a station is being purchased out of receivership or bankruptcy inasmuch as the receiver or trustee may be unwilling, or legally unable, to make the customary representations and warranties. Even if the receiver or trustee provides representations and warranties, the survival period for those representations and warranties may be uncommonly short. For example, the receiver or trustee may be willing to make representations and warranties but they may expire as of closing. Moreover, even if the receiver or trustee is willing to make representations and warranties and have those representations or warranties survive for some period of time after closing, the fact that the receivership or trusteeship could cease existence as of closing, or shortly thereafter, could leave the buyer with no effective recourse if it subsequently discovers that the representations and warranties were false. Purchasing a station out of receivership or bankruptcy is thus a classic case of "buyer beware."

That said, there are certain steps that a diligent buyer can take to minimize the risks. First, the buyer must be scrupulous in performing its due diligence. The FCC records should be checked and more importantly, a qualified engineer should be retained to perform a due diligence inspection of the station. The engineering due diligence inspection would include an inspection not only of the transmission and studio equipment, but would also include an on-the-ground review of station operations. AM directional stations and community sites with multiple antennas (because of potential RF issues) bear special technical scrutiny and expertise. It is not uncommon for stations that are in receivership or bankruptcy to have been poorly operated and to have been subjected to slipshod maintenance. Is the tower properly lighted? Is it properly painted? Is the STL licensed? The engineer must visit the transmitter site and make sure that it is properly fenced and bears all requisite signage warning of RF and high voltage dangers and informing visitors of the antenna structure registration number that has been accorded to the facility. No on-site transmitter site inspection can be considered to be complete without a confirmation that the transmitter site is located at the correct coordinates. It is all too common for an on site inspection to disclose that a station's transmitter site is not accurately reflected on the station's license. That is particularly true in the case of stations that have spent their existence at the cusp of receivership or bankruptcy. In addition to performing a rigorous due diligence inspection, the buyer should also insist upon a holdback escrow so that if problems are discovered with the station after the closing, the buyer has a ready source of funds that can be used to remedy the situation.

It is not always possible to negotiate an agreement that provides for a holdback escrow in a receivership or bankruptcy context, however.

Under those circumstances, the buyer has no choice but to weigh the potential for problems with the station against the reduced purchase price that the buyer should be able to negotiate for the station. If the price of the station is low enough, it may make sense for the buyer to take the risk and purchase the station, especially if the chances of uncovering significant liabilities associated with the station are slim. A recently-constructed FM station using rented facilities likely carries far fewer risks for a buyer than an AM station that owns real property with a transmitter site that has been in use since before PCBs were essentially outlawed.

Conditions to the Buyer's Obligation to Close

This section sets forth the conditions that must be satisfied before the buyer will be required to close. Such conditions usually include:

➤ Seller is in compliance with its covenants, representations and warranties.

➤ Approval as to form and substance of instruments to be delivered to the buyer at closing (*i.e.,* the closing documents, including the purchase agreements and any related documents or agreements such as evidence of FCC consent, etc.).

➢ Legal opinion of the seller's counsel has been received.

➢ The FCC has issued consent to the assignment of license or transfer of control, and the consent has become a Final Order.

➢ All necessary third party consents to the assignment of contracts, leases, etc. to the buyer have been obtained.

➢ No legal proceedings that would affect the transaction or impair the value of the assets are pending or threatened.

➢ FCC licenses are in good standing.

➢ Assets are being transferred free and clear.

➢ There has been no material adverse change in the assets, business or prospects of the station.

Conditions to the Seller's Obligation to Close

This section, like the one discussed above, sets forth the conditions under which the seller will be required to close. Though shorter than the list of conditions that qualify a buyer's obligation, the seller's list contains several of the same elements, such as:

➢ Buyer shall have paid the purchase price.

➢ Buyer is in compliance with its covenants, representations and warranties.

➢ The FCC has issued consent to the assignment of license or transfer of control, and the consent has become a Final Order.

➢ Approval as to form and substance of instruments that will be delivered to the seller at the closing.

➢ Legal opinion of the buyer's counsel has been received.

Mutual Conditions to Obligations

This section describes the obligations of the parties with respect to the filing of an application on FCC Form 314 (for a sale of assets) or FCC Form 315 (for a sale of stock) to obtain the consent of the FCC to the transaction. It usually sets forth the period of time within which the application is to be filed with the FCC, requires the cooperation of the parties in prosecuting the application, and establishes the duty of the parties to prosecute the application in the face of objections. The section also sets a deadline date for the closing.

Documents to be Delivered by the Seller at Closing

The documents which the seller usually must furnish at the closing include bills of sale, officer's certificates, deeds for real property, assignments of licenses, contracts, leases, stock certificates (in transactions for the purchase of stock) and a legal opinion letter. In some transactions, the seller must also execute a post-closing indemnification and escrow agreement, a consulting contract, and a non-competition agreement (sometimes referred to as a

covenant not to compete). For a more complete discussion of closing documents, see Chapter Seven.

Documents to be Delivered by the Buyer at Closing

The documents to be furnished by the buyer at the closing include monetary consideration (usually by wire transfer of funds), officer's certificates, a legal opinion letter, promissory note, security agreement and guaranty agreement(s).

Further Covenants of the Seller

In most agreements, separate sections obligate the seller (and in some cases, its shareholders or principals) to take certain actions (affirmative covenants), or to refrain from doing something absent the buyer's consent (negative covenants). The affirmative and negative covenants regulate the activity of the seller between the time of the execution of the agreement and the closing.

Typical affirmative covenants include duties to:

> ➢ Operate the station in a manner consistent with the normal and prudent operation of a commercial broadcast station and in accordance with the rules and

regulations of the FCC and the station's authorizations.

➤ Use best efforts to maintain intact the station's staff organization and employees, to promote the business of the station and to preserve the business reputation of the station and the goodwill of the station's suppliers, advertisers, viewing audience, and others transacting business with the station.

➤ Keep and preserve the business records of the station in accordance with good business practice.

➤ Make reasonable efforts to endeavor to protect the service area of the station from interference from other stations, existing or proposed, of which the seller has actual knowledge, to the extent such interference is prohibited by the FCC's rules and regulations, and promptly to give the buyer notice of any prohibited interference.

➤ Maintain all of the tangible personal property and real property, so that when it is delivered to the buyer it will be in substantially the same condition as on the date of the contract, and will satisfy all the warranties in all material respects on the part of the seller set forth in the agreement, subject to reasonable wear and tear and replacements.

➤ Follow usual and customary policies with respect to extending credit for sales of time on the station and with respect to collecting accounts receivable arising from such an extension of credit.

➤ Provide buyer copies of monthly unaudited income statements and balance sheets prepared in the ordinary course of business commencing as soon as they become available.

➤ Maintain the inventory levels of the station as they exist on the date of the execution of the agreement (including office supplies, spare parts, tubes, equipment and the like) and replace inventory items expended, depleted, or worn out.

➢ Exercise all reasonable efforts to obtain, prior to the closing, the consent and approval (in a form reasonably acceptable to buyer) of any third parties whose consent or approval is necessary with respect to the contracts to be assigned to the buyer (in addition, the parties should specify any material contracts where consent to assignment is required to be obtained prior to the closing).

➢ Notify the buyer of any unusual and significant problems or developments not in the ordinary course of business with respect to the station's business or the assets so that an uninterrupted and efficient transfer may be made.

➢ Pay all premiums for and maintain in full force and effect all existing insurance policies.

➢ Give prompt notice to the buyer of any occurrence of which the seller has actual knowledge that constitutes a misrepresentation, breach of warranty, or non-fulfillment of any covenant or condition by the seller contained in the agreement.

➢ Provide the buyer (and its authorized agents) reasonable access during reasonable business hours to the assets of the station and furnish the buyer such information concerning the station's affairs as the buyer may reasonably request.

In contrast to affirmative covenants, which require the seller to take affirmative steps to accomplish some objective, negative covenants prohibit the seller from undertaking certain actions without the prior consent of the buyer. Negative covenants might include prohibitions on:

➢ Canceling, modifying, altering, amending, encumbering, or in any way discharging, terminating, or impairing any contracts, leases or agreements pertaining to the station except in the ordinary course of business.

- Surrendering, modifying adversely, forfeiting, or failing to renew under regular terms the FCC authorizations with respect to the station or giving the FCC grounds to issue a monetary sanction or institute any proceeding for the revocation, suspension or modification of any such FCC authorization, or failing to prosecute with due diligence any pending applications.

- Selling or disposing of any of the assets material to the operation of the station other than in the usual and ordinary course of business, unless replacement assets are acquired prior to the closing.

- Creating, suffering or permitting the creation of any mortgage, conditional sales agreement, security interest, lien, hypothecation, pledge, encumbrance, restriction, or other liability on the assets.

- Increasing the compensation, expense allowance or other benefits payable or to become payable to any employee or to any agent of the station other than in the ordinary course of business consistent with the seller's historical practice.

- Failing to repair or maintain any of its transmitting, studio, and other technical equipment or any other equipment, supplies, and other tangible personal property used or usable in the operations of the station in accordance with the normal standards of maintenance applicable in the broadcast industry.

- Taking any action that would allow a material adverse change in the financial condition of the station.

- Making any material changes in the format or programming policies of the station except such changes as in the good faith judgment of the seller are required by the public interest, and then only upon reasonable notice to the buyer of the change.

➤ Shopping the station. Such a "no shop" provision prohibits the seller and its principals from shopping the station in the hope of procuring a better offer. A seller who has found a new buyer willing to pay more for the station might well be predisposed toward making pretextual claims concerning the buyer's compliance with the terms of the purchase agreement in an effort to scuttle the original agreement – thus permitting the unscrupulous seller to enter into a purchase agreement with the new buyer and depriving the original buyer of the benefit of the bargain that it had struck. Even if the seller can find no basis to claim that the original buyer is in breach of the purchase agreement, such a recalcitrant seller is likely to do everything in its power to delay the closing in the hope that it will be able to terminate the agreement upon the purchase agreement's "drop dead" date. Including a no shop provision in the purchase agreement eliminates the disincentive to close that would exist if seller had a new buyer waiting in the wings. A well-drafted no shop provision should be broadly drafted so that the seller cannot easily do an end run around the provision. It should thus prohibit seller and any of seller's principals from directly or indirectly soliciting, entertaining, negotiating with any person or entity, or accepting any proposal to acquire the station, the seller or any of the station assets in whole or in part. Read in conjunction with the other limitations placed in the purchase agreement, it should also prohibit the seller from terminating the purchase agreement if seller has violated the "no shop" provision. Otherwise, seller could violate the no shop provision with impunity simply by engaging in obstreperous conduct that makes it impossible to close until after the drop-dead date.

Further Covenants of the Buyer

Some agreements devote a section to describing covenants of the buyer, including that the buyer is financially and legally qualified (*e.g.*, compliance with the FCC's character policy, the radio multiple ownership rules, alien ownership restrictions) and has agreed to file promptly an application for assignment of license or transfer of control with the FCC.

Restrictive Covenants

In many transactions, the seller and/or some or all of its principal shareholders or executives agree not to compete with the buyer for a specified period in a specified market area. In many cases, a separate covenant not to compete or non-competition agreement is attached as an exhibit.

Risk of Loss

Unless otherwise specifically negotiated, this section makes clear that the seller bears the risk of any loss, damage, or impairment of any of the assets that takes place prior to the closing. It usually obligates the seller to replace, repair, or restore such assets to their prior condition as soon as possible. This provision might provide representations concerning casualty insurance and specifically require the seller to assume the risk for all deductibles.

Termination or Breach

This section discusses the rights of the buyer and the seller to terminate the agreement, as a matter of right or due to breach or default by the other party. There are usually different provisions in this section depending on whether the termination or breach of contract is caused by the seller's breach or default, the buyer's breach or default, or events beyond the control of either party, such as the FCC's failure to grant consent. Termination is usually effected after the provision of written notice (usually 30 days), which gives the breaching party an opportunity to cure the breach. Some agreements specify a fixed, pre-determined amount, referred to as liquidated damages, which the buyer must pay to the seller in the event buyer fails to close. Generally, the courts will uphold the amount agreed upon by the parties as liquidated damages if they are a reasonable estimate of the actual damages that the parties could suffer in the future.

As noted earlier, the "earnest money escrow deposit" usually serves as an available liquid asset pool to secure the payment of at least a portion of the liquidated damages for the seller. One contract contained the following provision detailing the basis of liquidated damages:

> The Buyer and the Seller acknowledge that in the

event that the transactions contemplated by this Agreement are not closed because of a default by the Buyer, the Adverse Consequences to the Seller as a result of such default may be difficult, if not impossible, to ascertain. Accordingly, in lieu of indemnification pursuant to Section 7(c), the Seller shall be entitled to receive from the defaulting Party for such default the Earnest Money Deposit as liquidated damages without the need for proof of damages, subject only to successfully proving in a court of competent jurisdiction that the Buyer materially breached this Agreement and that the transactions contemplated thereby have not occurred. The Seller shall proceed against the Earnest Money Deposit as full satisfaction of liquidated damages owed by the Buyer and as its sole remedy for a failure of the transactions contemplated hereby to occur as a result of a material breach of the terms of this Agreement by the Buyer.

The liquidated damages provision may not pass court muster, however, unless the damages resulting from a breach are incapable or difficult to estimate and the stipulation of damages in the provision is a reasonable forecast of just compensation.

Most agreements include a specific performance clause that entitles the buyer to obtain a judicial order requiring the seller to sell the station to the buyer in the event of breach or default by the seller. Such clauses usually contain a statement that the seller stipulates that the assets include unique property that cannot be readily obtained on the open market and that the buyer will be irreparably injured if the Asset Purchase Agreement is not specifically enforced. In addition, there is typically a provision that the seller agrees to waive the defense in any lawsuit that buyer has an adequate remedy at law and to interpose no objection to the propriety of specific performance as a remedy. Because of the many variables that can delay the grant of an application by the FCC (*e.g.*, the filing of a petition to deny or an informal objection), many agreements provide for a contract expiration date (typically nine months to one year from the filing of the application) and permit either party to withdraw if the FCC designates the application for a hearing, regardless of the timing.

Survival of Representations and Warranties

This section specifies the period of time that the representations and warranties of the buyer and the seller will remain effective beyond the closing. This is an important issue for both the seller and the buyer. There is a natural tension between the parties on the survival period. From the point of view of the buyer, the seller's representations and warranties should survive the closing to the extent of the applicable statute(s) of limitations for pursuing breaches or violations of the agreement. The seller, by contrast, generally wants to limit the length of time that its representations and warranties will remain effective. A lengthy survival period may mean that the seller (or its business entity) will be required to remain in existence longer than the seller's principals wish. In fact, the buyer may insist that the purchase agreement include a provision requiring that the seller remain in existence until the expiration of the survival period to help ensure that the seller will be available and able to stand behind its representations and warranties.

Various approaches can resolve the tension and determine the survival period of representations and warranties. Typically, the parties will agree on a fixed period of time within which the representations and warranties survive, and after which no claims can be made for breach. The shortest typical deadline is generally six months after the closing. Two years is typical of the longest deadline, with certain representations (such as those for taxes, environmental liabilities, title, fees to brokers, and the Employee Retirement Income Security Act (ERISA), if applicable) continuing through the applicable statute of limitations. Some agreements provide that the representations and warranties will survive for one audit period (typically not more than 18 months). The deadlines may vary depending on the nature of the warranty. There may be several categories into which warranties are allocated. For example, some agreements provide for no time limitation on the representations of the seller concerning its authority to engage in the transaction or its title to the real estate. In some instances, the asset purchase agreement places no limitations on survival: "All representations, warranties, covenants and agreements contained in this Agreement, or in any certificate, agreement, or other document or instrument, delivered pursuant hereto, shall survive (and not be affected in any respect by) the Closing, any investigation conducted by any party hereto and any information which any party may receive."

Indemnification by the Buyer and the Seller

This section describes the procedures and the limitations for indemnification in the event of a breach of contract. ("Indemnification" refers to the obligation to reimburse a party for all or some part of the expenses and damages sustained). The indemnification section typically requires the seller (and sometimes, its shareholders and principals) to indemnify the buyer not only for breaches of warranties, representations and covenants but also for other kinds of claims (such as tax or environmental liabilities) that may occur after the closing but were not assumed by the buyer. In some transactions, the indemnification obligation is secured with an escrow of a portion of the purchase price or an offset of payments relating to a non-competition agreement or a promissory note. Also, the indemnification section creates liability for the seller after the date of the closing even for matters that the seller had no knowledge of before the closing. For example, a typical indemnification clause may require the seller to indemnify the buyer from any post-closing claim resulting from a pre-closing "act, omission or event."

Some clauses provide for unlimited indemnification but must be qualified by a number of requirements. Other indemnification provisions specify a "cap" or maximum amount of coverage, an amount which frequently equals the total purchase price. Others provide for a safety net, or "basket," which is a minimum amount of loss that the indemnified party must exceed before the obligation of the "indemnitor" (the party who is obligated to indemnify the other party against the loss or damage) becomes effective – it is, in effect, a deductible. One of the purposes of such a threshold deductible is to avoid disputes over insignificant amounts of money. The amount of the basket usually depends on the size of the transaction – the larger the purchase price, the more likely the basket will be greater. Some buyers negotiate for a "threshold" deductible that, once crossed, entitles the indemnifying party to cover all damages rather than just the losses that exceed the amount of the basket.

The parties should keep in mind that an indemnification is worth only as much as the indemnitor. Some companies may not be able to stand behind their indemnification. If the seller plans to dissolve or disband after the closing, special arrangements should be made to specify who will be responsible under the indemnification section of the agreement (*e.g.*, the main stockholders or principals of the seller) Also, some buyers insist on the execution of a post-closing indemnification escrow agreement to secure indemnification rights and also obtain set-off rights with respect to the collection of seller's accounts receivable and payments under promissory notes. In recent years, some sellers have negotiated for the use of new insurance products to insure representations and warranties to back indemnification, although the premiums for such policies can be quite expensive.

As discussed more extensively in Chapter Three, if the transaction and the parties are of sufficient size, a filing is required under the Hart-Scott-Rodino Antitrust Improvements of 1976. The filing fee is quite significant (currently, $45,000.00 for transactions between $65.2 million and $130.3 million) and must be paid by the buyer in full to the Federal Trade Commission. The parties usually negotiate whether the fee will be paid by the buyer or split (in some percentage) by seller and buyer.

Fees and Expenses

Typically, each party bears its own expenses in connection with the preparation, execution and performance of the agreement. The seller and the buyer usually split FCC filing fees. Additionally, in some cases, parties each agree to pay one-half of any sales tax

and any realty, transfer, recording or documentary stamp charges. In other agreements, the parties agree to pay such taxes and fees in accordance with local custom.

Collection of Accounts Receivable

In transactions where the buyer agrees to collect the accounts receivable on behalf of the seller, this section specifies the procedures for collection and the timing of payments.

An issue commonly addressed is what happens when the buyer receives payment from an advertiser or agency that placed advertising on the station prior to the closing. The following is a typical provision contained in an asset purchase agreement:

Common Accounts. During the Collection Period, if Buyer receives a payment from an advertiser or agency ("Account Debtor") who has (i) placed advertising on the Station both prior to and after the Commencement Date, and (ii) has been invoiced both as a [Seller's] Receivable and as an account receivable of Buyer (a "Common Account"), such payment shall be applied to the oldest outstanding balance due from that Account Debtor, unless such payment is specifically identified

39

(by check, correspondence or accompanying invoice) as a payment on a specific receivable owed on a Common Account, in which case such payment shall be applied as directed (provided, however, that Buyer shall not encourage or solicit any Account Debtor to direct that a payment be applied to an account receivable of Buyer while any Receivables owed by such Account Debtor remain outstanding). Following expiration of the Collection Period, Buyer shall not be obligated to apply any payment received from a Common Account to the oldest outstanding balance due from that Account Debtor, and Buyer may apply such payment first to its own receivables, unless such payment is specifically identified (by check, correspondence or accompanying invoice) as a payment on a specific receivable owed on a Common Account, in which case such payment shall be applied as directed. If such payment is directed to a specific Receivable of Seller after the Collection Period, Buyer shall forward the proceeds of such payment directly to the Seller.

Brokerage and Brokerage Fees

This section indicates whether a broker or finder is involved and, if so, identifies the person or company entitled to a fee and the party responsible for payment of the fee. Usually, the seller pays any broker's or finder's fee. For a broader discussion of broker's fees, see "Before and After Signing the Contract," Chapter Five.

Bulk Sales Compliance

Some states still have bulk sales notification laws that require the buyer to notify the seller's creditors of the intended sale of substantially all of an entity's assets in advance of closing but these laws are usually applicable only to the sale of a business that is based on sales from inventory – and are thus not applicable to a sale of a radio station. It is unlikely that the purchaser of a radio station's assets must notify creditors of the seller but counsel should be consulted to determine whether there is any such requirement.

Many states, however, have laws that impose certain outstanding tax liabilities of the seller on the purchaser of a business. These states allow a purchaser to protect itself against such successor liability by obtaining from the seller a certificate from the state's taxation authority declaring that the seller has no outstanding liability for the types of taxes for which successor liability is imposed.

Notices

This section lists the name and address of parties to whom notices concerning the agreement should be sent and specifies the manner of giving notices (*e.g.*, by hand, email, facsimile, registered mail, or overnight courier).

Governing Law

This section specifies which state's or commonwealth's law will govern the interpretation and enforcement of the agreement. The clause will specify the particular state's substantive law while expressly excluding the state's conflict of law rules. Such an approach avoids the uncertainty that the selected state might, in turn, refer to the laws of another state unanticipated by the parties. Finally, the governing law clause may also include a "forum selection" provision which dictates the state, and perhaps the court, in which any lawsuit must be filed, as well as a waiver of a right to trial by jury by each of the parties.

Confidentiality

This section describes the agreement of the parties to respect the confidentiality of information received from the other party during the transaction. Many agreements contain a provision concerning how publicity or other disclosures of the existence or terms of the transaction will be handled.

Successors and Assigns

This section provides for the assignment of rights and obligations under the agreement. Most agreements provide that the buyer may not assign its rights and obligations without the prior written consent of the seller. A common provision allows the buyer to assign the agreement without the seller's consent to an entity controlled by or under the common control of the buyer.

Entire Agreement

This section, also known as a merger or integration clause, recites that the terms of the asset purchase agreement (including schedules, exhibits and closing and ancillary documents) constitute the entire agreement of the parties. It is intended to clarify the terms of the parties' relationship by excluding or superseding any earlier agreements or understandings between the parties that do not appear in the final definitive agreement, such as any letter of intent.

Amendment

Most acquisition agreements provide that the agreement may

not be amended except in writing signed by the parties. A typical provision is worded as follows:

> This Agreement may be amended, modified or superseded, and any of the terms, covenants, representations, warranties or conditions hereof may be waived, only by a written instrument executed on behalf of all of the parties or in the case of a waiver, by the party waiving compliance.

Severability

Sometimes in the course of litigation or a regulatory proceeding, a court or governmental agency may hold that a particular provision of the parties' agreement is unenforceable. This section provides that the remainder of the agreement shall not be affected by any provision that is declared invalid or unenforceable.

Time Is of the Essence

Courts generally will not find that time is of the essence in a contract unless it is specifically provided or the circumstances clearly indicate that it was the intent of the parties. In the absence of a "time is of the essence" clause, a "reasonable" time for performance will be implied by the courts if a problem arises as to any timing issue. To avoid this problem, parties customarily include such a clause in the contract. It enables them to take advantage of "drop dead" termination provisions and other contractual requirements where timing is critical.

Arbitration

Some agreements provide that any dispute that the seller and the buyer are unable to resolve by themselves will be settled by arbitration. This section sets forth how the arbitrator or arbitrators will be chosen, the standards to govern the arbitration, the venue for the arbitration, and how the costs of the arbitration will be allocated among the parties. Court litigation is time-consuming, expensive, and often involves unwanted adverse publicity. For this reason, arbitration has become an increasingly popular way of resolving contract disputes. An arbitrator has the authority to enter into a binding, court-enforceable judgment from which only the most limited kind of appeal will be allowed.

Many contracts specify that the arbitrator must use the commercial arbitration rules of the American Arbitration Association. For example, one asset purchase agreement provided that "[i]f any dispute should arise with respect to the interpretation of any provision of this contract, it shall be resolved by arbitration pursuant to the Uniform Arbitration Act as adopted by Maine, 14 M.R.S.A. §§ 5927 *et seq.*, pursuant to the Commercial Arbitration Rules of the American Arbitration Association."

Another asset purchase agreement provided for the settlement of contract disputes in Washington, DC by a panel of three arbitrators. The agreement provided that "Seller and Buyer shall each designate one disinterested arbitrator, and the two arbitrators so designated shall select the third arbitrator." In order to assure that arbitration is handled by persons familiar with radio, the agreement states that persons selected as arbitrators "need not be professional arbitrators, and persons such as buyers, accountants, brokers and bankers shall be acceptable." The agreement also provides that "[t]he arbitration hearing shall be conducted in accordance with the commercial arbitration rules of the American Arbitration Association" and that "[t]he written decision of a majority of the arbitrators shall be final and binding on Seller and Buyer."

Arbitration can save both the seller and buyer time and money because the rules and deadlines for collecting and revealing information relevant to the dispute are less formal than in a traditional lawsuit. In addition, many broadcasters prefer arbitration over litigation because the disputes are heard by "neutrals" who decide cases on fairness and equity and often know the radio business better than

judges. On the other hand, some broadcasters prefer the courts to adjudicate disputes based on their belief that arbitration generally results in compromises with neither party winning outright. There is also a belief that arbitration provisions can encourage buyers to contest relatively trivial matters as disputes that might not be worth litigating might be worth the lesser time commitment and expense of arbitration.

No Third Party Beneficiary

This section usually specifies that the agreement confers no rights, remedies, rights or obligations on any parties (*e.g.*, employees, brokers, etc.) other than the seller, the buyer and their permitted assigns.

Counterparts

This section provides that the agreement may be executed in one or more counterparts as if the signature on each counterpart were on the same document. Delivery of signatures by facsimile or other electronic means such as an Adobe Acrobat ® (pdf) document may be authorized.

Schedules and Exhibits

Most acquisition agreements include extensive schedules (sometimes called "disclosure schedules") that identify the specific assets (equipment inventory, contracts), and that support or list any exceptions to the representations and warranties. Failure to disclose a matter on a schedule could be grounds for the buyer's refusal to close or, in the event that the representation or warranty survives the closing, for the seller's liability under the indemnity provisions of the acquisition agreement. Generally sellers will seek to absolve themselves of responsibility for items that they have scheduled and disclosed to the buyer (e.g., defective studio equipment, a threatened lawsuit, etc.). On the other hand, buyers want to avoid responsibility for anything that occurred prior to the closing and may require language in the purchase asset that disclaims such liability. Where an item disclosed in the schedule is significant, the parties will need to negotiate who is responsible for the disclosed item after the closing.

The disclosure schedules are normally prepared in advance of signing the acquisition agreement in order to allow the buyer sufficient time to review them. Sometimes when the parties desire to sign an agreement before the preparation of the schedules, the acquisition agreement will provide that the schedules must be submitted to the buyer within a fixed period of time (usually 30 days) and will set forth the conditions under which buyer may terminate the agreement if certain conditions relating to the information to be supplied are not satisfied. The buyer's rights under such a provision can range from an absolute right to terminate if the disclosure schedules are not provided at the agreed-upon time, or if buyer is not satisfied with the information supplied in the schedules, or as a result of its due diligence to a more limited right to terminate, if for example, the schedules reveal any material adverse information or material adverse change.

Typical Schedules

FCC Authorizations
Other Authorizations, Permits and Licenses
Description of Tangible Personal Property
Description of Real Property
Contracts, Agreements and Leases
Required Consents
Intangible Assets
Allocation of Purchase Price (parties often wait until the closing or later)
Pending or Threatened Litigation

Financial Statements
Labor Agreements and
Compliance
Employee Benefit Plans
Insurance
Tax Obligations and Returns

"The devil is in the details" is a phrase with particular applicability to the schedules. Hard-fought representations and warranties negotiated by the buyer can be undone by a lack of care and focus in the review of disclosure schedules. Similarly, the seller needs to take special care in the preparation of schedules to make sure that exceptions to general representations and warranties are expressly disclosed.

Exhibits contain the proposed form of ancillary documents that the parties intend to sign in connection with the acquisition agreement and the closing on the acquisition.

The following list identifies exhibits that typically accompany, and are made a part of, the acquisition agreement:

Typical Exhibits

Escrow Agreement
Post-Closing Indemnity
Escrow Agreement
Local (or Time Brokerage)
Marketing Agreement
Non-Competition Agreement
Consulting Agreement
Promissory Note
Guaranty Agreement(s)

Security Agreement
Rescission (or Unwind)
Agreement*
Opinion Letters of Buyer's
Counsel and Seller's Counsel**

Some acquisition agreements also contain as exhibits the form of certain closing documents (*e.g.*, assignment and assumption agreements, bills of sale, lease estoppel certificates, certificates, opinion letters).

---

* See Chapter Three for a discussion of rescission or unwind agreements. Appendix H contains a sample Rescission Agreement.

** For guidance on the drafting of opinion letters by communications lawyers, see *Report of the Subcommittee on Legal Opinions of the Transactional Practice Committee of the Federal Communications Bar Association*, 48 FEDERAL COMMUNICATIONS LAW JOURNAL 389 (1996).

CHAPTER THREE

GIVING THE DEAL ITS DUE (DILIGENCE)

Generally speaking, the due diligence process consists of the investigation and evaluation of the financial condition and operations history of a business enterprise. The purpose of due diligence is to obtain information about the strengths and weaknesses of the target enterprise, potential legal or other obligations or vulnerabilities, cash flow and future profit potential, competitive position, and other matters that can help the buyer decide whether to go forward with a purchase. If the acquisition is completed, the same information derived from the due diligence process can provide the buyer critical guidance for initial operating decisions. An acquisition is certainly one of the more complex and risky business activities a businessperson can undertake. A thorough due diligence review will help a buyer define acceptable levels of risk.

The due diligence process involved in the acquisition of a radio station should include a review of the general economic and operating conditions as well as such areas as the financial and accounting systems, sales, programming, technical facilities, legal matters, marketing, FCC compliance, employee benefits, taxes, personnel and environmental matters. The objective of the due diligence review is to obtain information that will not only help decide whether or not to proceed with the acquisition but also assist in determining the amount of the purchase price or projected working capital adjustment. This chapter discusses the legal and engineering due diligence process but does not cover the extensive business due diligence that each buyer necessarily must accomplish.

The extent of the due diligence investigation depends on the experience and needs of the buyer, the magnitude of the purchase price, time constraints affecting the transaction and various other factors. For example, the financial scope of the effort may range from reviewing the prior year's financial statements and tax returns to a complete audit examination as of a specified date.

The scope and intensity of the due diligence effort should be balanced against the potential losses associated with an unsuccessful acquisition. The scope of the buyer's investigation prior to the execution of the agreement or the closing will depend in part on the nature of the representations and warranties contained in the acquisition agreement, whether the representations and warranties will survive the closing, the strength of the indemnification provisions and the financial ability of the seller to meet any event calling for indemnification. If the representations will not survive the closing or there is no effective provision for indemnification spelled out in the acquisition agreement, a more exhaustive investigation is warranted.

Timing

The more information you gather in the early stages of an acquisition the better position you will be in to understand the strengths and weaknesses of the target station, to anticipate crucial issues and to determine the areas that will affect the purchase price. Common "deal breakers" that may be uncovered in the first stage of the due diligence process include inaccurate financial representations, legal and environmental contingencies, title to and condition of the assets, onerous employment and/or union contracts, tower leases which have a short remaining term or are not assignable, under-funded pension plans and other burdensome post-employment obligations which the buyer would assume.

The Due Diligence Team

The buyer's investigation should be a team effort and should encompass an examination of business,

engineering, accounting and financial, and legal issues. Ideally, the due diligence investigation and development of the business plan should be conducted by a team of executives and professionals who will continue to be associated with the buyer if the deal goes through. In selecting outside advisors, it is very important to inquire about their previous experience in buying or selling radio stations and confirm their track records and references. Because broadcast executives or acquisition consultants, engineers, lawyers and accountants each have a tendency to focus solely on their individual areas of expertise, it is important that the evaluation in these specialized areas be coordinated with one another. A failure to appreciate the roles of the others may result in the failure to pass on essential information and to make a complete assessment of problems that arise; rarely do problems encountered in an acquisition review affect solely one particular area (*e.g.*, engineering). Each investigator should strive to keep other members of the team informed, and the coordinator must see to it that there are frequent exchanges of information.

One person should be responsible for coordinating the due diligence investigation and ensuring that the work is completed in a timely manner. The coordinator can be an experienced transaction lawyer, an acquisitions consultant, or a seasoned officer or employee of the buyer. Such a person should serve as a central point of communication and should be familiar with all of the data accumulated in order to answer any questions that may arise. He or she must identify significant problem areas and promptly bring them to the attention of the buyer's decision-makers.

Legal Review

The legal due diligence process is a team effort, employing primarily the expertise of lawyers and accountants specializing in different areas, such as corporate, tax, labor, employment benefits, FCC, environment and real property, all working together with the buyer. The legal due diligence process often begins prior to reaching an agreement in principle with the seller, and continues throughout the acquisition process. Indeed, a major objective of the definitive acquisition agreement (particularly the warranties and representations) is to obtain information necessary for, and to verify the results of, a due diligence investigation. It may save time once an agreement in principle is reached to request copies of the documents which you will eventually attempt to elicit for the definitive agreement. Most buyers will not sign the definitive agreement until satisfactory due diligence has been conducted, or

in the alternative, a provision is included in the agreement which allows the buyer to terminate the transaction in the event that the results of due diligence review are not satisfactory.

The acquisition agreement should provide the buyer with the opportunity to undertake business, engineering and legal investigations. The scope of the due diligence investigation prior to closing may depend in part on the nature of the representations and warranties contained in the acquisition agreement, whether the representations and warranties will survive the closing, and the strength of the indemnification provisions. If the representations will not survive the closing, or if no effective provision for indemnification exists, completing an exhaustive investigation will be more important. While all acquisition agreements contain representations and warranties and usually indemnification provisions, it is far more preferable to unearth all possible liabilities before the buyer executes the agreement, rather than resort to a lawsuit after the sale.

The results of the due diligence investigation will assist the buyer in evaluating the transaction and providing needed protection. Even though the due diligence process is generally the same whether stock or assets are acquired, what is discovered in the process may lead the buyer to decide whether an asset or a stock acquisition is preferable. If a stock purchase agreement is entered into, a prudent buyer will negotiate for stronger representations and warranties to secure protection against hidden liabilities.

It is the responsibility of the lawyer to prepare an acquisition agreement tailored to the facts and circumstances of the particular transaction. For example, if in reviewing financial data the accountant uncovers past income-tax deficiencies of the seller, the buyer's lawyer should include in the agreement a provision stating that the buyer is not liable for the tax obligations of the seller. Also, the buyer should undertake a comprehensive legal investigation, which should include the seller's litigation history, any FCC problems, contractual obligations, liabilities, ownership of realty and personalty, labor relations obligations, copyrights, trademarks and licenses, and obligations to brokers and finders.

Checklist of Legal Issues

The following checklist highlights some of the issues that might be included in the legal due diligence process:

A. The Seller as a Business Entity

☐ If the seller is a corporation, partnership, or limited liability company, ascertain the identity of the shareholders, partners or members and what rights each possesses. If the shareholder group is numerous, the mechanics of a stock transaction may be quite complex and an asset deal may be preferable. Check whether there have been agreements imposing restrictions on the sale of ownership interests (such agreements must be filed with the FCC).

☐ Obtain copies of the appropriate charter documents and shareholder, partnership or membership agreements, if any, in order to ascertain, among other things, any difficulty in obtaining consents to the transaction, priority rights of preferred holders and acceleration of obligations. Ascertain whether there are unusual provisions in any of these documents.

☐ Determine the existence and terms of any options (including any on outstanding stock), warrants and convertible securities. A large number of shareholders can create problems in having documents executed and gives additional bargaining power to minority holders.

☐ If the selling corporation is publicly owned, inspect the reports required to be filed with the Securities and Exchange Commission and with state Blue Sky commissions. Such records include corporate annual reports, applications for the listing of securities on stock exchanges, proxy statements and annual and other reports to shareholders.

☐ If the seller has operations in another state or is an entity formed under any law other than the state in which the buyer's lawyer practices, buyer's counsel should discuss the transaction with an experienced lawyer in the other state so as to ascertain whether there are any legal provisions applicable to the transaction of which he or she is not aware. For example, California has very restrictive laws with respect to non-competition agreements. In general, if the non-competition agreement is entered into by a person employed in California who is not an owner of the seller, the agreement might not be enforceable in California – a California court may not enforce the non-competition agreement even if it contained a choice of law provision selecting the buyer's jurisdiction where it would be enforceable.

☐ Ascertain in which states the seller does business or owns and leases property and whether, if a corporation, limited liability company or partnership, it is in good standing with appropriate governmental agencies.

☐ Check the applicable state laws as to whether compliance with the bulk sales laws is required in connection with the purchase of assets of the seller and, if so, how compliance is achieved. Determine the effect of noncompliance and whether there is a need to place in escrow a portion of the purchase price.

❑ Ascertain whether there are any corporations, limited liability companies or partnerships owned or affiliated with the seller, what their function is, who else owns an interest, and obtain copies of all charter documents.

❑ Obtain information concerning the size of the seller and of the transaction in order to ascertain whether pre-notification filing is required under the Hart-Scott-Rodino Antitrust Improvements Act of 1976 (HSR). HSR requires the parties to certain transactions to provide the Federal Trade Commission (FTC) and the Antitrust Division of the Department of Justice with information about the operations of the companies involved and of the details concerning the proposed deal. Transactions with a total value of under $65.2 million need not be reported. Transactions with a total value in excess of this threshold, but less than $260.7 million, must be reported only if the seller's annual sales equal or exceed $13 million and the buyer has annual sales or assets of $130.3 million or more. All transactions with a total value of $260.7 million or more must be reported regardless of the size of the participating parties.* If a filing is required, both the buyer and the seller must file a Notification and Report Form with the FTC and the Justice Department's Antitrust Division. The filing begins a 30-day waiting period during which the FTC and the Department of Justice

---

* Under HSR, the dollar thresholds are required to be adjusted each fiscal year beginning with fiscal 2005, for the percentage change in the gross national product compared with fiscal 2003. The thresholds stated above took effect on February 12, 2009.

will review the proposed transaction. The parties may not close the sale or merger during this 30-day period, although they may request an early termination of the waiting period.

B. The FCC's Files

☐ Since a station's file at the FCC is open to the public and copies of the documents in the files can be obtained from the Commission without the seller's knowledge, examination of the contents of such a file is a good place to start the due diligence process. The FCC's files are located at the main office of the Commission, 445 12th Street, S.W., Washington, D.C. Also, much information concerning the seller may be obtained by surfing the FCC's website (www.fcc.gov). Although most of the information contained in the FCC's files will also be available at the station in the "local inspection file" that licensees are required by the FCC to maintain, buyers generally prefer the anonymity of obtaining information directly from the Commission.

☐ The FCC's files will contain information with respect to (a) how and when the station was acquired by the seller, (b) the license, (c) complaints, (d) any construction permits obtained or applications pending with respect to the station (including coverage contour maps), (e) biennial ownership reports, (f) option agreements, management agreements, trust documents, partnership agreements, articles of incorporation, bylaws, stock pledge agreements, and (g) license renewal applications, which will include a statement concerning the station's compliance with the American National Standards Institute (ANSI) guidelines governing RF radiation. A review of the FCC's files will also reveal seller's compliance with FCC reporting and notification requirements and whether any conditions or qualifications have been attached to the licenses and other authorizations.

☐ Ascertain whether the persons in control of the seller have had any difficulties with the FCC or any state or other federal agencies. Unresolved character issues involving the seller can create severe timing problems and may jeopardize a transaction. The records on file at the FCC include a "complaints file" which will indicate whether any pending problems exist that would be likely to impede FCC approval of the sale. An examination of the complaints file will also indicate whether the licensee of the station has paid attention to compliance with FCC requirements. Also, as discussed further in Chapter 4, check whether an application is pending to renew the license of the station — the FCC generally will not act on an assignment or transfer application until it disposes of the renewal application. In addition, the Commission now

conditions grants of assignment applications such that the parties cannot close on the transaction while the station's renewal application is pending. The FCC schedules the dates when licenses expire and the renewal deadlines such that all stations in a particular state are required to file at the same time. Appendix F contains a table listing the license expiration dates and renewal application filing deadlines for radio stations in each of the 50 states, the District of Columbia, and U.S. territories and possessions. Timing of the submission of an assignment or transfer application can be critical if the station being sold is approaching the date for the filing of its renewal application. Filing the assignment or transfer application close to, or shortly after, the date for filing the station's renewal application can result in a delay in the closing by several months.

❐ The FCC's files also contain copies of any prior assignment of license or transfer of control applications. These applications are of particular value to potential buyers since they contain a copy of Asset Purchase and Stock Purchase Agreements. These agreements can provide a prospective purchaser with key information, such as the amount paid for the station by the current owner, and can alert the prospective purchaser to problems with the station, such as environmental problems or technical deficiencies that were required to be corrected as a condition of a previous proposed sale.

❐ Also in the FCC's files are copies of facilities modification applications and requests for special temporary authority filed by the station. These applications and requests can provide insight as to technical problems encountered by the station or coverage deficiencies. Not all of the material in the FCC's files is routinely available to members of the public through an examination of the station file available at the Commission's main office. Most notably, certain information concerning complaints on file with the Commission's Enforcement Bureau, EEO matters, and political complaints and investigations can be obtained only by sending letters requesting such information to the Enforcement Bureau, the Equal Employment Opportunity Branch, and the Office of Political Programming. It is the policy of the Enforcement Bureau to respond to such inquiries in writing through an email sent to the requesting party. In addition, the Enforcement Bureau now posts its orders at http://www.fcc. gov/eb/Orders/Welcome. html. The Commission's field offices also post the Citations, Notices of Violation and Notices of Apparent Liability issued by them at http://www.fcc. gov/eb/Orders/Welcome. html.

C. FCC Licenses

☐ Since the most important asset the buyer will be acquiring is the FCC license, diligence must be exercised in identifying the licenses held by the seller, their expiration dates, any matters which might impede or delay transfer of the license, and any restrictions imposed on the seller.

☐ The broadcasting industry is faced with environmental issues concerning antennas and radio frequency (RF) radiation. In order to renew a license, the licensee must conduct an RF study at the time of renewal. It is important to ascertain whether the seller, at the time of the filing of its application for renewal of the license, advised the FCC that the station complied with RF guidelines. The buyer must also report whether it has been sanctioned or fined by the FCC in the preceding license term for violations of FCC rules.

☐ Finally, the buyer must perform some due diligence on itself to determine whether it complies with FCC rules and policies governing alien or foreign ownership, multiple ownership restrictions, and character qualifications.

D. Real Property

☐ Ascertain whether real property is owned or leased by the seller and whether there are any encumbrances, liens or charges, including tax liens, mortgages, rights of way and easements, restrictions and reversionary rights.

☐ Review the deeds or certificates of title on the land and buildings.

☐ Obtain copies of all real property leases for leased property or title reports with respect to real property owned by the seller. The location of the tower, antenna and studio and the length of the term of leases for these premises should be verified. The length of the remaining term of a tower lease is a matter of critical importance where the target station operates with a directional antenna or is in an environmentally sensitive area. Lenders generally require that the term of the lease be equal to or longer than the term of the loan; buyers may desire even longer leases to ensure the salability of the station in the future.

☐ If the tower being used to support the station's antenna is guyed, it must be determined whether the guy anchors are located on the property and whether the guy wires pass over property belonging to another party.

☐ Check leases to make certain they are assignable without the lessor's consent. Determine the requirements for consent and whether there will be any change in terms upon the assignment. Some states have upheld provisions in leases that prohibit assignment without the consent of the lessor; other states construe such provisions to require that consent cannot be unreasonably withheld. As noted above, assignability is particularly important for tower leases of directional stations. Where the landlord consents to the assignment of the leases, consider obtaining an estoppel certificate or its equivalent confirming the basic terms of the lease as well as the fact that the lessee is not in default, that the lease has not been modified, and that it is in full force and effect. If the lender has particular requirements concerning the lease or the landlord's waiver of rights, make sure that the lease can be amended to comply with those requirements and ensure that the landlord is willing to enter into such a waiver of rights.

☐ If the seller owns the tower site, check whether there are subleases and the type of equipment on the tower.

☐ Check zoning or other local laws to see if they restrict expanding the studio or increasing the size of the tower or antenna or contain any other conditions which may adversely affect the operations of the station in the future.

☐ Check for neighborhood restrictions or covenants relating to signage, antenna placement, lighting, traffic and architectural styles that may restrict the buyer's flexibility and thus affect the price it is willing to pay.

☐ Determine if there are any easement or encroachment issues.

☐ Assess environmental problems (*e.g.*, hazardous waste, asbestos, PCBs, etc.).

E. Personal Property and Intangibles

☐ Ascertain what personal property is used in the operation of the station and whether it is owned, leased or subject to lien. Also determine the condition of those assets.

☐ Conduct a Uniform Commercial Code

search with the relevant office of the state (*e.g.*, the Secretary of State) and county or counties in which the station is located for any financing statements filed against the seller or any of the properties of seller.

☐ Ascertain whether the seller owns or uses any trade names, websites, domain names, trademarks, copyrighted material or other intellectual property in connection with the operation of the station. If so, and if the buyer wants to acquire these assets, determine whether there are license agreements or state and federal registrations covering them. If the seller's station has a website, Facebook page or other social networking presence, make sure that the purchase agreement includes a provision requiring the seller to assign all such rights to the buyer. The buyer may also want to consider securing additional domain name protection by obtaining the rights to domain names that are similar to seller's domain name, are a common misspelling of seller's domain name or are offensive variants of seller's name (e.g., "WWXPsucks.com").

❏ Consider whether to obtain an appraisal of the assets for tax purposes. The Internal Revenue Service requires a buyer and seller to allocate the purchase price to determine the basis and tax consequences in an asset acquisition or a stock acquisition treated as an asset acquisition. For a broader discussion, see Chapter Two.

❏ Determine whether vehicles are owned or leased. If leased, obtain details. If owned, obtain copies of the certificates of title.

F. Contracts and Leases

❏ Review existing contracts and leases to which the seller is a party to determine whether (a) they are assignable, (b) their terms are burdensome, and (c) they are terminable and the termination conditions.

Also, determine whether any of seller's contracts or leases must be assumed and analyze the consequences of terminating a major contract or lease.

❏ Carefully review contracts or leases that involve significant amounts of money or time periods. Determine the beginning and end dates and details of contracts and leases. Ascertain whether the seller is in breach or in default of any principal contract or lease. Contracts can sometimes be rewritten before the acquisition of the station, especially during times of economic stress, to provide savings and possibly new depreciation/ amortization opportunities for the buyer.

❏ Check network, syndication and other programming contracts. Make sure that the seller has provided a complete copy of each contract, including all side letters and addenda. It is not uncommon for networks and programmers to vary the terms of their "boilerplate" agreements by entering into side letters rather than by modifying the boilerplate (thus permitting the programmer to say to the next station with which it negotiates that they "never change that language"). Frequently, those side letters provide the seller with beneficial terms that are not assigned to the buyer. It helps to know, for example, that the seller has been able to avoid any fee for preempting network programming, but that buyer will not be able to take advantage of that side letter provision. It puts the seller's statement of revenues into perspective.

❏ If your company is the owner of a group of radio stations, determine whether the assumption of some contracts (*e.g.*, Arbitron or rep agreements) could affect the other stations in the group and their contracts.

❏ Investigate programming commitments, especially the amounts prepaid

for programming, obligations to run the same, terms and assignment provisions.

❏ Ascertain the amount and types of barter obligations and trade deals, and to whom they are owed. Find out whether the seller will comply fully with or reduce these obligations before closing.

❏ Ascertain whether the station has any sales representative agreements. Check the term of any agreement, its coverage and whether it may be assigned without consent.

❏ Examine loan agreements, bank agreements, and all security agreements, especially if such debt is to be assumed by the buyer.

❏ Review contracts for lease or maintenance of communications equipment (*e.g.*, telephone systems, fax machines, computer systems, wireless phones, PDA's, automation systems).

☐ Ascertain if there are any news service and/or jingle agreements.

☐ Ascertain whether there are any agreements restricting the conduct of the station's business (*e.g.*, non-competition agreements or non-competition clauses in prior purchase agreements that restrict the seller or benefit the buyer).

☐ Obtain a listing and copies of any other material agreements, including any made outside the ordinary course of business.

☐ Check whether a written or oral brokerage or finder's fee agreement has been entered into and, if such an agreement has been executed, review its terms. (From the viewpoint of both the buyer and seller, a written agreement with a broker or finder is desirable in order to eliminate the risk of unintended obligations or litigation.)

G. Insurance

☐ Check what insurance coverage exists — make certain that it is adequate. Review all insurance policies, including the carrier, amounts, limits and significant conditions and benefits for each (including deductibles).

☐ Check whether insurance policies are assignable.

☐ Determine the extent to which the seller is self-insured against risks. If the seller's insurance cost was excessive, the insurance expense may have to be reduced to permit a better approximation of past earnings.

☐ Ascertain if there is any life insurance on principals and who is the owner and beneficiary.

☐ Obtain a claims history for the last few years.

H. Litigation and Other Contingencies

☐ Check for any pending lawsuits. If any are pending, obtain names and addresses of counsel and copies of pleadings.

☐ Obtain and examine copies of lawyer responses to tax audit inquiry letters.

☐ Check if there is any threatened litigation and correspondence with governmental authorities.

☐ Obtain copies of all consent decrees, judgments, orders, settlement agreements and other agreements to which the seller is a party or is bound, and which require or prohibit any future activities.

I. Personnel

☐ Identify and obtain copies of all employment, consulting, commission, termination and severance agreements or other arrangements with personnel.

☐ In reviewing employment agreements, obtain details concerning the individuals, their duties, items and conditions, any fringe benefits included (*e.g.*, automobile insurance, club memberships) and termination arrangements (*e.g.*, severance pay and parachute payments).

☐ Obtain a copy of all management, consulting or talent contracts.

☐ Obtain an employee organization chart and a schedule or a list of all salaried personnel, including position, compensation, date of hire and status (*i.e.*, whether the employee is on a leave of absence and if so, what type and when the employee is expected to return).

☐ Determine whether a company employee manual exists and what other materials are given to prospective or new employees. The company's policy or personnel records should be checked.

☐ Ascertain whether any employees are covered by union contracts or, if not, whether there has been any union organizing activity. If so, determine whether there have been any union difficulties during the past five years (including dates, duration and settlements). Determine whether there are any formal charges pending or threatened before federal or state labor agencies.

☐ If a union contract is in place, review it for the following: term of contract, employees covered, vacation policy, sick leave policy, job security clause, successorship, arrangements concerning payment of benefit costs, restrictions on the employer's ability to change group benefit medical plans or pension plans and any unusual terms or conditions.

☐ Obtain a list and description of pending, threatened and settled grievances under any collective bargaining agreements.

☐ Ascertain the history of worker's compensation claims, including their disposition, and determine whether any claims are pending.

☐ Obtain a copy of affirmative action plans and where applicable, current form EEO-1.

☐ Review severance and vacation pay obligations to determine their impact on the buyer and whether such obligations have been properly reflected in the financial records of the target and in employee manuals.

☐ Determine whether there is any possible liability under the Federal Labor Standards Act requiring payment of time-and-a-half for overtime and minimum wage.

J. Unwanted Assets

☐ Ascertain whether there are any assets owned or leased by the seller which are unrelated to the station. These can take the form of an unrelated business or in the case of small closely-held companies, automobiles, airplanes, ships or condominiums. The existence of these items will either necessitate an asset deal excluding the transfer of these properties or a distribution of the same to the selling stockholders immediately prior to the sale of the stock.

☐ If certain real estate holdings pose environmental risks, consider excluding such property from the acquisition.

K. Environmental Audit or Assessments

☐ Obtain a copy of any documents relating to any environmental permits, investigations, orders, etc., pertaining to the real estate owned by seller.

☐ Ascertain the seller's environmental compliance history for the last five years, including the existence and status of any violations and whether any litigation has been pending or threatened with respect to any environmental matters.

☐ Ascertain the prior non-broadcast uses of all real property to be acquired.

☐ Obtain copies of any reports or site assessments prepared by environmental engineers or consultants during the past five years.

☐ Consider conducting a Phase I environmental assessment.

☐ Check if there have been any safety inspections conducted during the past five years by the Occupational Safety and Health Administration (OSHA) or state authorities. Obtain copies of any reports concerning these investigations.

☐ Check with a consulting engineer to determine whether the transmitting equipment or old equipment at the site contains any PCBs.

☐ Obtain the seller's records for the disposal of PCB materials by a qualified/certified disposal agent.

☐ Check if there is any asbestos insulation or tiles on the property.

☐ Check whether any underground or other storage tanks occupy the seller's property, and, if so, ascertain the substances contained therein (*e.g.*, No. 2 heating oil, kerosene, etc.) and the respective capacity and date of installation of each. Consider whether there is a need to obtain soil borings to determine if contamination is present.

☐ If the station's tower was constructed or modified in 2005 or more recently, did the tower owner adhere to the National Programmatic Agreement procedures? Those procedures in many cases require liaison with state historic preservation offices and Native American tribes.

L.   Problems of Disclosure

If the contemplated transaction is a stock purchase rather than an asset purchase and the company to be acquired is a publicly-traded corporation, the acquiror should be aware of the many requirements of the securities laws applicable to a stock acquisition. For example, Sections 13(d) and (g) of the Securities Exchange Act of 1934 require any person, including a group of persons acting together, to file a statement with the Securities and Exchange Commission (SEC) when that person acquires more than five percent of the equity securities or beneficial ownership of a publicly-traded entity. The acquiror must file the statement with the Commission within 10 days after the acquisition, and also send the statement to the issuer of the security and to each exchange where the security is traded. Under Sections 13(d) and 13(g), the definition of "acquires" is very broad and may be triggered by the execution of the definitive agreement, thereby requiring a filing within 10 days of signing and an amendment of the 13(d) or 13(g) filing at the closing. Information which must be disclosed includes the following:

☐ The background and identity of all persons by whom and on whose behalf the purchases have been or are to be effected.

☐ The source and amount of the funds or other consideration which was used in making the purchase.

☐ The plan or proposals for any major change in the business or corporate structure

64

of the corporation whose securities were purchased, if the purpose of the purchase or prospective purchases was to acquire control.

☐ The number of shares of the security which are beneficially owned and the number of shares of the security which the acquiror has a right to further acquire.

☐ Information as to any contracts, arrangements, or understandings with respect to any securities of the issuer.

The federal securities laws may require disclosure early in the process of carrying out the purchase. If the stock purchase is to be effectuated through a tender offer, Section 14(d) of the 1934 Act requires any person who makes a tender offer in which the person would become a beneficial owner of more than five percent of any class of an equity security registered with the SEC to file a disclosure statement at the time or invitation is first published or is first transmitted to security holders. Section 14(d) also regulates the offeror's communications to the holders of the shares for which the tender offer is made and governs certain terms of the tender offer itself.

M. Tax Liabilities

☐ Check whether all required federal, state and local tax returns have been filed, examined, and settled, including:

a. Income and excess profits taxes

b. Franchise and capital stock taxes

c. Sales and use taxes

d. Real and personal property taxes

e. Other excise taxes

☐ If a tax service is used, verify that the service has made all withholding remittances.

☐ Review correspondence to or from taxing authorities.

☐ Ascertain what taxes, if any, remain unpaid and withhold that amount at closing. If the buyer does not take this precaution, it may be held liable for the taxes under certain state statutes which impose such liability as a tax enforcement measure regardless of the good-faith intention of the parties.

Business and Financial Review

Any due diligence review of a station must include a careful analysis of the seller's business practices and financial records. At a minimum, that review should include:

- ❏ As a starting point, the buyer must be intimately familiar with the terms and conditions of the station's affiliation agreement if the station is a network affiliate. When does the affiliation agreement expire? How strong is the relationship between the station and the network? Has the relationship been mutually beneficial? Has current management been considering a change in affiliation? Is there the possibility of modifying the agreement? Are there any restrictions on the ability of the seller to assign the agreement to a third party?

- ❏ All programming agreements also must be closely reviewed to determine the profitability of the arrangements and the length of the commitment. Is the station saddled with paying fees for programming that it no longer airs? Is the station about to lose the rights to its most profitable program or personality?

- ❏ The buyer should inspect the station's accounts receivable. Are the accounts bona fide? Have there been extensive prepayments? Are there any advertisers that account for a disproportionately large share of the station's business? Are any advertisers being given unusually large discounts and has that practice extended over a protracted period?

- ❏ The buyer must also carefully assess the situation with respect to the seller's payables. Is the seller current on fees owed under its programming agreements? Is it current on its Arbitron payments? If it is streaming, is the station current on payments to SoundExchange? Are royalty payments current to ASCAP, BMI, and SESAC?

❏ Although more difficult to assess, the seller's standing in the community must be analyzed. A buyer that purchases a station that traditionally has been behind in making payments to vendors or that has a history of heavily relying on trade arrangements may find it necessary to engage in a public relations campaign to alter the community's perception of the station.

❏ All of the station's financial records must be analyzed to determine the extent to which the records are not being maintained in accordance with generally accepted accounting principles (GAAP) and to assess the impact of such noncompliance upon the station's financial outlook.

Engineering Review

A due diligence engineering review goes beyond the nuts and bolts of station equipment. While it is important to know the general condition of equipment in order to plan future purchases, other factors can have a far greater impact on station value than the condition of a control board. For example, can the power of the station be increased? Can the tower be moved to a location to serve the market better or to allow the sale of valuable real estate?

Aside from equipment and upgrade concerns, it must be determined whether the station is in compliance with the FCC's rules and regulations. There are also environmental issues including the presence of PCBs and radio frequency radiation.

The concerns in the due-diligence engineering review can be broken down into four areas: *analysis of the station's upgrade potential*; *assessment of potential competition in the market*; *operation in accordance with FCC rules and authorizations*; and *inspection of equipment.*

A. Analyze the Station's Upgrade Potential and Limitations

A qualified technical consultant can determine the potential of upgrading the coverage of a radio station without seeing the station.

❏ More power generally means more coverage and better in-building penetration. For FM stations, antenna height and location come into play as well. However, compared to FM, AM has the greatest difficulty overcoming atmospheric and man made noise. An engineering study can determine what would be needed to improve the coverage of an AM station. This might require adding towers to a directional array or changing transmitter sites to get a better signal over desired areas. A technical study can determine the improvement that is possible and what is required in terms of equipment and land to implement the improvement.

❐ The FCC encourages interference reduction among AM stations through the use of contingent applications. It may be now possible to buy a second station, turn it off, and expand coverage of the first station into the second station's former service area, provided that interference protection to other AM stations is maintained. Therefore a small, foundering AM station might be a turn-off target for a larger facility. The engineering review could include a study of stations that might be shut down in order to expand coverage, or conversely, stations that might be interested in paying to turn off the purchased facility. The FCC's AM technical assignment criteria may limit improvement potential.

❐ In FM, a channel study can help determine the upgrade potential of the facility. If an upgrade is possible, it may not be "clean." It may be necessary to change transmitter sites or pay for the frequency change of another station or a group of stations. It may be possible to use alternative coverage showings more accurate than the Commission's traditional methodologies to demonstrate that a distant transmitter site actually provides the requisite coverage of the community of license. In addition, FCC rules allow a change of the community of license of an FM station under fairly strict criteria. These rules can be used in an attempt to upgrade a station moving to a site that meets the increased separation requirements, but is so far from the city of license that the station no longer provides the requisite coverage of the community of license. Alternative coverage showings using propagation models more accurate than the models used by the FCC have sometimes been used to provide relief from these coverage criteria.

❑ If an upgrade is not possible through changing the class of a station, an upgrade within the station's class may be feasible if the station is operating with less than maximum facilities. There may be economy in co-locating with other radio stations in an area, especially if the old tower site could be sold and the new site offers a better transmitting location. Even with FM stations, directional antennas may provide increased flexibility in determining

areas to locate a new transmitter site. Newer FCC rules permit simultaneously-filed and cross-referenced minor change FM station construction permit applications that may increase options for improving a station.

❑ Some AM operators have seen their transmitter sites, once in rural areas, become surrounded by development. Through relocating the site, an improved facility might be able to be built, financed by the sale of the old site. There may be a tradeoff, however, in terms of reduced signal strength into the city from the more remote site.

❑ When studying upgrade possibilities involving a change in the location of a tower site, there are more concerns than can be easily addressed in a due diligence engineering review. Environmental constraints must be considered when investigating a new transmitter site. In addition to concerns about human exposure to radio frequency radiation, the FCC has environmental rules restricting towers in officially designated wildlife areas, flood plains and residential neighborhoods. The FCC is also concerned with facilities that could cause significant change in surface features, such as wetland fill, deforestation, or water diversion. FCC rules on the impact of tower construction on historic preservation require review and approval by state and tribal officers. Increasingly, there are state and local regulations impacting all aspects of tower lighting and construction. A competent technical consultant can help sort out the factors which are important for consideration.

❑ In evaluating any upgrade, the FCC isn't the only agency that must be satisfied. The Federal Aviation Administration (FAA) may evaluate a proposed structure both with regard to physical impact on the airspace and from the standpoint of electromagnetic interference. Increasingly, state aeronautical agencies are adding their own tower restrictions. An aeronautical consultant can be retained to help evaluate the feasibility of tower construction or modification. Local zoning boards may also restrict tower construction. A well-connected local attorney or real estate agent may be helpful if the buyer anticipates objections to tower construction.

❑ Digital audio broadcasting, or HD radio, is a transmission system developed by iBiquity Corporation that enables AM and FM radio stations to simulcast digital and analog audio within the same channel (a hybridized digital-analog signal) as well as add new FM channels and text information. Thorough evaluation of a station's HD radio experience should be undertaken in order to assess the reach and integrity of the digital signal, any adverse effects of the digital signal on the station's analog signal or the analog signal of stations on adjacent channels, and the prospect for improvement through power increase or relocation.

B. Assess Potential Competition

Along with examining the upgrade possibility of the prospective acquisition, the upgrade potential for the market as a whole should be considered to determine the prospects for increased competition. This can cover two areas: 1) upgrade possibilities of existing stations, and 2) the potential for new stations to be created in or moved to the market.

- ❐ FCC databases can be reviewed to determine which existing stations are operating with maximum potential. The databases can reveal if any station has applied for permission from the FCC to modify its facilities.

- ❐ Computer analyses can be made for FM channel availabilities. But caution must be used

because there is still a limited potential for new competition through swapping of station frequencies and changing communities of license. An experienced technical consultant familiar with the target market may also provide some insight on past efforts to provide new service.

- ❐ The Commission's Electronic Comment Filing System should also be reviewed to determine whether anyone has filed any rulemaking proposals that would have the effect of increasing the number of stations in the market.

- ❐ New technology also presents the possibility of increased competition for radio stations. Video and audio compression technology continues to improve, making programming available through increasingly narrower bandwidth channels, both wired and wireless. This technology could increase the competition from internet-provided programming, including "customized radio" such as Pandora.

❏ Digital cable radio companies offer subscribers dozens of channels of CD quality audio. Satellite delivered formats provide CD quality audio services to mobile and stationary receivers.

❏ The Low Power FM service for noncommercial and public safety entities, while probably not posing a significant competitive threat, has increased the interference level in the FM band, thus somewhat reducing the coverage of full power stations.

C. Determine Compliance with FCC Rules and Authorizations

Once the upgrade potential has been analyzed, an on-site inspection should be conducted to help determine whether the facility is operating in accordance with the FCC's rules and regulations and as specified by the station's license. Some rule infractions may be minor and cost little or nothing to correct. This knowledge is important

because a new owner may be liable for violations of the former licensee.

❏ A copy of the station's authorizations can be obtained from the FCC or the station. The license will specify operating parameters for the station. To verify that an FM station is operating legally, first check the output power and modulation. AM stations with directional antennas have additional parameters that must be monitored. Also, with directional AM stations, there is a requirement to not exceed specified field strength at one or more monitoring points at some distance from the antenna. These readings should also be verified. Directional AM stations are also required to make additional field strength measurements to demonstrate the performance of the antenna systems; these proof of performance reports are required to be retained in the station's records. For both AM and FM, depending on the height of the tower, the license may specify lighting or marking requirements. Tower lighting should be checked to make sure all lights are functioning properly. The condition of the tower marking (painting) should be noted and evaluated as to when repainting will be necessary (seven years is average).

☐ The station license may also specify an FCC antenna structure number. A copy of the registration should be on hand, posted with the station license. The registration number must be posted on the tower prominently enough to enable it to be seen from the point of restricted access to the transmitter site. The FCC will assess heavy fines for violations of tower lighting, marking, and registration requirements. The FCC has an inspection checklist for AM and FM radio stations that can aid in this technical review. This checklist is available on the Commission's website.

☐ Compliance with environmental rules, including those for human exposure to radio frequency radiation (RFR), should be confirmed. Most stations meet the FCC's RFR exposure guidelines. But the station is required to make its own determination, and there is some misinformation in the industry as to exactly what is required. A qualified tower contractor, or preferably a structural engineer, should make an independent evaluation. This is done by making sure that the public, employees, and contractors including tower workers are restricted from exposure in excess of the FCC's guideline values. The guidelines used can be those published by the FCC indicating acceptable distances from an antenna to publicly accessible areas. Those guidelines employ some worst-case assumptions; measurements of radio frequency radiation will usually show a less restrictive RFR environment. Specific antenna types can often be used in conjunction with FCC formulas to demonstrate compliance if it is not possible to do so under the worst-case assumptions. At antenna sites with multiple users, written RF exposure policies should be provided to each of the users.

❏ The presence or absence of polychlorinated biphenyls (PCBs) should be determined. The Toxic Substances Control Act of 1976 directs the Environmental Protection Agency (EPA) to regulate PCBs. Though PCBs are no longer used in the manufacture of broadcast equipment, they may exist in equipment manufactured before 1979, where they are usually found in transformers and capacitors.

❏ It is still permissible to use PCB items in many pieces of broadcast equipment. But if they are kept, they must be managed according to EPA rules covering record keeping, repair, storage and disposal. Worse, if there is a fire, the released PCB toxins may render a transmitter building or studio unusable for months. It is best not to acquire PCB items, or to obtain assurances from the seller that it will be responsible for the proper disposal of any PCB items. This has been a condition of sale at some stations.

❏ Underground storage tanks (USTs) that are used by broadcasters for emergency power generation fuel storage pose another potential hazard. USTs are regulated by the Environmental Protection Agency. Federally regulated USTs must be registered, meet leak detection requirements, and meet upgrade requirements that were effective December 22, 1998. Owners of USTs are required to meet financial responsibility requirements and to perform checks and corrective action in response to any leaks or spills.

❑ Asbestos is another environmental concern. It was used in most buildings constructed between the early 1900s to the mid-1970s. Since 1976, the Occupational Health and Safety Administration (OHSA) has required the removal of asbestos when the density of asbestos fibers in the air exceeds a certain threshold. In some instances, asbestos is permitted to remain if it is encapsulated or in a location where it can't be disturbed. The most trouble-causing form of asbestos is loose, wrap material that more easily disintegrates; asbestos board may pass under the threshold.

❑ Other safety concerns are mainly those of common sense. For example, areas of high voltage should be inaccessible to unauthorized workers to protect against electric shock. Towers should be fenced to prevent climbing by unauthorized personnel. If there are OHSA or other safety reports concerning the facility, they should be examined.

Because of the critical nature of environmental regulations and concerns, a Registered Professional Engineer should be consulted.

D. Inspect the Equipment

The first phase of equipment inspection can be done without setting foot in the station. Observations of the station's signal quality can be made at several locations in the primary service area with comparisons made to other stations. Often, this informal survey will reveal particular problems areas that need examination.

Once in the station, the general condition of equipment can be evaluated. Some buyers have found it useful to document the condition of equipment with a video camera.

❑ The useful life of the equipment should be estimated, along with information concerning the cost of replacement. The timing of new purchases will not necessarily depend on the condition of the existing equipment; a station may be outfitted with the latest in equipment, but a new owner may want to make further conversions to digital technology.

☐ Towers and guy wires should be inspected, preferably by a qualified structural engineer. The transmission line or waveguide should be examined to determine that it is securely attached to the tower and that there is no severe flexing in the line.

Consideration might be given to having a consulting engineer evaluate the transmission lines and antenna with more sophisticated equipment such as a network analyzer and/or thermal imaging equipment to check for "hidden" problems for festering bad internal connections, water intrusion, or other problems that may not be visible to the naked eye.

Appendix G contains sample due diligence requests for information. One is based on a request prepared by a financial institution. The other two were prepared by prospective buyers.

CHAPTER FOUR

KEEPING THEM HAPPY AT THE FCC

The sale of a radio station and the transfer of its license involve legal considerations that are not present in the transfer of most other business enterprises. Unlike unregulated businesses, the closing of a radio station sale cannot take place unless the Federal Communications Commission (FCC) gives its blessing. Many potential FCC pitfalls may adversely affect both the buyer and the seller. This chapter presents some practical suggestions for avoiding such pitfalls and making sure that the terms of the purchase agreement satisfy FCC rules and policies.

Requirement of Prior FCC Approval

The Communications Act of 1934 provides that a broadcast station construction permit or license may not be assigned nor may control of an entity holding a license be transferred, except upon application to the FCC and a finding by the Commission that the "public interest, convenience and necessity will be served thereby." This prohibition applies equally to transfers of *de jure* (legal) and *de facto* (actual) control. "Control" in FCC parlance encompasses any means whereby an individual or entity can "dominate" or "determine" the licensee's policies and/or corporate affairs, especially those relating to personnel, finances, and programming. Premature transfers of control have resulted in the disapproval of assignment and transfer applications, large fines, and in some cases, the initiation of proceedings to revoke the station's license. Accordingly, the asset purchase agreement should specifically provide that consummation of the transaction shall be subject to the prior written approval of the FCC.

For example, one asset purchase agreement included the following provision:

> The consummation of this Agreement shall in all respects be subject to the prior consent by the FCC to the terms and conditions of this Agreement, and in particular to the assignment of the Licenses to Purchaser. Purchaser and Seller shall use their best efforts to prepare and file as promptly as practicable, but in no event later than ten (10) business days after the date hereof, with the FCC all applications and other necessary documents to request the FCC Order.

After these applications and documents have been filed with the FCC, Purchaser and Seller shall prosecute the applications with all reasonable diligence to promptly obtain an FCC Order.

Some contracts condition the closing on the grant of FCC consent becoming final and no longer subject to review. The following is a definition of a "final order" commonly contained in the acquisition agreement:

"Final Order" means an order or action of the Commission as to which, under FCC Rules, the time for filing a request for administrative or judicial review, or for instituting administrative review <u>sua sponte</u>, shall have expired without any such filing having been made or notice of such review having been issued; or, in the event of such filing or review sua sponte, as to which such filing or review shall have been disposed of favorably to the grant and the time for seeking further relief with respect thereto under the applicable FCC or court rules shall have expired without any request for such further relief having been filed.

Licensee Control

The Communications Act requires that the licensee retain control over the station up to and until the closing and the buyer to assume control immediately upon closing. To meet this requirement, the asset purchase agreement provides that: "[b]etween the date of this Agreement and the Closing Date, Buyer, its employees or agents, shall not directly or indirectly control, supervise or direct, or attempt to control, supervise or direct, the operation of Stations, and such operation shall be the sole responsibility of and in the complete discretion of Seller, except as may be provided in this Agreement."

Avoiding an Unauthorized Transfer of Control

The FCC requires that station owners exercise sufficient control over major management decisions (finances, personnel, and programming) to ensure that the licensee retains ultimate responsibility for station performance. The Commission regularly has advised prospective buyers to refrain from the premature exercise or assumption of control of the stations involved. Because the presence of the prospective owner's employees at the station on a day-to-day basis lends itself to situations which could easily result in the premature exercise of control, the FCC repeatedly has advised prospective buyers to refrain from the day-to-day participation in the station's affairs while the application awaits Commission approval.

Under such circumstances, how can a buyer ensure that prior to the closing, the target station is being operated to its expectations? Four devices for dealing with this problem are (1) a consulting contract, (2) a services agreement, (3) a joint sales agreement (if the buyer currently has a radio station in the market), and (4) a local marketing agreement. Under the first option, the seller and buyer enter into an agreement pursuant to which the seller retains the buyer as a consultant. Under the auspices of this agreement, the buyer as consultant acts as the licensee/seller's contractor and may provide services touching upon the operation of the station to the extent spelled out in the agreement and always subject to the oversight and control of the licensee. Under the consulting agreement, the seller usually pays the buyer some specified sum in exchange for the consulting services. The expense needs to be considered in setting the purchase price for the station. A sample consulting agreement appears at Appendix C.

Under the local marketing agreement (LMA, also known as a Time Brokerage Agreement), the buyer buys the broadcast time of the target station on a wholesale basis pending the closing. Buyer provides the programming for the station and sells advertising. As in the case of the consulting agreement, the LMA must unequivocally reserve to the licensee/seller the unlimited right to suspend, cancel, or reject any programming furnished or recommended by the lessee/buyer. Additionally, the licensee remains responsible for the salaries of certain employees and certain other costs of the station's operations, as well as for compliance with all regulatory requirements such as maintenance of the public inspection file and political file. In contrast to a consulting agreement, under the LMA, the broker/buyer customarily pays the licensee/seller for the lease of the airtime. These payments can also stand on their own or be treated as advances that will reduce the purchase price stated in the purchase agreement. In addition, an LMA between the seller and buyer of a station must be filed with the FCC as part of the assignment application.* LMA's are discussed in more detail in Appendix D (ABCs of LMAs

---

* The Federal Trade Commission regards the execution of an LMA as a reportable transaction under the Hart-Scott-Rodino Antitrust Improvements Act if the buying and selling companies meet the statutory tests (see Chapter Three).

and Time Brokerage Checklist for the Licensee) and two sample agreements are shown in Appendix E. Buyers and sellers should also consult Worksheet #3D to the application for consent to assignment of license (FCC Form 314). Some buyers are reluctant to enter into an LMA (a) because the Media Bureau usually processes assignment and transfer applications in about 45 days and (b) due to the concern that a competitor of the station might file a petition to deny alleging that an unauthorized transfer of control has occurred.

Whether it is a consulting agreement or an LMA, a carefully drafted document should include a provision that "nothing in this Agreement shall be construed to prevent or hinder the licensee from retaining and exercising full and complete control over the station, including, but not limited to, control of its finances, personnel, and programming." The wording of these agreements is critical in situations where the General Manager is buying the station or a "workout team" plans to assume a managerial role. But words alone will not necessarily immunize the station from a determination by the FCC that an unauthorized transfer has occurred. The parties must maintain continuous oversight to ensure that the seller makes all key management decisions, particularly those relating to station financing,

programming and employment. A contemporaneous written record of each approval is recommended.

Yet another approach to the problem is to include a provision whereby the seller agrees "to allow Buyer an observer who will have full and free access to the Purchased Assets so that Buyer's organization shall have an opportunity to study existing operations and prepare for a smooth transition to ownership." Such an opportunity should also make clear that "the observer shall have no role in the operation of the Station prior to the Closing." This provision, however, provides only a minimal amount of protection to the buyer. In those situations where there is concern about the continuing viability of the station, a consulting contract might provide greater protection.

It is also important to guard against violating the FCC's prohibition on an unauthorized transfer of control before signing bank or other financing agreements. Banks use a variety of techniques to place pressure on borrowers who are in default. In some instances, this pressure comes perilously close to violating the Communications Act by unduly restricting the discretion of the licensee of the station. For example, one bank was rumored to have ordered the owner of a group of radio stations to cut costs by firing each of the General Managers and by having the Sales Manager at each station also act as General Manager. Some banks also have tried to induce borrowers in default to execute a power of attorney giving the lender the authority to sign an application to assign the license of the station to a new buyer. One bank tried to include the following provision in a Forbearance Agreement: "Simultaneously upon the execution of this Agreement, the Borrower shall complete (but not date) and execute an FCC Form 314 -Assignment of License - in blank and deliver the same to the Bank, such that the Bank shall possess an undated current and effective FCC Form 314 for the transfer of the Station's FCC licenses at all times." The FCC staff has taken the position that both a power of attorney of the kind just described and the signing of blank application forms clearly violate FCC policy and constitutes an unauthorized transfer of control as of the date of the signing.

Radio broadcasters should not, indeed may not, sign away their rights as licensees. Such action jeopardizes their licenses. Some broadcasters have taken the position that they will sign an assignment application in only two situations: either when an asset purchase agreement with a buyer of their choice has been executed, or if (and when) the bank secures a court order forcing them to sign an assignment application.

If the parties do decide to enter into an LMA, the seller must take particular pains to make sure that the buyer's actions under the LMA do not result in a situation where seller is in technical breach of the purchase agreement because of buyer's actions under the LMA. For example, many purchase agreements include a representation by the seller that the station is being operated in material compliance with the FCC's rules and regulations. If the buyer provides programming under the scope of the LMA that the FCC deems to be indecent, however, the seller's representation concerning the station's compliance with the FCC's rules and regulations will no longer be correct. This could lead to the anomalous situation wherein the buyer could terminate the purchase agreement because of the failure of that representation even though the buyer is the party that caused the representation to no longer be true. To avoid precisely this kind of situation, the parties to a recent agreement included the following provision in their purchase agreement:

> Notwithstanding anything contained herein to the contrary, the Seller shall not be deemed to have breached or otherwise failed to fulfill any of its representations, warranties, covenants or agreements contained herein

or to have failed to satisfy any condition precedent to Purchaser's obligation to perform under this Agreement (nor shall the Seller have any liability or responsibility to Purchaser in respect of any such representations, warranties, covenants, agreements or conditions precedent), in each case only to the extent that the breach of or failure to fulfill any such representation, warranty, covenant or agreement or the inability to satisfy any such condition precedent is due, directly or indirectly, to (i) any actions taken by or at the direction of Purchaser or its Affiliates (or any of their respective officers, directors, employees, agents or representatives) in connection with the Purchaser's performance of its obligations under the [LMA] or (ii) the failure of Purchaser to perform any of its obligations under the [LMA].

Although LMAs have been in use for nearly 20 years, there is always the possibility that the FCC could decide to forbid their use in the future or could rule as a matter of policy that certain standard LMA provisions are not in the public interest. As a result, it is incumbent upon the parties to the LMA to make provision for either or both of these possibilities. For example, in one Local Programming and Marketing Agreement, the parties included a provision that stipulated that "[e]ither party to this Agreement may terminate this Agreement if the FCC's policies or rules change in a manner that would require such termination by providing the other party with ten (10) days advance written notice." Although this type of provision addresses the question of what is to happen in the event that the FCC forbids LMAs, it does not address the more likely scenario of the FCC adopting regulations that would require the parties to change their operations pursuant to the LMA. The following is a more comprehensive provision addressing this issue:

In the event of any order or decree of an administrative agency or court of competent jurisdiction, including without limitation any material change or clarification in FCC rules, policies, or precedent, that would cause this Agreement to be invalid or violate any applicable law, and such order or decree has become effective and has not been stayed, the parties will use their respective best efforts and negotiate in good faith to modify this Agreement to the minimum extent necessary so as to comply with such order or decree without material economic detriment to either party, and this Agreement, as so modified, shall then continue in full force and effect. In the event that the parties are unable to agree upon a modification of this Agreement so as to cause it to comply with such order or decree without material economic detriment to either party, then this Agreement shall be terminated . . .

Disclosure of the Purchase Price

In many transactions, the buyer and seller may wish to keep the purchase price confidential. For a short period of time several years ago, the FCC staff allowed the parties to delete the amount of the purchase price from the acquisition contract filed with the Commission. The FCC later reversed this policy, and the policy was tested again in 1990. In the Agreement between KCOL Corporation and University Broadcasting Company, L.P., for the sale of Stations KCOL(AM) and KIMN(FM), Fort Collins, Colorado, the purchase price section read as follows:

The Purchase Price for (a) the Property to be sold, (b) the non-competition covenant, and (c) other agreements,

warranties and representations of the Seller shall be the amount stated in Schedule No. 1, and shall be paid as specified therein. The parties expressly agree that the Purchase Price is Confidential Information which shall not be made publicly available unless required by law or specifically requested by the Commission.

Neither the Communications Act nor FCC rules explicitly requires disclosure of the purchase price. The FCC arguably has no regulatory reason or public interest justification for requiring applicants to submit this information. Nonetheless, the FCC staff rejected the parties' request to keep the purchase price confidential and insisted that the purchase price information be submitted for the KCOL/KIMN transaction.

FCC Fees

Since expenses will be incurred for FCC filing fees (currently, $940.00 for each station), compliance with the Commission's local publication requirements, and preparation of the assignment application, the agreement should include a provision apportioning such expenses. For example, the following is a common provision in Asset Purchase Agreements: "[e]ach party will be solely responsible for the expenses incurred by it in the preparation, filing and prosecution of said Application. The FCC filing fees shall be paid one-half by Seller and one-half by Buyer."

The Rule Against Reversion and Reservation of Time

Question 3 of Section II, the assignor's portion of FCC Form 314, asks the seller of a station to certify that the purchase agreement and related agreements submitted to the Commission "embody the complete and final understanding between licensee/permittee and assignee . . . and [that they] comply fully with the Commission's rules and policies." As the instructions to the application observe, an applicant must consider "a broad range of issues" in order to make this certification. To help applicants navigate through these issues, the FCC has added a number of worksheets to Form 314.

Worksheet #2 of Form 314 aids applicants in determining whether their agreements satisfy Commission requirements. Item 4 on the worksheet inquires whether the agreements provide in any way "for a reversion of the license(s) in the event of default or any right to reassignment of the license in the future[.]" The worksheet specifically notes that "[t]he response to [this question] must be 'No' in order to certify that the contractual

documents comply fully with the Commission's rules and policies. If 'Yes,' the applicant may not make the appropriate certification."

Section 73.1150, which is the Commission's "rule against reversion" prohibits clauses in contracts (a) providing for reversion (i.e., reassignment of a license) or "reacquisition" of station control in the event of default by the purchaser and (b) reserving to the seller any rights to use the facilities of the station as a condition of the sale. In interpreting its prohibition against reversions, the Commission has consistently refused to grant transfer and assignment applications where the former owner retained the right to regain the status of licensee through reversion of stock control or reassignment of the license. FCC policy demands that the buyer be free to dispose of the control of the corporation or the station license without the former owner's consent.

Where the deal contemplates a stock transaction, the exchange may involve either positive stock control (that is, a sale of a voting interest in the company exceeding 50 percent) or negative control (that is, a voting interest of exactly 50 percent that can act as a veto on actions by the shareholders holding the remaining 50 percent of the voting shares). Regardless whether the sale involves positive or negative control of a corporate licensee, however, the sale must be absolute, with no reversionary rights in the event of default. The voting rights to the stock must immediately be transferred to and remain with the buyer until other disposition is made of the stock with the prior consent of the Commission. The buyer may pledge the stock with a pledgee, including the seller, but, title to the stock and any related voting rights may not revert to the seller under any circumstances. However, provision may be made for allowing the stock to be sold at a public auction in the event of a default, or in a private sale to a buyer found after the default, at which time the seller could also be a bidder.

The Commission's prohibition against reversionary interests most often comes into play in situations in which seller financing is used. A seller naturally wants to make sure that it will receive full consideration for the station and that it is protected in the event the buyer defaults on the note. The temptation will be to include in the purchase agreement, the security agreement or even in the note itself a provision whereby the seller will get the station back if the buyer were to default. This, however, is a classic example of a prohibited reversionary interest. The temptation to provide the seller with a reversionary interest in the event of a default on a note is so great that the Commission staff frequently will ask the parties to a

transaction involving seller paper to confirm that the transaction does <u>not</u> give the seller the right to get the station back in the event that the buyer defaults on the note.

The rule against reversionary interests not only prohibits the blatant form of reversionary interest that would arise if the sales documentation simply stated that the seller gets the station back in the event of a default by the buyer. The rule also prohibits any reservation of rights to "use the facilities of the station for any period whatsoever." This provision has been interpreted by the Commission staff to mean not just that a seller cannot retain the right to use the physical facilities of the station, but also that the seller may not enter into a local marketing agreement with the buyer that would permit seller to provide programming to the station. Although case precedent addressing the point is sparse, the Commission staff has stated that, in the context of a television LMA, a provision whereby the seller would be able to provide programming over the station after closing "would appear to violate the plain language" of the reversionary rule to the extent that the LMA is "either a condition of, or consideration for, the proposed transaction." Nexstar Broadcasting, Inc., and Mission Broadcasting, Inc., 23 FCC Rcd 3528 (2008).

Hypothecation and Security Provisions

It is important to understand the distinction between the station's license and the station's non-licensed assets.

The FCC consistently has held that a broadcast license (as distinguished from other assets of a station) may not be encumbered by mortgage, lien, pledge, or lease. The rationale for this principle is that the license belongs to the government and such an encumbrance endangers the independence of the licensee who must be at all times responsible and accountable to the Commission. A licensee should also be free to assign the license of the station or transfer control to anyone of his or her choice without the consent of creditors or others (subject, of course, to the prior consent of the FCC).

Thus, when Item 5 of Worksheet #2 asks whether there is "any provision in the agreements which provides for a security interest in the station license(s), permits or authorizations," you should know the correct answer. In fact, a note to Item 5 states: "Under existing precedent, it is permissible to grant a security interest in the proceeds of the sale of a station license, permit, or authorization, but not in the license, permit, or authorization itself."

Where the agreement specifies that Commission approval must be obtained prior to any assignment of voting control, the FCC has allowed loan agreements to require a pledge of the capital stock of the licensee corporation as security. The FCC also has allowed security provisions prohibiting the purchaser from making major expenditures not contemplated in the ordinary course of a broadcast operation without the lender's approval. The FCC permits the loan documents to require the borrower, in the event of a default, to cooperate with the lender in the appointment of a receiver. Although neither a station's license nor control of a licensee corporation may be the subject of a security agreement, a station's physical assets may be foreclosed or sold without the prior consent of the Commission.

FCC Processing of Assignment and Transfer Applications

Because the Communications Act requires FCC approval of *any* change in the control of a licensee, an entity controlling a licensee, a sole proprietorship, or the holder of a majority voting interest, assignments of license and transfers of control can take many forms. An assignment or transfer can be voluntary, as in the case of the consensual sale of a station between two parties, or involuntary, as where a corporate licensee becomes bankrupt or a sole proprietor licensee dies. Likewise, an assignment or transfer can involve a change in ultimate control of the licensee, or it can merely be *pro forma*, such as changing the ownership structure of a licensee without actually changing the party ultimately in control. Applications for FCC consent to involuntary or *pro forma* assignments or transfers of control follow "short form" procedures. That is, they utilize FCC Form 316 (the "short form"), are subject to less stringent public notice requirements, and are processed more quickly.

For the most part, the discussion in this book relates to voluntary assignments or transfers of control that result in a *de facto* and a *de jure* change in the ownership and control of the license or the licensee. These types of deals are called "long form" transactions. That is, parties to such agreements must file a long form application – FCC Form 314 in the case of assignments, FCC Form 315 in the case of transfers of control – to seek FCC consent to the transaction. If the buyer proposes to employ five or more full-time employees, it must file together with the assignment or transfer application a model EEO Program Report on FCC Form 396-A. In considering such applications, the Commission does not permit the filing of competing applications for the station's assigned frequency, but instead evaluates only the "basic" qualifications of the parties (especially the transferee or assignee) to dispose of and to acquire the license that is the subject matter of the application.

Although the discussion in this book focuses on voluntary assignments or transfers of control, there is one form of involuntary action about which every prospective seller or buyer needs to be aware. Specifically, the Commission treats any action whereby a federal or state court appoints a trustee, debtor-in-possession or a receiver as an "involuntary" assignment or transfer even if the licensee is a willing participant to the proceeding. Because such bankruptcy and receivership actions are treated as being "involuntary," not voluntary, FCC consent can be obtained by filing for such consent on the "short form," FCC Form 316. Short form applications are not subject to the statutory 30-day period for the filing of petitions to deny discussed below and it is not uncommon for the Commission staff to grant short-form applications within days of their being filed. Because the Commission need not observe the 30-day period for the filing of petitions to deny and because such applications are frequently acted on within days of filing, it is unusual for objections to be filed with respect to short-form applications.

Simply put, the logistics are such that interested parties may be unable to get an objection on file before the FCC staff acts on the application.

In addition, it is customary for the short form application that is submitted in response to a bankruptcy or receivership proceeding to be filed *after* the court has appointed the debtor-in-possession, trustee or receiver. In fact, the normal procedure is to include a copy of the court order appointing the debtor-in-possession, trustee or receiver as part of the short form application. The court order can also serve as the signature of a recalcitrant licensee/assignor. In most cases, the FCC staff will defer to the decision of the court – unless that decision is at odds with the Communications Act or the Commission's rules or policies.

Once a new buyer is found for the station through the bankruptcy or receivership process, another application seeking FCC consent must be filed. In this case, however, the Commission requires that a "long-form" application, namely an FCC Form 314 or an FCC Form 315, must be used. The long-form application is required in order to permit the Commission staff to examine the proposed licensee and its principals to ensure that their ownership of the station would be consistent with the Communications Act and the Commission's rules and policies.

The Commission formerly required applications for consent to assignment of license or for transfer of control to be filed in hard copy and in triplicate. However, the Commission no longer accepts paper versions of FCC Forms 314, 315 and 316. Instead, these forms must be filed electronically. The electronic filing system can be accessed via the Internet at the FCC Media Bureau's Web Site: http://www.fcc.gov/mb/ elecfile. html. Instructions for using the Consolidated Database System (CDBS) for such filings may be found at: http://svartifoss2.fcc. gov/ prod/cdbs/forms/prod/cdbs_ef.htm.

Because an application for consent to assignment or transfer of control is "feeable" (subject to a filing fee), the Commission's electronic filing regulations specify a procedure for remittance of the applicable fee. The amount of the fee assessed for the application may be found in either the FCC Fee Filing Guide, or as specified in special electronic filing Public Notices. As noted above, the filing fee for FCC Forms 314 and 315 is presently $940.00 per station for which consent is sought. Applicants must pay the FCC filing fee at the time their application is electronically filed or shortly thereafter. The Commission offers an electronic fee payment system which allows immediate payment by credit card and facilitates faster processing of the application.

Payment also may be made by check or money order sent to the FCC's lockbox bank, U.S. Bank in St. Louis, Missouri. This will delay application processing by several days, however, and if there is an error in processing the check, the application may risk being dismissed for failure to pay the filing fee on time.

An FCC Registration Number (FRN) is required for the filing of all FCC forms. Pursuant to the Debt Collection Improvement Act of 1995, the FCC is required to request this ten digit entity identifier from anyone doing business with the Commission. An FRN can be applied for and obtained from the FCC Commission Registration System (CORES), which is linked on the FCC's homepage, http://fcc.gov. An FRN can also be applied for manually by submitting FCC Form 160.

When an applicant submits its application, CDBS displays a confirmation page containing the Application Reference Number (ARN) and time of filing, and noting the filing fee requirement. It provides a link to initiate the FCC Electronic Form 159 (Remittance Advice) system. The system will calculate the appropriate fee and provide for launching a browser for completion of the Electronic Form 159.

The applicant may print the completed Form 159 and send it to U.S. Bank by mail or courier, or may pay electronically. The Commission cautions that payment of the fee must be received by the bank within 14 calendar days of the date that the application is officially received by the Media Bureau's electronic filing system as indicated by the ARN assigned to the application. This deadline applies whether payment is submitted electronically or by a paper check. If payment is not received in time, the filed application will be considered to be **not paid** and the Media Bureau will not process it.

An applicant may elect to submit an application without immediately initiating the fee filing process. Applicants can submit their applications and then defer the submission of the filing fee. This arrangement can be useful if the applicant paying the filing fee does not have readily at hand all the information required to be included on the Form 159. The downside to this arrangement is that it increases the risk that the applicant will fail to timely submit the filing fee and risk dismissal of its application.

After the seller and buyer file the application, and the filing fee is recorded, the Commission staff begins processing it. If the staff determines upon this initial review that the application is complete, within five to ten days after the filing, the Commission will issue a public notice announcing that the application has been accepted for filing.

Following the release of this initial public notice, a statutory 30-day period must elapse during which interested parties may file "petitions to deny" against the application. Challenges to the application may also be submitted at any time in the form of "informal objections." Such objections do not carry the same procedural protections as formal petitions; however, objections that raise material concerns will often receive the careful attention of the Commission staff. If, at the end of the 30-day period, a petition to deny or other objection has been filed, the timing of final Commission action on the application becomes quite uncertain. Such filings can add several months, and in some cases even years, to the processing time for an application.

In the absence of any objection, an application becomes ripe for Commission action at the close of the 30-day period, and the parties can typically expect to receive a grant between five days and one month after the comment period. Customarily, the staff will make an action granting an application immediately effective although the public notice announcing the action will be issued about three business days after the grant.

Upon release of the public notice announcing the staff's action on the application, another statutory 30-day period opens within which aggrieved parties (unsuccessful petitioners to deny or new third parties in the case of a granted application and the applicants themselves in the event of a denial) may petition the Commission staff to reconsider the decision if the grant is made pursuant to delegated authority. The Commission, for its part, has an additional 10 days (for a total of 40 days) within which it may review the staff's action on its own motion. As with a petition to deny, the filing of a petition for reconsideration can make it very difficult to forecast accurately the timing of final action on the application. This is particularly true because the staff's decision on reconsideration itself then becomes subject, potentially, to further review by the Commission or by the United States Court of Appeals. If no petitions for reconsideration are filed, and the Commission takes no action on its own, a grant of the application is deemed to be "final" by operation of law and is no longer subject to legal challenge, on the 41st day after public notice of the grant.

Deadline Date for FCC Approval

Some agreements provide that either the buyer or the seller may declare the agreement null and void if the Commission has not granted its consent to and approval of the assignment or transfer by a certain date. Commonly referred to as an "upset date" or "drop dead date," this provision allows either party to terminate the agreement without penalty. Parties should be aware, however, that Section 309(b) of the Communications Act provides that no application for assignment or transfer of control may be granted until 30 days after the FCC issues a public notice accepting the application for filing. In addition to this statutory waiting period, the parties should allow ample time when selecting an "upset date" for the processing of the application by the Commission staff. Many agreements provide that the grant of the application and the closing must take place within nine months to a year after execution of the acquisition agreement. A typical provision in an asset purchase agreement provides:

> [i]f for any reason, closing hereunder does not occur on or before [the specified date], including failure of the Commission to enter a final order consenting to the renewal and assignment of the license … this Agreement shall be rendered null and void. For purposes of this Agreement, an order becomes final when, by lapse of time

or otherwise, it is no longer subject to administrative reconsideration or judicial review.

The agreement also provided that if a final order granting the assignment application was not secured by the agreed-upon deadline:

> [t]his Agreement may be terminated at the option of either party upon ten (10) days written notice to the other, and the Deposit (and any interest thereon), shall be returned to Buyer, provided, however, that neither party may terminate this Agreement if such party is in default hereunder, or if a delay in any decision or determination by the Commission respecting said application has been caused or materially contributed to by any failure on the part of such party to timely furnish, file or make available information within its control within the period provided by the Commission for the submission of such information, by the willful furnishing by such party of incorrect, inaccurate or incomplete information to the Commission, or by any action taken by such party or inaction of such party for the purpose of delaying any decision or determination respecting said application.

Delays in Obtaining FCC Approval

Section 309(b) of the Communications Act provides that the FCC cannot approve an application for a voluntary transfer of control or assignment of license until the expiration of a 30-day period "following issuance of public notice by the [Commission] of the acceptance for filing of such an application or any substantial amendment thereof." In addition to the statutory 30-day waiting period, an FCC staff policy could result in a delay of up to an additional four months in processing an assignment or transfer of control application. Specifically, the FCC staff will not grant an assignment or transfer of control application while the renewal application of the station being sold is pending and potentially subject to petitions to deny. The processing cycle for license renewal applications is a minimum of four months. In situations where action on an assignment or transfer of control application might be delayed as a result of the FCC staff's policy, the parties should take this policy into account in negotiating the provisions of the asset purchase or stock transfer agreement. Appendix F contains a listing of the license expiration dates and renewal application deadlines.

There will be delays in the processing of the assignment or transfer application if it is not complete. One FCC staff member suggests that the seller and the buyer review the other party's application for completeness before it is filed with the Commission.

Closing Before a Final Order

The grant of an assignment or transfer of control application is not "final" until after the disposition of all applications for review, petitions for reconsideration and judicial review and the passage of the 40-day period during which the Commission can revisit a staff grant of an application. Most contracts provide that the closing shall not take place until the FCC's grant of the transfer or assignment application has become a "final order." However, there is no legal barrier to closing before finality. The FCC's grant is effective immediately. The Commission has stated that parties that elect to close a transaction exercise their own business judgment and proceed at their own risk with the full understanding that they may ultimately be required to undo the transaction.

Many parties take the risk and close before the grant becomes final. How can the seller and the buyer protect themselves if they close before a final order and the FCC subsequently rescinds the grant? One way of handling this rare occurrence is for the parties to include an "unwind" or rescission provision in the asset purchase agreement. The following is an example of such a provision:

> If the Closing occurs prior to a Final FCC Consent, and prior to becoming Final, the FCC Consent is reversed or otherwise set aside, and there is a Final order of the FCC (or court of competent jurisdiction) requiring the re-assignment of the FCC Authorizations to Seller, then Seller and Buyer agree that the purchase and sale of the Station Assets shall be rescinded. In such event, Buyer shall reconvey to Seller the Station Assets, and Seller shall repay to Buyer the Purchase Price and reassume the Seller Contracts assigned and assumed by Buyer at Closing. Any such rescission shall be consummated on a mutually agreeable date within thirty (30) calendar days of such Final order (or, if earlier, within the time required by such order). In connection therewith, Buyer and Seller shall each execute such documents (including execution by Buyer of instruments of assumption of the Seller Contracts assigned and assumed at Closing) and make such payments (including repayment by Seller to Buyer of the Purchase Price) as are necessary to give effect to such rescission. Seller's and Buyer's obligations under this section shall survive the Closing.

In some transactions where the parties dispense with the need for a final order in order to close, they enter into a rescission · agreement (also called an "unwind" agreement) at the closing which sets forth the procedures and ramifications in the event that the FCC were to rescind the grant. Such agreements normally provide for the return to the <u>status quo ante</u> in the event of a later final FCC or court order vacating the FCC consent. Appendix J contains a sample rescission or unwind agreement.

Speeding Up the FCC Application Process

Where an assignment or transfer application is unopposed, it usually takes about 50 to 60 days from the time the application is filed until the grant by the FCC staff. As noted earlier, one way to expedite the processing of the application is to pay the requisite filing fee by credit card (rather than by check). Another way to speed up the process is to file the application with the FCC before the definitive asset or stock purchase agreement is signed by the parties. In such cases, the application should contain an exhibit indicating that the definitive document will be supplied shortly as an amendment to the application and including as an attachment a copy of the letter of intent and a statement that the letter of intent embodies the principal terms of the proposed transaction. As long as the amendment transmitting the definitive agreement is filed within the next 10 to 15 days, there should be no delay in the processing of the application. However, if the definitive document is submitted 30 days after the issuance of a public notice announcing the acceptance of the application, the FCC will issue a public notice announcing the date the definitive agreement was filed and deferring action until a later date in order to give interested parties the opportunity to review the contract and comment. The late submission of the definitive agreement is treated by the FCC as the submission of a major amendment and starts anew a 30-day period for the filing of petitions to deny.

Most sellers are reluctant to file an application until the contract is signed because of the disruptive consequences of announcing a sale to the station's staff and the public which does not materialize.

Buyers, however, usually want the transaction to proceed as quickly as possible. One middle ground is to file the application when the contract is signed but before completion of the schedules (*e.g.*, a description of the inventory, a listing of the contracts and leases being assigned, etc.). In one asset purchase agreement, the parties agreed that the seller had 15 days to deliver the schedules to the buyer. To make sure that the schedules contained no unanticipated problems, the agreement provided that "Buyer shall have the right to declare the Agreement terminated if, within fifteen (15) days after the delivery of the Schedules, Buyer reasonably believes that the Schedules materially adversely affect Buyer's original estimate of the value of the Stations." By adopting this approach, the parties shortened the timetable for the processing of the assignment application by about two weeks.

The parties' desire to file the application in advance of the completion of the purchase agreement and the associated schedules and exhibits must be balanced against the delays in FCC processing of the application that could occur if the purchase agreement and related documents are not on file by the time that the FCC staff begins reviewing the application, which usually occurs before expiration of the 30-day period for the filing of petitions to deny. Any such documentation that is not provided could well lead to a phone call from the Commission staff asking for the missing documents. Crucial time can be lost while the documents are compiled, the application is amended to provide the staff with the omitted documents and the staff then reviews the missing documents.

In deciding which documents must be filed with the Commission, it is important to consider that the application form itself specifically requires the applicants to certify that the contracts and agreements provided to the staff as part of the application process "embody the complete and final agreement for the sale of the station(s)." Despite the breadth of this representation, there is an exception to the general requirement that the Commission staff must be provided with a complete copy of the purchase agreement, including all schedules and exhibits. The Commission well understands that many of the schedules and exhibits that are appended to a purchase agreement have no bearing on the Commission's consideration of the proposed assignment or transfer. For decades, FCC practitioners omitted the schedules and exhibits but nevertheless felt no qualms whatsoever about having their clients certify that the documents

submitted to the Commission were "complete."

As the result of a petition to deny asserting that the parties to an assignment application were guilty of a misrepresentation to the Commission because the submitted documents did not include the schedules and thus could not be considered to be "complete," the Commission devised a compromise solution. That solution provides that, if an applicant submits complete and final copies of all the transaction documents, including all schedules and exhibits, the applicants may certify that they have complied with the requirement to file "a complete and final agreement." If, however, the applicants omit transaction documents containing information that is not germane to the Commission's processing of the application, the applicants must respond "No" to the applicable certification item. In that case, the applicants must submit an exhibit describing each of the omitted documents and stating both the specific reason for omitting those documents and the basis upon which the applicants contend that the omitted documents are not relevant to the Commission's consideration of the application. Application of LUJ, Inc., and Long Nine, Inc., 17 FCC Rcd 16980 (2002). In reaching this compromise solution, the Commission emphasized that the applicants bear the risk if they wrongly conclude that certain documents are not required to permit the Commission staff to process an application. As the Commission pointed out, the failure to submit documentation that contains all of the material terms of a proposed assignment or transfer of control will delay processing of the application and could even result in the bureau providing the public with an additional 30-day period, following the submission of such documentation, for the filing of petitions to deny.

CHAPTER FIVE

HOW TO AVOID SELLER'S REMORSE: SELLING WITHOUT SELLING OUT

To use Charles Dickens' often-quoted phrase, selling a radio station can be "the best of times" if the seller finds the right buyer who is willing to pay the best price at optimal and secure terms in a transaction structured to maximize the after-tax benefits to the seller. But it can be "the worst of times" if there are strategic mistakes in the pricing or presentation of the station, if administrative snafus prevent the transaction from moving forward in a timely manner, or if important details are left undone. This chapter discusses some of the business considerations that a seller should address before placing a station on the market and suggests some contractual provisions to protect the seller's interests. Although this chapter is written from a seller's perspective, prospective buyers who would like insights on how to deal with the party on the other side of the bargaining table will also find it valuable.

Overall Business Strategy

Time spent planning and preparing for the sale of a radio station is time well spent for the seller. The first important decision any seller has to make concerns timing. If you can avoid it, don't attempt to sell in the midst of an economic downturn. Make sure that prospective buyers understand your station's current economic value as well as its future growth potential. Another important threshold step is determining the method you will use to find the right buyer. Do you want to use confidential bids? An open auction? Selecting an aggressive and creative media broker and/or investment banker is another key preliminary task. Some of the most significant preliminary business considerations are discussed below.

❑ Check and double-check your reasons for selling. If you are selling for tax reasons, make sure your tax advisor agrees. If you are cashing out an investment to accommodate your passive partners, determine if it would be preferable to buy them out rather than sell completely.

❑ Analyze whether the time is right to sell. This determination involves consideration of the local economy, the current level of interest rates, the general market for radio station acquisitions, the station's financial condition, and your own financial needs.

❑ Establish solid relationships with media brokers and/ or investment banking firms. Even if you do not plan to sell now, it is good to know brokers and investment bankers who will give you an idea of the state of the market and the current value of your station; you, in turn, will be in a better position to evaluate their knowledge and ability.

❑ Decide how you wish the station to be marketed and sold. Your choices include an auction; a relatively public advertising and selling campaign; or a quiet, private marketing to select potential buyers. Your choice will depend on the speed and confidentiality with which you want to sell. Before making a decision, consider

your basic objective for selling (in other words, consider the result you want to accomplish).

❑ Consider having your station valued by a consultant specializing in station valuation before you speak with brokers or potential buyers. An independent appraisal of your station's value may be the best way to set a price that is neither too low nor too high.

❑ Decide on a realistic price range in consultation with your partners and broker before going to market. Do your homework before going to the market and find out what similar properties are selling for.

❑ Decide what you are selling. Do you want to retain the real estate or towers? The domain name and domain leases? Some of the equipment?

❑ Be sure that any broker and/or investment banker you may use is reputable, smart, and aggressive. If you are selling real estate and/or stock, make sure the broker or agent has the proper licenses to do so. These professionals are helpful in many areas — qualifying prospects, showing the property, establishing a fair price, negotiating the terms of the transaction, and securing financing for prospective purchasers.

❐ If you want to maintain the confidentiality of your station's listing and/or if you want the broker to clear prospects with you in advance of contacting them, be sure you have a clearly written agreement with the broker, and let the broker know how important you consider the need for confidentiality.

❐ Establish a realistic time frame to develop a packet of information, screen prospects, conduct inspection tours, solicit bids, analyze offers and negotiate the deal. Be prepared for a long wait to sell the station. Even if the sale documents are signed quickly, it usually will take at least three months from the first discussions until FCC approval and the closing. Moreover, if marketing or negotiating the deal proves to be difficult, the entire process could take up to, or more than, one year.

❐ Keep your financial partners and key management aware of your progress. Do not let them discover your plans to sell from outside sources. You should advise your investors, lenders and any other parties who may have a special need to know about your planned sale.

❐ Expect that word of the prospective sale will leak out no matter how carefully guarded, and act accordingly. The broadcast trade press is extremely adept at sniffing out new deals.

❐ Have your tax advisors and attorneys carefully assess tax implications (both federal and state) of a sale of stock and/ or a sale of assets. Know the tax consequences first. Try to eliminate "double taxation" of the net proceeds. If any major tax problems exist, look for solutions early.

❏ Decide which employees (general manager, sales manager, etc.) should know of your decision to sell. Get ahead of the grapevine. Consider offering key employees a bonus or some other financial incentive to continue working at the station and to maintain the station's performance through the closing. Be sure to disclose these compensation arrangements to the buyer, who usually will not object.

❏ Determine up front whether you have a deadline by which to close. If so, that date may influence your choice of selling methodology. You should emphasize the deadline with your broker, accountant, and attorney.

Finding the Right Buyer and Getting the Station in Order

Once you have decided to sell, be prepared to find the right buyer, and spend time getting things in order before talking to qualified prospects.

❏ Look at your station from the buyer's perspective. Determine what features will be attractive to a potential buyer and what problems could elicit concern.

❏ Before offering the property, prepare a detailed information package. Consider using a financial spreadsheet to track your station's revenues and cash flow; such an approach makes it easier to reflect new information in your package. A detailed information package demonstrates the value of the property and makes it more attractive to potential buyers; it is also helpful in educating the broker of the strengths of your station.

❏ If the property includes more real estate than the buyer needs to operate the station, consider whether the excess real estate can be sold separately from the station. Get an appraisal of the fair market value of the excess real estate.

- Identify any possible major problem areas. Be ready to turn the buyer's objections into the buyer's opportunities.

- Upgrade your station's facilities to maximum technical specifications allowed under law, or at least apply for a construction permit to upgrade in order to protect the station's options.

- Inspect and maintain the tower, transmitter, master control room, studio(s) and other equipment on a routine schedule. Be prepared for a technical inspection by prospective buyers.

- Conduct an audit of the local public inspection file and the station's compliance with FCC rules and licenses.

- Make appropriate leasehold improvements and repairs. Acquire decorative furniture, plants and wall hangings to improve the office's appearance. Present a professional, attractive facility. Many buyers look at the station like someone shopping for a first home.

- Maintain an up-to-date inventory of station equipment as well as a file of all current contracts and lease obligations. Buyers will want to review this information.

- Show why the buyer is paying a lower multiple of cash flow than might appear to be the case from the financial statements. Develop an "adjusted cash flow" to show the cash flow ratio available to a buyer for debt service.

For example:

→ *If one or more owners are on the payroll, indicate this amount as an excess expense of the present owner. This amount then reduces operating expenses and increases cash flow.*

→ *Accounting reclassifications can make a big difference to a buyer in calculating cash flow or operating income. The more deductions that can be excluded by classification, the better for the seller.*

→ *Point out items that distort performance. For example, theft, fire, equipment failure or an unusual one-time expense. Also, note any accounting or engineering fees that were above the norm.*

❒ Target and focus on positive performance. For example, when releasing ratings information, show the share in target demographics, not 12+ figures. Explain your audience and sales strategies, and demonstrate how they are working. Bar graphs and other charts work particularly well to depict audience growth or trends.

❒ Think about your station's future sales potential. It is often better not to concentrate on past figures. Instead, emphasize the future.

❒ Show total market revenue projections. Then outline your station's potential, based on projections of the station's share of market revenues.

❒ Allow the buyer maximum flexibility regarding long-term commitments. If possible, obtain favorable options on long-term leases, contracts, and the like. Also, make certain that you understand the impact of long-term commitments on the buyer of the station (*e.g.*, leases, union contracts, unfunded pension and/ or profit sharing plans, program contracts, etc.).

❒ Clear up tax problems (*e.g.*, the filing of sales, income tax and withholding returns).

❒ Put all oral agreements in writing. Facilities leases or subcarrier agreements should be in writing so that a value can be assigned to them.

❒ Calculate "hidden" costs such as severance and accrued vacation obligations.

❒ Clean up any current litigation now. It may cost money, but it is better (and in the long run, less expensive) to deliver a clean slate. Have your law firm(s) prepare a summary of all pending and threatened litigation.

☐ Verify the financial and legal qualifications of a prospective buyer early to eliminate unqualified "tire kickers." Require the buyer to provide you with financial information establishing the ability to pay the purchase price. Where possible, interview other sellers who have closed deals with your prospective buyer. If a broker is used, assessing a buyer's qualifications should be their first priority.

☐ Find out whether the buyer intends to offer employment to existing employees. In the case of the sale of a station with a large number of employees or a group of stations, federal or state plant closing statutes could be implicated. The timing of layoffs associated with the transaction could give rise to liability under those statutes and negotiating with the buyer for an indemnification provision against any liability of this sort may be worthwhile.

☐ Determine whether the buyer will be willing to assume all of the station contracts. If the buyer is unwilling to assume a contract, the seller may be in the worst of all worlds – be forced to eat the fees under a programming agreement, but have no way to offset the expense through revenue from the programming. Programming agreements are of particular concern, of course, but nonprogramming agreements that cannot be assigned to the buyer may also present a significant burden to the seller. Who eats the cost if the ownership of a skybox cannot be assigned? What happens if the buyer decides that the lease for a 2009 van is too rich for its blood? Is there another station to which the seller can assign the lease? Does the seller own another station that can use the van?

❐ If there will be seller financing, check whether the prospective buyer has adequate equity and has management capability to operate the station profitably and, therefore, to retire debt.

Before and After Signing the Contract

❐ Use proven professionals — brokers, consultants, lenders, accountants and attorneys — to assist on the deal. Each should be accessible and understand your business situation.

❐ Explain your objectives up front and establish all fees. While a broker's commission is usually paid by the seller, it often is an item of negotiation between the parties. In some transactions, the buyer and seller each pay half of the broker's commission. Traditionally, a broker's commission is based on the so-called Lehman Formula, namely, 5% of the first million dollars of the sales price; 4% of the second million dollars; 3% of the third million dollars; 2% of the fourth million dollars; and 1% of the fifth million; any balance is negotiated. Some brokers have adopted a fee schedule of 5% of the first $2-3 million, plus 1-2% on any sales price in excess of the first $2-3 million. For deals under $1 million, it is not uncommon for the intermediary to charge a higher percentage (e.g., 10%) or a fixed fee ($25,000-$50,000). Some brokers use a "reverse Lehman" (1, 2, 3, 4, 5) as a way of giving them a greater incentive to obtain a higher sales price. In recent years, a number of larger firms charge 5% of the first $3 million; 2% between $3 million and $25 million; 1.5%, between $20 and $50 million; and one percent, above $50 million. Although not publicized, it is not uncommon for brokers and sellers to negotiate the fee formula.

❐ Get all offers in writing, and insist on as much detail as possible.

- After receiving a letter of intent (see Chapter One), set a short date (*e.g.*, 14 to 30 days) for the execution of a definitive purchase and sale agreement. It may take longer, but push for tight deadlines to keep the transaction moving forward.

- Establish a positive relationship with the buyer. Try to avoid taking an adversarial approach in negotiating the transaction.

- Negotiate an adequate deposit that will compensate you in the event the buyer fails to obtain financing or otherwise reneges on the deal. A deposit of 5% of the total sales price is typical.

- Evaluate the tax risks of an installment sale. If you provide financing to the buyer, make sure that the purchase price reflects your willingness to accept a deferred payment. Also, be certain that the buyer gives you adequate security. Determine whether the buyer has sufficient equity investment and the management ability to own your station and to retire the debt. Think through all the various possibilities for when and how a default by the buyer might occur, and protect yourself in each scenario. Be aware that a buyer who has bank financing is likely to negotiate for a provision that your financing will be subordinated to that of the financial institution. Such subordination puts the seller in a much less secure position. Remember that it is time consuming and expensive to foreclose on a radio station. Insist on the personal guaranty of the buyer or buyer's parent company in addition to a security interest in the station's physical assets and any other assets the buyer will pledge as collateral. Ask the buyer to provide you with a pledge of the stock of the licensee corporation.

- Assure yourself prior to signing the contract that the buyer has the requisite financial and legal qualifications (*e.g.*, compliance with FCC rules and policies governing multiple ownership, character, alien ownership) to pass muster with the FCC. Some sellers interview the principals and former employees of the buyer, its lenders, suppliers and competitors and where possible, other sellers who have closed transactions with the buyer. In addition, make sure the contract includes representations and warranties relative to the buyer's financial and legal qualifications.

❐ Begin the preparation at the earliest possible time of the disclosure schedules that will be appended to the definitive agreement.

❐ Include a provision in the contract limiting the time which the seller's representations and warranties survive the closing. Consider a limitation of six months.

❐ After signing a purchase and sale agreement, set a very short date for the filing of an assignment or transfer application with the FCC (*e.g.*, three days).

❐ Develop a plan for informing all of the station's employees of the sale. Determine who should know at each step of the process, recognizing that word of the sale may leak out and that some employees may leave the station before the closing. It is preferable to explain the proposed sale to key employees early. Rumors hurt. Introducing the buyer to the staff soon after contract signing can be a positive step in maintaining staff continuity. Understand the insecurity a possible sale engenders in employees and counter it with positive plans and reinforcement. You will need to develop a strategy and incentives to keep your team of people in place and enthusiastic through the closing.

Before and After the Closing

A smooth, uneventful closing usually results from deliberate planning.

☐ Deal with all of the paperwork and potential areas of dispute ahead of time, and prepare a closing checklist well in advance of the date scheduled for the closing. Chapter Seven outlines the tasks to be accomplished at the closing and the various agreements and other certificates and documents that typically are exchanged between the buyer, seller and other interested parties (*e.g.*, the escrow agent).

☐ After the application for the sale has been filed with the FCC, start assembling the documents needed for the closing. Be sure to obtain assignments of contracts and leases. For an extensive discussion of closing preparation, see Chapter Seven.

☐ Get the accounts receivable in order. Collect as much as possible prior to the closing, and write off uncollectible receivables.

☐ Pay the payables and leave a reserve for contingencies. Ask your accountant to prepare the financial statements and the final tax returns.

☐ Plan in advance how you will invest the funds you will receive at the closing.

Contract Provisions Protecting the Seller's Interests

Typically the buyer's counsel prepares the initial draft of the definitive acquisition agreement. The following is a listing of the negotiating approaches often taken by counsel for the seller in responding to the buyer's initial draft:

◆ diluting the strength of the seller's representations and warranties by adding phrases such as "to seller's knowledge" or "to the best of seller's knowledge" and including materiality exceptions (*e.g.*, phrases such as "in all material respects"); the addition of "knowledge" qualifications to the representations and warranties can significantly limit the buyer's post-closing indemnification rights by shifting to the buyer the economic risks of unknown facts.

- placing a "basket" (the dollar losses that must be suffered by the buyer before the buyer's claims for indemnification are asserted and then whether all damages may be recovered or just those in excess of the agreed amount), a "ceiling" or "cap" on the seller's liability for indemnification (the total amount of damages for which the seller may be liable) and the type of damages to which the buyer is entitled (whether consequential or punitive damages are excluded or modified in some ways)

- avoiding the inclusion of overly broad provisions which enable the buyer to terminate the agreement or its obligations to close in the event of a minor breach by the seller or its failure to fulfill a minor condition

- limiting the period of time for the survival of the seller's representations and warranties

- negotiating against the inclusion of a "material adverse change" clause

- limiting the type of conditions to the buyer's obligations to close beyond those that are "normal and customary"

- not allowing the buyer to terminate the acquisition agreement without a penalty

(e.g., loss of earnest money deposit) as a result of its failure to obtain financing or approval of its governing board or shareholders

- insisting on the assumption of all contracts by the buyer so that the seller is not burdened with paying off any agreements

The remainder of this chapter provides specific examples of provisions in the acquisition agreement that are designed to protect the seller's interests.

A. Assuring that the Buyer Is Financially Qualified

The seller's primary concern is whether the proposed buyer will have the funds available at the closing to purchase the station. Thus, sales contracts typically contain a provision such as "Buyer represents that it is, and at the closing shall be, legally and financially qualified under rules, regulations and policies established by the Commission to be the licensee of Radio Station _____."

The seller should not allow the buyer to include a provision in the acquisition agreement that permits it to "walk away" from the purchase if it is unable to obtain financing. In some transactions, the seller negotiates for a provision which renders the buyer's failure to close because of the lack of funds a breach of contract. For instance, one asset purchase agreement stated that "Buyer intends to finance a portion of the purchase price through borrowing of funds from one or more third parties, [and] Buyer knows of no reason why such third parties should not fund the loan to Buyer." The agreement also provided that:

> Any failure of the Buyer's lenders to fund the loan to acquire the assets to be conveyed hereunder shall be treated as a breach by Buyer of its obligations hereunder, regardless of what cause may in such event be stated by Buyer's lenders or Buyer, including the quality of the Personal Tangible Assets or Seller's corporation.

B. Making Sure of the Buyer's Legal Qualifications

FCC approval of a transaction might be delayed or even denied if the buyer does not possess the requisite legal qualifications to be a licensee of a radio station or is deemed to have excessive concentration of media interests in the market. A broadly worded provision such as the following covers the various legal qualifications required by the FCC:

> The Purchaser is legally and financially qualified under the Communications Act to enter into this Agreement and the Purchaser Documents, and to consummate the transactions contemplated hereby and thereby. It is not necessary for the Purchaser or any Affiliate of the Purchaser (or any person in which the Purchaser or any Affiliate of the Purchaser has an attributable interest under the Communications Act) to seek or obtain any waiver from the FCC, dispose of any interest in any media or communications property or interest, terminate any venture or arrangement, or effectuate any changes or restructuring of its ownership, including, without limitation, the withdrawal or removal of officers or directors or the conversion or repurchase of equity securities of the Purchaser or any Affiliate of the Purchaser or owned by the Purchaser or any Affiliate of the Purchaser (or any person in which Purchaser or any Affiliate of the Purchaser has any attributable interest under the Communications Act). The Purchaser is able to certify on an FCC Form 314 that it is financially qualified.

In a like vein, a sales agreement provided as follows:

Buyer is legally, financially and otherwise qualified to acquire and own the Station and operate the Station's Business under all applicable federal, state and local laws, rules and regulations, including the Communications Act. The filing of the Assignment Application will not require any waiver of the FCC's rules, regulations and policies, with respect to Buyer or any Person having an attributable interest in Buyer pursuant to the Communications Act or the rules, regulations and policies of the FCC. To Buyer's Knowledge, no fact or circumstance exists relating to the FCC qualifications of Buyer that (a) could reasonably be expected to prevent or delay the FCC from granting the Assignment Application or (b) would otherwise disqualify Buyer as the licensee, owner, operator or assignee of the Station.

C. Selling Assets But Obtaining the Benefits of a Stock Sale

In some situations and especially for tax reasons, the seller of a radio station might insist on a sale of stock (rather than assets). Buyers generally prefer to purchase assets rather than to risk assuming hidden liabilities by acquiring stock and in order to get the tax benefits of a stepped-up-basis of the assets. One seller devised an unusual and creative solution by persuading the buyer to agree to the following provision:

> The Purchase Price will be increased by an amount equal to the amount by which, all else being equal, the income taxes of the Stockholders resulting from this sale of assets exceeds the income taxes of the Stockholders which would have been payable upon a sale of stock of the Seller, as reasonably determined by Seller's accountants, plus $10,000.00 to compensate Seller for additional attorney's and accounting fees, provided that Seller, Seller's accountants and the Stockholders will make available to Buyer such information as Buyer shall reasonably request for purposes of verifying the determination of Seller's accounts, including income tax returns if needed.

D. Limiting Personnel and Promotional Obligations

Most asset purchase agreements require the seller to use its best efforts to retain existing employees and to maintain the same levels of expenditure for advertising and promotion. However, one seller negotiated the inclusion of the following provision:

Except for the level of Sales Department employees (which Seller intends to reduce shortly after execution of this Agreement), Seller will use its best efforts to maintain its staff levels; however, Seller shall be under no obligation to hire employees to replace any employees who may voluntarily resign between the period from execution of the Final Sale Agreement and the Closing.

The Agreement also provided that "Seller shall be under no obligation to maintain the same levels of expenditures for advertising and promotional efforts as expended prior to execution of this Agreement."

In another asset purchase agreement the seller obtained the following provision: "It is understood and agreed that the defection of any of the Stations' present employees following the execution of this Agreement and prior to the Closing Date shall not constitute a material adverse change in the business of Seller."

E. Easing the Pain of the Buyer's Default

How can the seller be protected if the buyer "walks" from the deal?

Most agreements provide for the collection of liquidated damages by the seller (usually, the total amount of the escrow deposit) in the event of a breach of any material representation, warranty, covenant, or condition. Typically, the liquidated damages provision makes clear that the seller has no other remedies in the event of a breach. For example, one asset purchase agreement stated that "[r]ecovery of liquidated damages from the Escrow Account shall be the sole and exclusive remedy of Seller against Buyer for failing to consummate this Agreement on the Closing Date and shall be applicable regardless of the actual amount of damages sustained."

In some situations, sellers have been able to negotiate a provision which gives them the option of collecting the escrow deposit as liquidated damages or going to court to collect compensatory damages. For example, an asset purchase agreement provided that in the event of a material breach by the buyer of any of its representations and warranties, the seller had the option of treating the escrow deposit as liquidated damages or, at seller's option, waiving the right to liquidated damages and bringing "an action at law or in equity to cover its actual compensatory damages, if any, sustained as a result of such default."

F. Selling the Equipment "As Is"

Sometimes the seller of a station tries to obtain a provision that, in effect, states that the buyer is acquiring the equipment and the buildings on an "as is" basis. One asset purchase agreement provided that "Buyer and Seller agree that Seller expressly disclaims any warranties of merchantability or fitness for a particular purpose, and that Buyer has obtained the advice of independent engineers employed by Buyer as to the usefulness or fitness of the personal tangible assets for Buyer's purposes."

G. Turning Adversity into a Tax Deduction: A Charitable Donation

Are there any alternatives to bankruptcy for a deficit-ridden radio station that cannot attract buyers? One alternative carrying potential tax benefits for the owner is for the licensee to donate the assets of the station to a qualified Section 501(c)(3) charitable corporation. For example, a licensee donated the assets of the station to a local college. The Agreement for Donation of Station provided that the donor intended that "the transfer of STATION to COLLEGE shall be a contribution to enhance COLLEGE's public educational services" and stated that the "Donor values the equipment, facilities and other elements of this donation of STATION to COLLEGE at [specified sum]." One cautionary note: the Internal Revenue Service requires an appraisal that documents the value attributed to the assets of the station.

H. Profiting From a Material Positive Change: The Flip Side of Material Adverse Change

A "material adverse change" provision is included in some contracts to protect the buyer in the event that the station performs poorly between the date of the execution of the acquisition agreement and the closing. Generally, sellers take the position that a "material adverse change" provision is not appropriate if a Local Marketing Agreement (LMA) is entered into on the ground that an LMA shifts the operating risk to the buyer.

By contrast, some agreements provide for an upward adjustment of the purchase price for the seller in the event the station performs significantly better than anticipated. For example in one asset purchase agreement the parties agreed that the cash payment to be paid by the buyer to the seller at the closing would be increased on a dollar for dollar basis, by the increase in working capital during the term of the time brokerage agreement into which the parties were entering contemporaneously with the execution and delivery of the purchase agreement. Conversely, the parties also agreed that the cash payment to be paid by the buyer would be decreased, on a dollar for dollar basis, in an amount equal to any decrease in working capital that occurred during the term of the time brokerage agreement.

A "material positive change" clause can be very useful for a seller when there is clear reason to expect that the station will increase in value following the closing. For example, say you're the licensee of a small market radio station and you have a construction permit application on file with the FCC to relocate the station closer to a major metropolitan center. You've decided to sell the facility before completing the upgrade, but you would still like to realize an upside from the increased value the upgrade is likely to deliver. How do you achieve that objective?

One approach to this problem can be found in an asset purchase agreement in which the parties established a base purchase price for the station of $7 million, which was subject to upward adjustment if the buyer, within three years of acquiring the station, successfully completed the upgrade and sold the station to a third party for a net profit in excess of $10 million. The specific amount of the adjustment depended on the amount of the net profits from the resale. Specifically, in the event that the net profits on the resale of the station were between $10 million and $30 million, the seller, was to receive a 10% share of the net profits in addition to the base price. If the net profits exceeded $30 million, the seller, would be entitled to 25% of the net profits over that figure.

To effectuate these provisions, the agreement required the buyer to notify the seller in writing within five days of entering an agreement for the sale of the upgraded station to a third party. The notice was required to include the amount of the purchase price adjustment to which the seller, was entitled. Moreover, because the agreement provided that the net profits were to consist of the buyer's net proceeds for the resale minus all of its direct costs related thereto (including, e.g., legal and engineering fees, filing fees, build out costs, and any costs associated with the third party purchase agreement or any channel change agreements), the buyer was also required to furnish an itemized breakdown of the costs used to calculate net profits, which breakdown was subject to audit by the seller. Finally, the agreement directed the buyer to instruct the third party purchaser to distribute the purchase price adjustment directly to the seller at the time of the closing of the resale of the station. The caution to the seller in this kind of arrangement is that the buyer may either wait to sell the station until after the negotiated period of time or may never sell the station.

I. Using Warrants

The use of warrants also enables the seller of a station to reap some benefit from an increase in the value of the property after the station is sold. For example, in one transaction, the purchase price for the stations was one million dollars. The letter-agreement for the purchase of the stations provided that the buyer would deliver to seller "a warrant for five percent (5%) of the accretion in the stations above the $1,000,000 price." The warrant was made exercisable when the stations were sold to an independent third party or at the maturity of the bank loan taken out by buyer (namely, five years from the closing). In the event that the stations were not sold prior to the maturity of the loan, the parties agreed to engage an appraiser to determine the stations' value. The letter agreement provided that in the event of a disagreement between the appraisers, they would choose a mutually-acceptable third appraiser whose opinion would be binding.

J. Obtaining Added Value for Seller Paper

"Seller paper" (a purchase money mortgage) can be used as a means of financing the purchase if mezzanine financing or subordinated debt is difficult to obtain. Seller paper is usually subordinated to senior bank debt and often takes the form of a loan at two to three times cash flow for a five-year period at a fixed interest rate at or below prime. Some agreements give warrants to the seller to provide the seller with the benefit of the possible upside of a transaction. In other transactions, all or some seller paper takes the form of a covenant not to compete. In some deals, the seller is given stock in the acquiring company as well as a promissory note.

In one transaction, the seller agreed to take a promissory note in the amount of $400,000 with the following terms: (a) the entire principal balance (including any deferred interest accrued during the first year) would not be due until five years after the closing, and (b) the note would be deemed paid in full if on or before a fixed date, the buyer paid the seller $250,000 plus all accrued interest. This promissory note reflects a negotiated discount for early payment which provides a significant benefit for both the buyer and the seller.

In addition, the buyer agreed to deliver another promissory note with a principal balance equal to the lesser of the face amount of all of the accounts receivable or $150,000.00. The asset purchase agreement provided that prior to full payment, the seller could put the note to the buyer in exchange for a 5% stock interest in another broadcast station owned by the buyer "plus the payment of all accrued interest, including any deferred interests accrued during the first year."

To protect the seller, payment of both promissory notes was secured by a security interest in the tangible and intangible personal property used in the operation of the station. To benefit the buyer, the agreement provided that the buyer's obligations were subordinate and junior with regard to its obligations (including any refinancing) to one or more institutional lenders up to a maximum principal balance of $2,500,000. Also, to make sure that the seller helped the buyer obtain financing, the asset purchase agreement provided that:

> Seller agrees to cooperate with Buyer, Buyer's underwriters, lenders, and their respective agents and representatives in connection with Buyer's financing arrangements, including without limitation providing such information and documents as Buyer may reasonably request for the purpose of obtaining the funds required to consummate the transaction.

This transaction illustrates how the seller can accommodate the buyer

by, in effect, providing working capital, by creating an incentive for early payment of a note, and by making it easier for the buyer to obtain financing. In turn, the buyer provides the seller with a subordinated secured interest in the physical assets of the station and an option to purchase stock in another broadcast licensee.

K. Securing Protection for Seller Paper

If the seller provides the buyer with seller paper, what protection can the seller obtain to make sure that the station will be operated properly and that financial and other information will be provided on a timely basis after the closing? One seller sold the station assets for $4,000,000 and received the buyer's promissory note in the amount of $3,200,000. Since the seller paper accounted for the lion's share of the sales price, the seller wanted protection in addition to a security agreement (accompanied by a UCC-1 filing), a trust deed on the real estate, and a pledge agreement from the three individuals who provided personal guarantees.

The asset purchase agreement provided for a series of "post closing covenants" by the buyer concerning the operation of the station in accordance with all laws and regulations, payment of all taxes, maintenance of the assets in good condition and repair, and keeping the assets free of liens and encumbrances. These covenants echo those that the seller provided for the period between execution of the contract and the closing. Also, the buyer was required to keep the assets fully insured against fire, theft or vandalism and to name the seller as an additional insured under the policy and to "insure the life of one of the principals of the buyer" in an amount equal to the unpaid balance of the Note with the Seller named as beneficiary." The buyer was also obligated to provide the seller with quarterly financial statements. The seller or an agent of the seller was given "the right at reasonable times during Buyer's normal business hours to inspect the assets and to inspect, audit and copy any books and records of Buyer relating to the Assets."

Although it would seem logical that the seller should be able to protect itself by providing that the station will revert to the seller in the event that the buyer defaults on the seller paper, this type of reversionary interest is prohibited by the FCC's rules. Section 73.1150 of the Commission's rules is broadly worded. It provides that, in assigning a broadcast license, the licensee "may retain no right of reversion of the license, no right to reassignment of the license in the future, and may not reserve the right to use the facilities of the station for any period whatsoever." Moreover,

the Commission staff takes the position that such a reversionary interest cannot be salvaged by including a requirement that FCC approval be obtained before the station is reassigned to the seller.

Section 73.1150 can also be read to prevent a seller from holding rights to provide programming over the station once the closing occurs. In an agreement for the sale of a noncommercial educational radio station, the parties included a provision whereby the seller would hold a right of first refusal to "prepare, produce, present on-air, and sell course materials for" college level courses to be aired on the station if the buyer ever proposed to offer such college-level courses as programming on the station. The FCC staff objected to this provision and the parties found it necessary to file an amendment to the purchase agreement that struck this provision. According to the amendment, the parties agreed to strike the provision because the FCC staff had advised counsel for the parties that the provision "must be deleted to bring the Agreement into compliance with FCC rules and policy."

L. Building a Margin of Error in Financial Statements

One of the most important provisions of a contract is the representation and warranty concerning the accuracy of the financial statements furnished by the seller. The seller should review its financials with its accountant(s) and other experts to identify problems. The wording is often the subject of intense negotiations. In some exceptional situations, the seller is able to negotiate a contract which contains no representations or warranties concerning financials, but the seller should beware. In a stock transaction, SEC Rule 10b-5 prohibits "... mak[ing] any untrue statement of a material fact or... omit[ting] to state a material fact necessary in order to make the statements made, in the light of the circumstances under which they were made, not misleading."

While most contracts provide that financial statements are prepared in accordance with "generally accepted accounting principles," sellers try to include a provision which allows for a margin of error. For example, in one asset purchase agreement, the sellers negotiated the following provision:

> The financial statements are not audited but are prepared substantially in accordance with accepted accounting principles consistently applied, are correct in all substantial and material respects and present fairly, the operating income and financial condition of the stations as of their respective dates and results of operations for the period then ended.

M. Providing Incentives for the Seller and the Seller's Key Executive

How do you provide an incentive to the hands-on executive of the seller who will be responsible for making or breaking the success of the acquired station? In one asset purchase agreement, an executive of the seller was given a lucrative compensation arrangement whereby he would have a substantial personal stake in the operation. First, he was given an opportunity to purchase stock in the corporation at a sweetheart rate and on sweetheart terms – while the price for the stock was specified as $100,000, the buyer agreed to loan the executive $66,667.00 of the $100,000, payable over a three year period. Secondly, the executive was given options to purchase an additional 15% of the stock: 5% at closing, 5% one year later and 5% in two years for one dollar each purchase. Third, if the stations were to be sold for more than $50 million, the executive would receive, as a bonus, 20% of the net proceeds, and if sold between $47.5 million and $50 million, a proportionate percentage. (A cautionary note: any executive compensation plan must comply with the strict requirements contained in Section 409A of the Internal Revenue Code.)

The asset purchase agreement also contained a creative way of assuring that a station would have sufficient funds to operate prior to the closing and of giving the seller a piece of the action if the station was very profitable the first year after it was sold. The buyer agreed to loan the seller $200,000 which would be credited against the sale price at closing. If the deal were to fall through, the buyer would take back $200,000 with interest plus $10,000 "to compensate Purchaser for its costs and expenses in making the loan." The contract provided for "an incentive profit payment" of $500,000 to the seller if the gross revenues during the first year after closing are greater than or equal to $4 million. The payment is a creative way of giving the seller a share of the profits without having to give away a stock interest.

N. Obtaining Some of the Benefit of Post-Closing Improvements.

Diligent broadcasters remain perpetually attuned to application and rule making activity at the FCC that could potentially affect their ability to seek an improvement in station facilities. The station's power may be able to be increased. The antenna may be able to be moved closer to a larger market. A rule making may be able to be filed that could lead to a significant improvement in coverage. Generally, these types of facilities improvements take a lot of time. Months and, frequently, years may be devoted to the upgrade project. Having invested substantial time, effort and money in the upgrade project, the seller does not want the buyer to reap the benefits of the project without rewarding the seller for its efforts. The buyer does not want to pay the seller for those efforts unless they produce results. Of course, at the time that the application is filed, the parties cannot be sure that the FCC will grant the application or the rule making that will lead to the improvement of the station's coverage or even that the improved facilities authorized by the FCC will receive local zoning approvals.

The compromise usually achieved in such cases is to include a provision whereby the buyer will make a payment to the seller above and beyond the purchase price if the upgrade project is successful. The difficulty in such cases is in reaching agreement as to what constitutes successful completion of the project. An initial grant by the FCC staff is subject to further review and consideration, so the issuance of a favorable staff decision is usually not a satisfactory point at which to consider the project complete. Even when the staff decision is final, other obstacles may arise that would prevent the station from ever achieving the facilities upgrade that had been contemplated by the parties. Zoning authorities may deny permission to build the new facility. The tower site may prove to be unsuitable for construction. The construction permit filed in response to the successful rule making may not be granted.

As each milestone in the process of upgrading the facility is reached, the risk that the project may fail decreases, but the length of time that the impatient seller must wait before it receives its payment increases. The seller may be forced to trade dollars for a more immediate payment. Whatever compromise ultimately is reached by the parties, it is vitally important that the payment be tied to a clear, demonstrable event, such as a final FCC decision, a final zoning board decision or the FCC's final grant of a covering license application for the facilities. The use of a well-defined triggering event helps to avoid disputes as to the timetable for payment.

In deciding which event will trigger the payment obligation, the parties may be tempted to use the final grant of the covering license application inasmuch as the issuance of that grant removes virtually all uncertainty as to whether the upgrade will become a reality. Sellers, nevertheless, would be well advised to take care in deciding whether to use the final grant of the covering license application as the triggering event. Processing of covering license applications has a very low priority at the FCC and as a result, it is not uncommon for many months to elapse before the covering license is granted. In the meantime, buyer is able to make use of the upgraded facilities while seller continues to wait for its payment. From seller's perspective, that is an unhappy situation. One alternative triggering event that could be used is the commencement of operations pursuant to Program Test Authority (PTA). Although commencement of PTA does not signal an absolute certainty that the covering license application will be granted, it reduces the likelihood of non-grant significantly. Stations routinely operate under the terms of PTA during the time the covering license application is pending. Although grant of PTA does not signal an absolute certainty that the license will be granted, it reduces the risk of non-grant to nearly zero.

CHAPTER SIX

HOW TO LEAVE THE PIG IN THE POKE: GETTING WHAT YOU BARGAINED FOR

Today's marketplace presents new challenges to many buyers attempting to buy stations while ensuring that the station's operations will not deteriorate between the contract signing and the closing, and that all of the equipment will remain in good condition while minimizing the risk of environmental liabilities and maximizing the likelihood that the seller will resolve any problems arising after the closing. These challenges require innovative solutions.

This chapter discusses creative contract strategies used by buyers in four areas: (1) making sure that there will be no surprises concerning the condition of the equipment, the status of the real property, the accuracy of the financial statements, any facilities upgrade promised by the seller, and the obligation of the seller to take care of the accounts payable; (2) engineering and environmental audits; (3) ways of dealing with a potential "material adverse change" in the operation of the station between the execution of the contract and the closing, including both positive and punitive approaches, and (4) creative uses

by the buyer of the seller's accounts receivable.

Avoiding Unpleasant (Translated: Costly) Surprises

A. Making Sure the Real Estate is "For Real"

How does the buyer of a radio station make sure that the real estate being purchased is free from any defects? The acquisition agreement should contain representations and warranties concerning the real property owned, leased or used by the seller. Typically, the seller will make representations as to title, proper zoning, condition and the lack of encumbrances.

In an asset acquisition, the buyer should obtain title insurance on any real estate to be purchased. If the transaction is structured as a stock purchase, the purchaser should determine if the seller has a valid title insurance policy. A standard title insurance policy will insure the buyer against loss or damage occasioned by (1) title to the property being vested in an individual or entity other than the insured; (2) any defect in or lien or encumbrance on title; (3) the lack of right of access to property, or (4) unmarketability of title.

One asset purchase agreement required the seller to purchase, at its own expense, title insurance which would "insure title to the Real Property to the Buyer subject to only standard printed exceptions normally contained in the owner's title commitment." The agreement concerning real estate, which prospective buyers might view as a checklist, also contained representations and warranties of the seller concerning (1) the lack of existing or threatened condemnation proceedings, (2) the sufficiency of the zoning for the uses of the property "as intended by Buyer;" (3) the location of towers, antennas, guy lines, anchors and other related structures within the confines of the real property; (4) the validity of the easements for the utilities required for the operation of the station; (5) the use of improvements on the real property and the conduct of business as having been in accordance with any laws, statutes, ordinances, rules or regulations of any governmental body "including, without limitation, those concerned with environmental and occupational safety standards"; and (6) the lack of any problems with respect to "adequate water supply, sewage and waste disposal facilities or air, water or land pollution."

☐ If the transmitter site and/or the studio is leased, the seller will need to make arrangements for the assignment of its lease(s) to the buyer. The landlord's consent to the assignment of such lease(s) should be a condition to the buyer's obligation to close. If the site is one that cannot easily be replaced, it is of critical importance that a lease with a substantial term (*e.g.*, a minimum of 10 to 15 years) be assigned to the buyer because of the difficulty of finding an alternative site. Given the importance of the continued availability of the site in such circumstances, the buyer may wish to consider obtaining a leasehold title insurance policy. The following extensive provision concerning real property leases was contained in a purchase and sale agreement:

Real Property Leases

(i.)   The <u>Asset Schedule</u> contains accurate descriptions of the Real Property Leases and the location of the real estate leased thereunder (the Leaseholds) and the type of facility located on the Leaseholds. Seller will as of the Closing have a valid leasehold interest in each of the Leaseholds.

(ii.) None of the Leaseholds is subject to any covenant or restriction preventing or limiting in any respect the consummation of the transactions contemplated hereby, except for any consent listed on Seller's Disclosure Schedule required of the landlords under the Real Property Leases. Seller's right, title and interest in and to the Leaseholds will at the Closing be held by Seller free and clear of all Liens.

(iii.) The use for which the Leaseholds are zoned permits the use thereof for the business of the Station consistent with past practices. The use and occupancy of the Leaseholds by Seller are in compliance in all material respects with all regulations, codes, ordinances and statutes applicable to Seller and the Business, and Seller has not received any notice asserting any material violation of sanitation laws and regulations,

occupational safety and health regulations, or electrical codes.

(iv.) There are no facts relating to Seller, and to the best of the knowledge of Seller, no facts relating to any other party, that would prevent the Leaseholds from being occupied and used by the Buyer and/or any assignee of the Buyer after the Closing Date in the same manner as immediately prior to the Closing.

(v.) There is not under any Real Property Lease any material default by Seller or any condition that with notice or the passage of time or both would constitute such a default, and Seller has not received any notice asserting the existence of any such default or condition.

(vi.) Each Real Property Lease is valid and binding and in full force and effect as to Seller and, to the best of the knowledge of Seller, as to each other party thereto, and except as disclosed on the Asset Schedule, has not been amended or otherwise modified.

(vii.) The Leaseholds constitute all of the real property in which Seller has a leasehold interest or other interest

122

or right (whether as lessor or lessee) and which is or will prior to the Closing be used in the operation of the Station.

B. Assuring Station Value

When the calculation of the purchase price is based upon a multiple of the station's cash flow, it is important for a buyer to assure against inaccuracies in cash flow estimates. One buyer utilized an interesting and effective device to shield itself from such cash flow discrepancies.

In that agreement, the buyer obtained a provision that if the station's broadcast cash flow for the calendar year of closing was less than a specified amount ($12,000,000), then the seller would be required to pay the buyer an amount equal to 20 times the shortfall as an adjustment to the purchase price. The buyer was required to calculate the amount of any broadcast cash flow shortfall and provide it to the sellers by a date certain. If the sellers disagreed with the buyer's calculation of the shortfall, then the parties had 10 business days to attempt to resolve the dispute in good faith, after which time, in the absence of a resolution, the matter would be submitted to binding arbitration by a private accounting firm designated by the parties. In addition, if the seller's supplemental financial statements to be provided to the buyer prior to the closing suggested that a shortfall in cash flow would be likely, then the buyer would be entitled to withhold, in escrow, an amount equal to 20 times the estimated shortfall from the purchase price at closing.

Also of particular interest, the parties excluded from the calculation of the broadcast cash flow shortfall any losses the buyer might incur in connection with a contract for the rights to broadcast certain National Football League games. Instead, the parties provided separate protections for the buyer for such losses, providing for reimbursement of any such losses as a purchase price adjustment, and also providing procedural mechanisms, including binding arbitration, for the resolution of any disputes that might arise.

C. Making Sure the Financial Statements are Accurate

The representation and warranty concerning the accuracy of the seller's financial statements constitutes one of the most important provisions in an asset purchase agreement. These financial records usually take the form of a comparative balance sheet, income statement and a statement of cash flow for the last three to five years and for the most recently available stub period. Preferably, the financial statements will come from the station's outside independent accountants.

Such outside financial reports come with three ascending degrees of assurance.

Compiled

"Compiled" financial statements simply reflect information provided by the station to its accountant. From the accountant's standpoint, this means that all figures are unverified; transactions have simply been "compiled" and categorized in accordance with generally accepted accounting principles.

Reviewed

The term "reviewed," when applied to financial statements, means that the accountant has systematically looked at the client's controls and original books of entry for some, but not all, of the transactions reflected in the financial statements and has formed a general conclusion that those transactions have been accurately presented.

Audited

The greatest level of assurance is provided by "audited" financial records. In conducting an audit, accountants examine all original records of revenue and expense and independently verify the existence of assets and obligations listed in the financial statements. Unfortunately for buyers, few companies undertake this substantial expense,

except publicly traded companies or where audited financial reports are required by lenders as a condition of loans.

With all financial statements, whether compiled, reviewed or audited, the "notes" following the statements are an integral part of the report and should be carefully reviewed to ascertain the accountant's reservations about the statements and the limitations on the report.

Most banks require independently prepared financial statements when reviewing a loan application. Depending on the size of the offering, when a buyer intends to resort to the private capital markets for financing, such as through a limited partnership offering, audited financial statements may be required. And when the acquisition is to be made through the purchase of stock rather than simply the purchase of assets, the availability of audited financial statements takes on added importance.

Where there are material doubts about a station's financial history, the buyer should insist on the opportunity to make what accountants refer to as a "businessman's review" of the financial records and seek to make the satisfactory completion of such a review (that is, verification of previously supplied financial reports) a condition of the buyer's obligation to complete a purchase.

The wording of the provision concerning the seller's financial records often generates intense negotiation between the buyer and the seller. In some exceptional situations, the seller can negotiate a contract containing no representations or warranties concerning the financials. Most contracts require financial statements to be prepared in accordance with "generally accepted accounting principles (GAAP)." Although the requirement that financial statements be prepared in accordance with GAAP provides some comfort to the buyer, the buyer should be aware of the wide latitude of generally accepted accounting practices within GAAP. GAAP describes a broad group of concepts and methods for preparing financial statements. Also, GAAP permits the exercise of professional judgment in deciding how to present financial results fairly. Thus, GAAP permits different methods of accounting for items such as inventory valuation (FIFO, LIFO, or average cost), depreciation (straight line or accelerated methods), and accounting for repairs and small tools. Some sellers try to include a provision which allows for a margin of error. For example, in one asset purchase agreement the sellers negotiated the following provision:

The Financial Statements are not audited but are prepared substantially in accordance with generally accepted accounting principles consistently applied, are correct in all substantial and material respects and present fairly, the operating income and financial condition of the Stations as of their respective dates and the results of operations for the period then ended.

By contrast, at the buyer's request, an asset purchase agreement contained the following provision:

The Financial Statements are prepared in accordance with generally accepted accounting principles consistently applied, are true and correct in all material respects, and present fairly the operating income and financial condition of the Station as at their respective dates and the results of the operations for the periods then ended. None of the Financial Statements understates the true costs and expenses of conducting the business or operations of the Station, fails to disclose all material contingent liabilities, or inflates the revenue of the Station because of the provision of services or the bearing of costs or expenses or the payment of fees by any other person, or for any other reason.

This provision protects the buyer more extensively than the phrase "generally accepted accounting principles" and provides stronger language in the event of a lawsuit. Similar language could also be used in those situations in which the seller's financial statements have not been prepared in accordance with GAAP, which is often the case with smaller licensees. In such situations, the seller should be required to explain precisely how its financial statements have not been prepared in accordance with GAAP, but should also provide the remaining representations and warranties set forth above.

As the price of a radio station increases, the possibility that the buyer may be required to audit the station increases. To facilitate that audit, it is helpful if the seller commits in the purchase agreement to cooperate in the conducting of such audit including, without limitation, by providing management representation letters that may be requested by the auditors. Such letters usually require the seller to confirm certain matters concerning the preparation of the seller's financial statements and the conduct of the seller's company. The letters, in turn, help the auditors to ensure that the seller's financial statements fairly present the financial position, results of operations, and cash flows of the seller.

D. Making Sure the Accounts Payable are Paid in Full

How can you make sure that the seller of the station pays all the accounts payable due at closing? In one asset purchase agreement, the buyer persuaded the seller, (a) to warrant that any accounts payable which were not paid at the closing would be taken as an offset against the funds to be paid to seller, and (b) to require the seller to place in escrow at the closing a sufficient amount of funds from the buyer's down payment "to pay all usual, ordinary or otherwise known expenses of the Station which occur prior to the Closing Date but which have not yet been billed to Seller as of the Closing Date." This provision assured the buyer that all station creditors would be paid, including those who had not submitted bills as of the closing, thereby eliminating situations which might create considerable ill will toward the station.

Undoubtedly, the most unwelcome surprise to confront a buyer would be to learn that the license for the radio station being purchased will not be renewed by the FCC without a significant amount of legal wrangling, uncertainty or delay. Although the FCC designates a renewal application for hearing only in the most unusual of cases, it is becoming increasingly common for the FCC to delay the grant of a renewal application while the Commission confirms that the station has complied with the Commission's various reporting requirements. To help minimize the likelihood of such delay, a prudent purchaser will insist upon a representation by the seller that the seller has made all requisite filings with the FCC on a timely basis and is maintaining the requisite public inspection files. The following is a typical representation concerning the seller's compliance:

> "All reports and filings required to be filed by the Sellers with the FCC and all material reports and filings required to be filed by the Sellers with any other agency of the Federal, State or local government ("Government Agency") have been timely filed. All FCC reports and filings are accurate and complete and all other reports and filings are accurate and complete in all material respects and from the date hereof to the Effective Time all will be filed on a timely basis. Each Seller maintains appropriate public files at the Stations as required by FCC rules."

E. Making Sure that the Seller Has Funding for Post-Closing Breaches of Contract

A buyer's major concern is how to collect monies from seller for breaches of contract discovered after the closing. Among the sources of funds to remedy a breach are accounts receivable payments collected by the buyer on the seller's behalf and payments owed to the seller pursuant to the terms of a promissory note, consulting agreement or covenant not to compete. An example is the following provision in the asset purchase agreement: "Buyer shall have the right to offset against either of the accounts receivable due under Section 8.6 of this Agreement, or against payments due the Shareholders under the Consulting Agreement, any and all amounts suffered or damages incurred by Buyer as a result of Seller's material breach of any of its representations or warranties under this Agreement."

In some transactions, the parties agree in advance to the specific amount of money to be deposited in an indemnification fund. One buyer successfully negotiated a provision entitling it to withhold at the closing payment of "such amount as may be necessary" to insure compliance with post-closing provisions and adjustments and with "all of seller's representations and warranties." The open-ended wording of this provision gave the buyer an unusual amount of latitude concerning the amount of the purchase price that it might withhold.

In an asset purchase agreement adopting a middle ground, the buyer was given a limited right of offset to the monies which it collected from the accounts receivable. The Agreement also stated that prior to offsetting any sums, "Buyer shall provide Seller with written notice of its intention, setting forth in reasonable detail the claim which is the reason for such action, within ten (10) days prior to taking such action." In the event the seller disagreed with the amounts to be offset and provided the buyer with notice of such disagreement within three business days, the agreement required the buyer to deposit the offsetting funds into an escrow account until its claim could be arbitrated. The agreement provided that "the party which succeeds in arbitration shall be entitled to receive any interest accrued on the escrowed amount during such escrow, and the party which does not succeed shall bear all costs (including reasonable attorney's fees and expenses) related to such arbitration."

F. Retaining Key Employees

Many acquisition contracts are silent on the fate of current employees of the station when the new owner assumes control. Some agreements deal with this situation directly. One asset purchase agreement, for example, contained a representation that "Seller has not received notification that any of the current [station] employees of Seller presently plan to terminate their employment, whether by reason of the transactions contemplated hereby or otherwise." The seller was obligated to "[i]ntroduce Purchaser to its [station] employees prior to the closing date and reasonably encourage these employees to become employees of Purchaser." The agreement also provided that "Seller shall arrange to terminate each of Seller's [station] employees, at no resulting expense to Purchaser, on or before closing unless Purchaser has advised Seller in writing at least forty five (45) days prior to closing that Purchaser desires to retain such employees." The buyer, the Agreement provided, "shall have no obligations to employ any of the current employees of Seller."

How does a buyer make sure that key employees of the station will continue to be employed by the seller? One asset purchase agreement required the seller to "use its best efforts to retain [John Doe and Jane Doe] as employees of the stations through the closing date, including offering them additional compensation contingent on their remaining as employees of the Stations." Since the seller owned other radio stations, the agreement provided that "seller shall not transfer either [John Doe and Jane Doe] to a position with Seller other than at the Stations and shall not offer either of them such a position."

Another approach to assuring the retention of seller's employees was contained in the following provision:

Employment Offers. Upon notice to the Seller, and at mutually agreeable times, the Seller will permit the Buyers to meet with its employees prior to the Closing Date. The Buyers may, at their option, extend offers of employment to all or any of the Seller's employees effective on the Closing Date. From and after the execution of this Agreement, the Seller shall use its best efforts to assist Buyers in retaining those employees of the Stations which the Buyers wish to hire in connection with the operation of the Stations by the Buyers subsequent to the Closing, and the Seller will not take any action to preclude or discourage any of the Seller's employees from accepting any offer of employment extended by Buyers.

The same agreement also included the following provision concerning severance benefits of seller's employees who were hired by the buyer:

Severance Obligations. In the event an offer of employment is extended by the Buyers to and accepted by an employee of the Seller pursuant to [the above] Section and such subsequent employment by the Buyers is terminated within sixty (60) days from the Closing date, the Seller shall be responsible for, and shall pay to such accepting employee, all severance benefits (if any, pursuant to the Seller's practices as in effect on the Closing Date) that may be due and owing such employee by reason of his or her employment with either the Seller or the Buyers.

Where the seller has a union contract in place, the hiring or retention of former employees of the seller in sufficient numbers as to constitute a majority of the new bargaining unit could obligate the buyer in an asset transaction to recognize the union as the employees' representative and to bargain with it under the "successorship" doctrine. However, the buyer would not necessarily be obligated to assume or be bound by the substantive provisions of the union contract, although care must be taken to ensure that the buyer's conduct after the transaction is not considered to be a tacit adoption of the contract. The buyer is free to select its own work force but may not refuse to hire the seller's employees because of their union membership or activities or in order to avoid having to recognize and bargain with the union.

G. Assuming Only Those Time Sales Agreements Made in the Ordinary Course of Business

Most asset purchase agreements provide that the buyer will assume all contracts for the sale of advertising time for cash. Some contracts provide that the buyer will assume only those time sales agreements entered into by seller in the ordinary course of business, consistent with the past practices of seller. However, one asset purchase agreement provided that among the assets being purchased is "each Time Sales Contract, which is in effect on the Closing, provided that the Purchaser need not assume any 'evergreen contract,' or any other contract which does not terminate within ninety (90) days following Closing unless Purchaser previously has consented thereto." This provision allows a buyer not to assume long-term, low rate "sweetheart" advertising contracts.

Especially in the case of radio stations that have not been profitable, trade accounts may constitute a significant portion of the station's advertising revenues. The seller may have accrued a substantial obligation to provide air time to the trade account advertisers and, in all likelihood, will have no way of satisfying these obligations other than by requiring the buyer to assume the obligations and to broadcast the commercials to which the trade account advertisers are entitled. This represents a drain on buyer's commercial inventory with no corresponding revenue. In other cases where a trade account may not have a negative balance, the buyer still may have little use for the good or service being provided by the trade account advertiser in return for the advertising being aired over the station. One custom that has arisen in dealing with trade accounts is for the purchaser to agree to air advertising for trade account advertisers up to a given dollar amount and to be reimbursed by the seller for any advertising required to be aired in excess of that amount. Typically, no payment is made by the buyer to the seller if the dollar value of the goods and services to be provided after the closing by the trade account advertisers to the buyer exceeds the dollar value of the advertising time to be provided by the buyer after closing. The following provision concerning trade accounts is typical:

The Sellers' trade and barter accounts, trade contracts and trade commitments receivable and payable (the "Trade Accounts") are listed in detail on Schedule 2.3(e), which lists the Sellers' gross dollar obligations to provide airtime by advertiser and the gross airtime assets available of the Sellers as of [date certain]. The Sellers will transfer all Trade Accounts to the Buyer at the Closing, effective as of the Effective Time, and the Buyer shall assume the Trade Accounts; *provided, however,* if the aggregate airtime liability of the advertising-for-advertising Trade Accounts to be assumed by the Buyer at Closing exceeds the value of advertising to be received by the Stations as of the Effective Time ("Value of Trades") by more than $10,000, all as determined in accordance with Sellers' customary bookkeeping practices, then the excess Trade Accounts shall appear as a debit to Sellers in the closing pro rations . . . provided, further, all such Trade Accounts assumed by the Buyer shall be subject to preemption for cash advertising.

H. Making Sure the Proposed Upgrade Is a Reality

Sellers often tell prospective purchasers that the station has the potential to be upgraded. In most acquisitions, however, the buyer purchases the target station on an "as-is, where-is" basis. That is, although the buyer may be investing with a view toward capitalizing on the target station's unrealized potential, the seller typically delivers the station only at its existing location, in its existing operating condition. A prudent buyer will make sure that the sales agreement expressly deals with any promised upgrade.

In some transactions, the buyer agrees to pay an additional sum for the station in the event that the FCC grants a construction permit (or amends the FM Table of Allotments) to authorize the upgrade. Thus, in one agreement, the buyer agreed to sign a promissory note to the seller at the closing in the amount of $200,000.00. The agreement provided that "Buyer's obligation to pay the Note shall be conditioned upon the FCC action issuing a report and order upgrading the station's facilities and that report and order becoming a Final Order (the "Approval Date"). The Note provided that $100,000.00 was payable within five business days after the Approval Date. The remaining $100,000.00 (plus interest) was to be paid on the latest of (1) the date on which the Commission Order granting the construction permit became final, (2) the date on which the buyer constructed the facilities, or (3) the second anniversary of the Approval Date.

To protect the buyer, the agreement provided that the second $100,000.00 payment need not be paid if the upgraded facilities had not been built or the FCC order granting the construction permit had not become final within five years of the closing. To make sure that the buyer acted in good faith, the seller negotiated for a provision that the buyer had to have "diligently prosecuted the Upgrade, the Construction Permit, and the construction of the Improved Facilities."

A potential shortcoming of this approach is that the purchaser is then left with the task of effectuating any improvements to the station's facilities that may be needed to maximize the station's performance --- a process that can delay, perhaps indefinitely, the buyer's ability to enjoy the full value of its purchase. One method for the buyer to avoid this problem is to make FCC approval of the upgrade a condition of closing. Thus, if the Commission does not approve the upgrade within a specified period of time, the buyer can walk away from the deal.

For example, in one asset purchase agreement, the buyer did not have to close unless a construction permit for a new transmitting facility and tower was issued by the Commission and assigned to the seller in form and substance satisfactory to the buyer, "which permit shall have been extended so as not to expire prior to [fixed date] or ninety days subsequent to the closing, whichever first occurs." If the seller had not complied with this condition, the buyer could have recovered its escrow deposit with interest.

Another buyer found a similar way of getting the station it desired by securing the seller's agreement to a condition in the purchase agreement that made the deal contingent on seller's ability to deliver the station with certain significant modifications of the station's facilities already completed. The contract stated that the deal could not be consummated until the FCC had approved the proposed change in facilities.

While the agreement provided that the seller would bear the cost and responsibility for preparing the necessary FCC filings, it set forth certain time limits within which the buyer had to prosecute each of the necessary filings with the FCC.

The agreement also provided that, notwithstanding all of the undertakings required of the seller, if the buyer (despite its best efforts) was unable by a specified date to obtain final approval (including, for example, land use, zoning, and environmental approvals) to construct its facilities, then the buyer could terminate the agreement without recourse and have its escrow deposit and all accumulated interest returned.

The contract for the purchase and sale of another station exhibits a less aggressive, but just as effective approach to the same problem. Here, the parties agreed to use their best efforts to close the transaction within 60 days of the execution of the contract. However for the first 45 days of that period, the parties provided for a "feasibility period" during which the "Purchaser [had] the right to conduct such tests, studies, and examinations of the Seller and the Assets as Purchaser shall deem necessary or advisable." At any time during this Feasibility Period, if the buyer determined for any reason that it did not want to purchase the station, it could terminate the agreement without further obligation by either party. The agreement further provided that the seller and its shareholders would cooperate with the buyer in the conduct of any tests or examinations, and would provide any information or records requested.

I. Avoiding Headaches in Bankruptcy Purchases

If you are buying a station from a debtor-in-possession in reorganization proceedings under Chapter 11 of the U.S. Bankruptcy Code, how do you make sure sufficient post-closing funds will be available to pay off all claimants? One buyer negotiated an asset purchase provision that required the seller to place $500,000 in escrow as a fund for the payment of any claims for which the buyer may be entitled to indemnification. The "Indemnification Escrow" was required to be maintained for a period commencing on the closing date and ending 120 days after the closing or on the "Administrative Claims Bar Date," whichever was later. The agreement defined the Administrative Claims Bar Date as "the date declared by the Bankruptcy Court as the date from and after which the Bankruptcy Court will refuse to entertain claims against the Seller for payment of any administrative costs, fees or other liabilities." The agreement also clarified that "Buyer and Seller acknowledge that Buyer's rights to indemnification are not limited to the amount of Five Hundred Thousand Dollars ($500,000.00)."

J. Paying Off the Seller's Bank

In troubled times, the price of some radio stations might be the buyer's assumption of the outstanding bank debt. One buyer purchased a station for $1,180,000. The purchase price included the assumption of lease payments in the amount of $65,000, the assumption of the indebtedness of certain stockholders in the amount of $32,000, and the assumption of bank debt in the amount of $1,015,000. To protect the buyer, the asset purchase agreement provided that if at closing "the Bank Debt is not at least $1,015,000, the Purchase Price shall be adjusted downward to reflect that the Bank Debt assumed is less than $1,015,000." As further protection for the buyer, the agreement provided that one of the conditions of closing was that "Buyer shall have renegotiated the terms of the Bank Debt in a manner that is acceptable to Buyer in its sole discretion."

To provide some benefit to the seller in the event that the buyer concluded that the renegotiated terms of the bank note were unacceptable, the agreement provided that the seller would keep the $100,000 escrow deposit if "Buyer's failure to close was solely because the condition relating to the Bank Debt is not satisfied." The agreement also provided that the buyer could get back its $100,000 escrow deposit "if the sole reason that the buyer does not close is that the lender materially changes the terms of the Bank Debt assumption at Closing, after committing the terms of the Bank Debt assumption in writing to Buyer prior to Closing." As a means of assuring that the bank rather than the buyer materially changed the terms of the bank debt assumption, the Agreement required that the buyer "furnish Seller a copy of the lender's written commitment for the Bank Debt assumption immediately upon receipt of same."

K. Making Sure the Equipment Works

How does the buyer make sure that the equipment and other technical facilities are in good working order? Typically, the buyer negotiates for a specific representation and warranty by the seller. For example, most agreements contain a representation and warranty by the seller that the tangible property "is in good maintenance, operating condition, and repair in accordance with generally accepted standards of practice in the broadcast industry, and to Seller's knowledge, is free from defects in materials and workmanship in all material respects." In some agreements, the seller represents and warrants that "all broadcast property being sold and transferred hereunder meets the standard of good engineering practices for radio stations and in all material respects is operated in compliance with the Commission's regulations and requirements and all Commission Authorizations and Other Authorizations." In other instances, contracts also contain an affirmative covenant that the seller will keep all the equipment in normal repair and operating condition consistent with the terms of the station's FCC licenses until the closing.

In practice, most station buyers won't want to wait until the closing for assurance that the station's technical facilities are in good operating condition. In one asset purchase agreement the seller represented and warranted that the "transmission equipment and other communications equipment to be transferred to Purchaser hereunder is in good repair and working condition and in material compliance with all current FCC requirements." The buyer negotiated for the right to inspect the facilities of the station "at a time prior to closing to be mutually agreed upon with Seller" and if it found that the equipment was not in good working condition, required the seller to make the necessary repairs and adjustments at its expense. The agreement also provided that if the seller disagreed with any of the buyer's statements concerning the condition of the

equipment, "a consulting engineer chosen jointly by Seller and Purchaser shall be the final arbiter of any disagreements."

As shown in the next section, more and more buyers now insist that engineering audits and facilities tours as well as environmental audits be conducted prior to the closing.

Environmental and Engineering Audits

Many asset purchase agreements include provisions requiring an engineering audit of the equipment and an environmental audit of the real property. In some agreements, the completion of such audits to the satisfaction of the buyer is made a condition to the buyer's obligation to close. The environmental audit usually covers PCBs,** air pollutants, asbestos, solid waste substances, hazardous or toxic materials, underground storage tanks, and compliance with any applicable federal, state or local

---

* Although PCBs are no longer used in the manufacture of broadcast equipment, they must be managed in accordance with rules adopted by the Environmental Protection Agency covering recordkeeping, repair, storage and disposal. Buyers should not acquire equipment containing PCBs or, at the very least, should obtain assurances from the seller that it will be responsible for the proper disposal of any PCB items.

environmental laws. Audits usually are conducted early in the due diligence process by engineering or environmental consultants. It can be disastrous to wait until the eve of the closing to conclude environmental and engineering audits.

The rules of landowner and lender liability are stated in the federal Comprehensive Environmental Response, Compensation and Liability Act (CERCLA). When purchasing contaminated land, the new owners are liable for the cleanup cost, and some states impose liability under their environmental laws (*e.g.*, New Jersey). As a result of CERCLA, many transactions for the sale and purchase of radio stations include environmental assessments. The following is a description of the three phases of an environmental assessment or audit:

A **Phase I** environmental audit is a preliminary assessment by an environmental engineer or consultant and usually includes a review of historical data on the property, review of available aerial photographs, and onsite facility inspection. A comprehensive report, with recommendations, is completed if warranted. A Phase I assessment of a transmitter site may cost in the range of $750.00 to $3,500.00 (assuming no unusual problems).

Phase II assessments, if required per the results of the Phase I assessment, are typically conducted to confirm and define the Phase I indications. Phase II evaluations consist of geophysical surveys, soil drilling and test hole excavation, soil analysis, and ground and surface water sampling and analysis. A Phase II report, with recommendations, including follow up activities, is completed if warranted.

Phase III covers the remediation of contamination detected in the Phase I/Phase II evaluation. This process includes preparation of the Remedial Action Plan (RAP), work plan and bid specification generation, comprehensive site safety and health plans, project supervision, and project closing reports.

As suggested in Chapter Three, the buyer should ask the seller if there has been an environmental audit and request a copy of the report. In determining whether a buyer should conduct its own audit, it may be necessary to check the qualifications of the consultant or engineer who prepared the report for the seller. Most lending institutions insist on a Phase I audit prior to the closing.

A. Environmental Audit

Environmental liabilities are like icebergs; a great deal that needs to be known about them is not immediately apparent, and what is unknown can be very dangerous. The following provision was included in an asset purchase agreement:

> Seller shall conduct a Phase I Environmental Audit of the Property to be Sold, employing Stewart Environmental Consultants or such other company, selected by Seller, competent to perform such audit, and the expense of the Phase I audit shall be paid by Seller; provided, however, that should the Phase I Environmental Audit (a) report the presence of Hazardous Materials or (b) recommend a Phase II Environmental Audit to be performed by Stewart Environmental Consultants or such other company selected by Seller that is recognized as competent to conduct such Audits, then the cost of the Phase I and Phase II Environmental Audits shall be paid by Buyer.

It is not uncommon for the buyer to engage and pay for an environmental consultant. One asset purchase agreement also included the following provision which provided both the buyer and the seller with an "escape clause" in the event that the Environmental Audit revealed a significant problem:

> In the event that an environmental audit of the Property to be sold discloses the presence of Hazardous Materials, Seller shall remove the Hazardous Materials or otherwise bring the Property to be sold into material compliance with existing Environmental Laws at Seller's expense. In the event that the Hazardous Material cannot be reasonably removed or otherwise brought into material compliance with existing Environmental Laws by Seller, then, at Buyer's election, this Agreement may be terminated by Buyer. Buyer shall not be obligated to Close under this Agreement until such time as any of the assets contained in and among the Property to be sold are in compliance with Environmental Laws. Seller shall have the right to terminate this Agreement without further obligation or liability in the event that the cost of conducting the Environmental Audit and/ or removing any Hazardous Materials or otherwise causing the Property to be sold to comply materially with Environmental Laws shall exceed Twenty Thousand and No/100 Dollars ($20,000.00).

B. Engineering Audit

Buyers and sellers can handle the engineering inspection and any disputes resulting from the inspection in many different ways. One asset purchase agreement permitted the buyer's engineer to inspect the equipment within 10 days prior to the closing. The agreement provided that "if Buyer's engineer reports that the equipment fails to meet the warranties, and Seller disputes the report, Buyer and Seller shall jointly hire and pay a consulting engineer to give a report on the disputed items(s)." The consulting engineer's report was considered final and the seller was required to repair any equipment that did not meet the warranties and conditions contained in the agreement as determined by the consulting engineer. This approach avoids any dispute at the closing as to the accuracy of representations and warranties concerning the equipment.

Another asset purchase agreement placed the burden on the seller to deliver to the buyer:

> a report by the Station's Engineer, dated as of a date not more than fifteen (15) days prior to the Closing Date, certifying to the best of his knowledge that (i) the tower antennae and transmitter of the Stations are in good operating condition, free of any material defects and consistent with their age and intended use, in compliance with applicable rules and regulations of the Commission, and consistent with good engineering practices; and (ii) on-line broadcasting and production equipment is in good operating condition and consistent with their age and intended use.

This departs from the usual practice of having the buyer's engineer conduct the inspection. Any buyer would be well advised to have its own engineer review the report and conduct a personal inspection where there is any doubt. For detailed suggestions on inspecting the equipment of a station, see Chapter Three.

Strategies For Dealing With "Material Adverse Change"

One of the sticking points in most transactions is the clause dealing with "material adverse change" in the operation of a station between the signing of the contract and the closing. Material adverse change clauses are typically set forth as representations, warranties and closing conditions by the parties, and also form the basis by which the acquisition agreement can be unilaterally terminated. These clauses range from a simple clause requiring that there be no material adverse change between the signing of the agreement and the closing on the business or operations of the seller, to heavily negotiated terms in which certain events or circumstances are excluded or in which a quantitative formula (*e.g.*, the use of a cash flow or a gross revenues formula) is used.

In one agreement the parties defined "Material Adverse Effect" to mean "any change or effect that is materially adverse to the assets, properties, operations, business, financial condition and/or results of operations of the Business, taken as a whole, or to the consummation of the transactions contemplated by this Agreement, except for any such changes or effects resulting directly from (i) the transactions contemplated by this Agreement, (ii) the announcement or other disclosure of the transactions contemplated by this Agreement, (iii) regulatory changes that affect the broadcast radio industry generally, or (iv) changes in conditions generally applicable to the radio broadcasting industry, or in general economic conditions in the geographic region in which the Business is conducted."

General "no material adverse change" clauses lack precision and sometimes result in litigation. In *The Borders* v. *KRLB, Inc.*, 727 S.W.2d 357 (Tex. App. 1987), the court held that a significant decline in Arbitron ratings (the station lost one half of its listening audience) did not constitute a material change because the provision did not specifically refer to a ratings decline and a ratings decline was not within the scope of the material adverse change provision at issue. It is important, therefore, to provide a clear definition of the phrase. Several standards are often used and are discussed below.

A. Gross Revenues and Cash Flow Standards

Some contracts define "material adverse change" in terms of gross revenues or net revenues during the comparable period in the year prior to the closing. One asset purchase agreement provided that "if Cash Flow for the period between the signing of this Agreement and the Closing Date is less than ninety percent (90%) of Cash Flow provided for such period in the Budget (the annual operating budget for the station for the prior calendar year) there will be an adjustment to the Purchase Price of eight dollars ($8) for every dollar the actual Cash Flow is less than ninety percent (90%) of Cash Flow provided for such period in the Budget." To keep pressure on the seller, the agreement also included a covenant that "Seller shall maintain advertising and promotion expenditures at levels substantially in accordance with the Budget." The above approach quantifies a material adverse change in easily measurable terms and provides incentives for the seller and safeguards for the buyer to make sure that the condition of the station at closing will at least equal the condition at the time the contract was signed. (Negotiating for the protection of downswings in gross revenue or cash flow may result in the seller negotiating increases in the case of upswings.)

Another asset purchase agreement contained a provision that if the station's gross sales between the date of the Agreement and the closing fell below gross sales for the same period during the previous calendar year, "a material adverse change shall have occurred, for which Buyer's sole and complete remedy shall be an adjustment in the settlement of the accounts receivable." If the Gross Sales for the year in which the transaction was closed fell below the previous year's Gross Sales by more than 10 percent but less than 20 percent, the buyer was entitled to retain $1 of the collected accounts receivable for each dollar of the shortfall. If Gross Sales fell below the previous year's Gross Sales by more than 20 percent, the buyer was entitled to retain $2 for each dollar up to the total of the collected accounts receivable.

In another asset purchase agreement, the ultimate purchase price and the consummation of the transaction were conditioned on the amount of total sales revenue and the cash flow of the stations for the 12 month period immediately preceding the closing date. If the sales revenue was less than $1,300,000, the purchase price ($3,650,000) was to be decreased by the product obtained by multiplying the shortfall by 2.81. In the event that the sales revenue was less than $1,150,000, the buyer had the option of reducing the purchase price in accordance with the formula or recovering its escrow deposit and terminating the Agreement. Similarly, if the cash flow was less than $475,000, the purchase price was to be decreased by the product obtained by multiplying the shortfall by 7.68. The buyer could take advantage of this price adjustment formula at the closing or walk from the transaction if the cash flow dropped below $475,000. The cash flow usually employed is "broadcast cash flow" which is commonly regarded as the operating cash flow of the radio station which does not include any cash items or deductions for other unrelated operations or assets. The agreement also provided that if the sales revenue fell below $1,300,000 and the cash flow was under $475,000, the purchase price would be reduced by the larger of the adjustment and not by the sum of the two.

In another transaction, a slightly different formula involving only cash flow was used. The asset purchase agreement specified that the purchase price of $5,000,000 would be reduced by the number obtained by multiplying the shortfall by 8.00 if the cash flow for the preceding 12 months fell below $620,000. The agreement also provided that in no event would the purchase price be reduced by more than $320,000. If the cash flow adjustment were to result in a purchase price reduction of more than $320,000, the buyer could opt to close the transaction with the reduction in purchase price capped at $320,000 or could terminate the deal.

B. Audience Ratings

The phrase "material adverse change" can also be defined in terms of audience ratings. In acquiring a radio station, the buyer negotiated for the following clause in the asset purchase agreement:

> Notwithstanding any other provision of this Agreement, this Agreement shall automatically terminate if the Station fails to achieve a total weekly metro share of at least 6.0 for all persons aged 12 or more in the Spring . . . radio ratings published by Company for the Little Rock, Arkansas market. Upon termination of this Agreement

pursuant to this Section, Twenty-Five Thousand Dollars ($25,000.00) of the Escrow Deposit shall be paid to Seller, the balance of the Escrow Deposit [$75,000.00] shall be returned to Buyer, and the parties shall be released and discharged from any further obligations hereunder.

C. Adjustment Formulas

In another asset purchase agreement, the purchase price of $5,250,000 was made subject to the application of four adjustment formulas: (1) a cash flow adjustment, (2) a ratings adjustment, (3) a net trade liability adjustment and (4) a tower adjustment. A careful study of each formula demonstrates for prospective purchasers how to make sure that the purchase price paid at closing reflects changes which occur after the signing of the agreement.

In this agreement, if the Adjusted Cash Flow were less than 95% of the previous year's Adjusted Cash Flow, the purchase price would be reduced by an amount equal to the product of (i) the percentage (rounded to the nearest hundredth of a percentage point) obtained by subtracting (a) the Adjusted Cash Flow as a percentage of the previous year's Adjusted Cash Flow, from (b) 95% (*e.g.*, if the Adjusted Cash Flow is 90% of the prior year's

Adjusted Cash Flow, then 95% minus 90%, or 5%), multiplied by (ii) $5,250,000. If the Arbitron Ratings were below 90% of the previous year's Arbitron Ratings, the purchase price would be reduced by an amount equal to the product of (i) the Arbitron Percentage, multiplied by (ii) $5,250,000. If the aggregate of all trade payables at closing "exceeded the sum of (i) the lesser amount of trade receivables on such date and $100,000, plus (ii) any trade receivables in excess of an aggregate of $100,000 which are approved in writing by Buyer," the purchase price "shall (x) not be reduced by the first $40,000 of such excess; (y) be reduced by an amount equal to 75% of such excess as exceeds $40,000 but does not exceed $90,000; and (z) be reduced by 100% of such excess as exceeds $90,000." Finally, if the seller moved the station's tower prior to closing, the purchase price would be "increased by one-half the amount in excess of $40,000 reasonably expended by Seller to move such transmission tower; provided, however, that any such increase in Purchase Price shall not exceed $20,000."

D. Maintaining Promotion and Advertising Budgets

If the seller is unwilling to agree to a provision in the asset purchase agreement which uses a quantifiable formula to define a "material adverse change," a prudent buyer will try to include covenants concerning promotion, advertising, and other aspects of station operation. One approach is for the buyer to negotiate for a general covenant that the seller shall continue all operations and policies, including maintaining normal expenditures for promotion. For example, in one asset purchase agreement the sellers agreed to "continue all practices, policies, procedures and operations relating to the Stations in substantially the same manner as heretofore, including without limitation, sales, promotions at normal expenditures, spot unit loads, bookkeeping and record keeping practices and policies."

Another approach is for the buyer to tie the level of promotional expenditures to the amounts spent by the seller during the preceding year. In one transaction, the seller made a covenant that "advertising and promotional efforts on behalf of the Stations will be continued at the same levels and in the same months as in the past twelve (12) months." Similarly, in another transaction, the seller agreed to "continue to make expenditures and engage in activities designed to promote the Stations and stimulate the purchase of advertising time on the Stations in a manner consistent with Seller's practice during the twelve (12) month period immediately preceding the date of this Agreement."

A tougher standard was included in an asset purchase agreement where the seller agreed to use its best efforts to "maintain Station promotion at a level consistent with, and at least equal to, past efforts, including, but not limited to, station advertising and promotion, and in accordance with Seller's budget," plus reasonable increases in promotional expenses if the closing was delayed (with such increases being in an amount at least equal to the changes in the Consumer Price Index).

Another asset purchase agreement took a novel approach. Since the buyer wanted the seller to accelerate its level of advertising and promotion, he placed $125,000 in a special "Advertising Escrow Agreement" and agreed to use these funds to reimburse the seller at the closing for advertising expenditures which were in excess of the previous year's budget of the stations.

Creative Uses of Accounts Receivable

A. Obtaining a Fee for Collecting the Seller's Receivables

The buyer, acting as agent for the collection of the seller's accounts receivable, holds two advantages.

First, the buyer has the use of the money received (albeit for a short period of time). Second, the buyer avoids the risk that the former owner will alienate the station's advertisers by taking an overly aggressive stance. One buyer negotiated an additional benefit, namely, a collection fee for its efforts: "In consideration of Purchaser's agreement to bill for, collect and remit the accounts receivable, Seller agrees that Purchaser shall be entitled to an administrative and collection fee of five percent (5%) of the gross amount of all accounts receivable of Seller collected by Purchaser and remitted to the Seller." Another agreement provided a "collection fee" for the buyer of 10% of any accounts receivable which the buyer collected. The Agreement also provided that the buyer had the right to set-off against the funds collected for the accounts receivable any amounts then owed to it by the seller.

In situations where commissions are paid by the station at the time of collection (as opposed to at the time of sale), the buyer should make clear in the acquisition contract that such commissions are the responsibility of the seller. Some contracts contain a provision which makes clear that "all commissions payable with respect to the accounts receivable of the seller (whether due before or after the closing) should be solely for the account and responsibility of the seller."

B. Holding the Receivables Hostage for Poor Station Performance

One asset purchase agreement defined a "material adverse change" as a drop in Gross Sales of more than 10% from the prior year. For purposes of this determination, Gross Sales excluded trade amounts and network revenue and the two periods consisted of the time beginning on the date of the asset purchase agreement and ending at 12:01 a.m. on the Closing Date and the same period during the prior calendar year. If such a material adverse change were to occur, the buyer's "sole and complete remedy" was an adjustment in the settlement of the accounts receivable. The adjustment formula provided in the agreement stated that if Gross Sales were to fall below the prior year's Gross Sales by more than 10% but less than 20%, the buyer would be entitled to retain one dollar of the accounts receivable for each dollar of the deficit. If Gross Sales were to fall by more than 20%, the buyer would be entitled to a one dollar adjustment for the amounts up to 20% and payment of two dollars for the amounts in excess of 20% up to the total amount of the collected accounts receivable. The agreement directed the buyer to collect the accounts receivable for 120 days

and to retain the sums collected until "four months and ten days after the Closing."

C. Using Accounts Receivable as Operating Capital and an Indemnification Fund

Accounts receivable may be used as a means of providing the buyer of the station with operating capital to fund initial operations and as security for the seller's breach of representations and warranties in the contract. One buyer negotiated for a provision in the asset purchase agreement whereby it collected the accounts receivable for a period of 180 days and did not have to provide the seller with any of the funds collected until the 185th day after the closing. On the 185th day, the buyer was allowed to deduct from the funds collected any sums owed by the seller as a result of the indemnification provisions of the asset purchase agreement. The agreement specifically provided that "Seller's Accounts Receivable collected by Buyer during the 180-day period shall be held by Buyer and may be used by Buyer as security to set-off Seller's obligation to pay any and all indemnifications due to Buyer." The buyer was allowed "to retain that portion of the Seller's Accounts Receivable representing the value of Buyer's claim as set-off against the sums claimed by Buyer, until a final determination of the validity of Buyer's claim thereto." This provision not only provided the buyer with working capital for six months but also ensured that funds would be available to remedy any breach of the seller's representations and warranties.

Another asset purchase agreement provided that "any sums collected by Buyer from the Accounts [Receivable] may be used in its business; provided, however, that ninety-five (95) days after the Closing Date, Buyer shall furnish Seller with an accounting of all sums collected on the accounts during said ninety-five (95) day period and shall deliver to Seller a cashier's or certified check in an aggregate amount equal to 80% of the Accounts, irrespective of the sum collected on the Accounts of Buyer." The agreement also provided that 155 days after the Closing, "Buyer shall deliver to Seller a cashier's or certified check in an aggregate amount equal to 10% of the Accounts, irrespective of the sum collected on the Accounts by Buyer, and shall have no further obligation to Seller with respect to the Accounts." This provision gave something to both the buyer and the seller as the seller received 90% of the accounts receivable whether or not they were collected and the buyer got the unrestricted use of the funds collected for at least 95 days. Due diligence is important

here — the buyer should get a good sense of the station's collection history and review a list of aging accounts receivable before signing the contract.

Some agreements provide the buyer with protection against a lawsuit by the seller for the manner in which the accounts receivable are collected. For example, the following is an example of such a provision:

> The Seller acknowledges and agrees that the Buyers are acting as collection agent hereunder for the sole benefit of the Seller and that Buyers have accepted such responsibility for the accommodation of the Seller. The Buyers shall not have any duty to inquire as to the form, manner of execution or validity of any item, document, instrument or notice deposited, received or delivered in connection with such collection efforts, nor shall the Buyers have any duty to inquire as to the identity, authority or rights of the persons who executed the same. The Seller shall indemnify Buyers and hold them harmless from and against any judgments, expenses (including attorney's fees), costs or liabilities which the Buyers may incur or sustain as a result of or

by reason of such collection efforts.

D. Using Accounts Receivable to Make Sure that the Station is Healthy

The Incentive Approach: In signing a letter of intent to acquire a station, the buyer agreed to increase the $20 million purchase price "by 50% of the amount by which the accounts receivable of the Station on the day of the acquisition exceed the accounts receivable of the station on the date" the letter of intent was executed. This approach has a downside risk since it may encourage the seller to do business with advertisers who are poor credit risks. To afford some protection, the letter of intent could stipulate that the seller shall not change its credit policies and shall not change the average age of the receivables. In this connection, the letter of intent obligates the seller to manage the accounts receivable and payables of the station in a manner consistent with past practices, taking no extraordinary measures to delay or to accelerate the collection of receivables. As a realistic concession to the seller, the letter of intent recognized that the seller "may continue to make ordinary collection efforts as would be prudent to a business of the size and scope of the Station."

The Penalty Approach: A buyer agreed to pay $6,500,000 for the assets of two stations which included all of the stations' accounts receivable. The asset purchase agreement included warranties by the Seller that (a) the face amount of the receivables at closing shall be at least $300,000, and if not, any shortfall will be deducted from the purchase price, and (b) at least 80% of the receivables at closing, "using reasonable collection practices," would be collected by the buyer within 120 days after the closing and if not, seller would be obligated to pay the shortfall. The 120-day provision protects the buyer against an abnormally high percentage of uncollectible receivables.

E. Splitting the Receivables

As noted above, the buyer usually agrees to collect the accounts receivable for a period of time (usually 90 to 120 days) on behalf of the seller or to purchase the receivables from the seller (often at a discounted price). One asset purchase agreement required that at the end of the 90-day collection period, the buyer was required to pay 50% of the sums collected on the accounts receivable, "less 50% of the commissions due on such accounts to current Station employees." The remainder of the collected accounts receivable belonged to the buyer. The agreement also provided that "[f]ollowing ninety (90) days after the closing date, Buyer's only responsibility shall be to account for and remit to seller on a monthly basis fifty percent (50%) of any payment of Accounts Receivable transferred to Buyer at the closing which Buyer actually receives, less fifty percent (50%) of any commissions due to sales personnel who continue as employees of Buyer."

In another asset purchase agreement, the buyer agreed to collect the accounts receivable on behalf of the seller for a period of 120 days following the closing. The agreement provided that "the first $50,000 collected shall be owned and used by the Purchaser" and "any amounts collected over $50,000 shall be distributed to the Seller or its designee."

F. Providing Safeguards in Purchasing the Seller's Receivables

In most radio deals, instead of acquiring the accounts receivable, the buyer acts as a collection agent for the seller for a 90 to 120-day period. In some transactions the buyer wants to assume the receivables and places a value on the accounts in negotiating a purchase price. An innovative approach was spelled out in an asset purchase agreement in which the buyer purchased the accounts receivable based on the following formula: 90% of face value for accounts receivable that are up to 30 days old, 85% for accounts 31-60 days old, 80% for accounts 61-90 days old, 75% for accounts 91-120 days old, 70% for accounts 121-150 days old or more and 25% for any other accounts that are 151 days old or more.

To protect the buyer, the agreement provided that the accounts receivable being purchased were limited to those (1) generated in the ordinary course of business, (2) not subject to known claims of disallowance or offset, (3) not turned over to third parties for collection, and (4) mutually acceptable by the buyer and the seller as "collectable accounts" on the closing date. Under the arrangement specified in the agreement, the seller remained liable for the payment of commissions to employees with respect to the accounts receivable which were purchased. Also, the Agreement provided that the seller would indemnify and hold the buyer harmless from and against any and all claims and causes of action related to the payment of such commissions.

As to the accounts receivable that the buyer would not accept, the agreement provided that they would be assigned to the buyer for collection purposes only for a period of 120 days. The buyer was required to remit collections from these remaining accounts to the seller every 30 days during the 120-day collection period. At the end of the collection period, the buyer had to reassign the uncollected accounts receivable to the seller who then became solely responsible for the collection of the remaining balance.

G. Purchasing of One Month's Receivables

The accounts receivable of a station are subject to negotiation as to whether the buyer purchases the receivables or collects them on the seller's behalf. A hybrid approach was taken in an asset purchase agreement which provided that the buyer purchased "[a]ll Accounts Receivable of the Station, billed or unbilled, for commercial spots broadcast on the Station during the thirty (30) days immediately prior to the Closing," including "all rights to payment for such spots, and all payments received by Seller for such spots." The seller was entitled to all rights and payments received for "Accounts Receivables of the Station, billed or unbilled for spots broadcast on the Station thirty-one days or more prior to closing."

H. Offering to Purchase Selected Receivables

Once the seller no longer owns the station, it no longer has an incentive to keep the goodwill of advertisers. In most transactions, the buyer collects the receivables for a period of 90 or 120 days and then turns

over the uncollected accounts to the seller. Buyers are concerned that the seller will then try to collect the unpaid accounts by referring to a collection agency or a law firm. One asset purchase agreement specifically provided that "[a]fter the expiration of the Collection Period, Seller shall not refer any of Seller's Accounts Receivable to a collection agency or an attorney for collection unless it has first offered to sell such Accounts Receivable to Buyer at fifty percent of their face value."

A different approach with the same objective was taken where the buyer was allowed to "compromise or settle for less than full value" the accounts receivable if it "[paid] Seller the full amount of any deficiency." The Agreement also provided that "buyer shall be entitled to purchase from Seller any Retained Receivables for the full amount thereof at any time during or at the expiration of the Collection Period."

CHAPTER SEVEN

HOW TO MAKE THE CLOSING LOOK EASY

The closing brings to a successful conclusion the long and sometimes ulcerous process of deciding to sell or purchase a radio station, finding a buyer (or seller), valuing the business, conducting due diligence and negotiating agreements reflecting the interests and intent of the parties. At the closing, the consideration (cash, notes or stock) is exchanged for the property. And if all has gone well, the buyer and seller walk away convinced that each got a good deal, and the lawyers finally smile with a sense of accomplishment, collect the papers and quietly leave the scene to the sweepers and shredders.

This short chapter briefly outlines the tasks to be accomplished at the closing and the various agreements, certificates and other documents that typically are exchanged between and among the buyer, seller and other interested parties. In the process of describing the typical closing documents, we will provide you with some practical suggestions on how to make the process a smooth one.

Let's start with a short reminder about the basics. A purchase and sale transaction can take the form of either a sale of the assets of the broadcasting property or a sale of the stock of the company that owns the broadcasting property by the selling stockholders. The principal tasks to be accomplished at the closing are to transfer title to the assets or stock being sold from the seller to the buyer and to deliver the consideration (the purchase price) to the seller. That consideration can take the form of cash, stock of the buyer or some other issuer, promissory notes, other assets (broadcasting or any other type of property), or some mixture of some or all of the foregoing. For simplicity, this chapter limits the consideration to the most common forms, cash and stock.

Also, we have assumed that neither buyer nor seller is a publicly-held entity and that no proxy or registration statement or the like must be filed with the Securities and Exchange Commission or the securities administrators of any state.

General Guidance

We can offer some general guidance to those contemplating a closing. Don't lose sight of the fact that, for the most part, once the deal has been struck, the buyer and seller share the same general objective:

Close the deal. No one – not the buyer, the seller, nor their lawyers - relishes surprises at the closing. Taking into account the differing interests of the buyer and seller, try to keep all parties informed as your preparations progress and be ready to solve problems, not just identify them.

On that note, a comprehensive document checklist can give you the memory of an elephant. First, analyze the requirements for the closing and then develop checklists describing the tasks to be accomplished, the documents to be prepared and signed, the persons responsible for each task or document, and the status of preparations and delivery. Secondly, circulate checklists to all parties early in the preparation period so that they may use them as the vehicle for coordinating the actions and preparations of the buyer, seller, their counsel and their other representatives.

The devil is in the details. The details for the closing are set forth in the acquisition agreement, and a typical agreement will contain sections that usually are titled "Conditions to Closing" or "Deliveries at Closing." One of the key conditions to closing the purchase and sale of a radio station in most agreements is the issuance of a final, non-appealable order by the FCC consenting to the transaction (the Final Order),

whether it is an assignment of the seller's license to the buyer in an asset transaction or a transfer of control stemming from the buyer's purchase of a controlling interest in the company which is the licensee of the station. The grant of an assignment or transfer application by the Media Bureau will become a Final Order by operation of law 40 days after the issuance of a Public Notice by the FCC announcing the grant, provided that no petitions for reconsideration or applications for review are filed and that the Commission does not rescind the Bureau's action on its own motion. For a more detailed discussion, see FCC Processing of Assignment and Transfer Applications, Chapter Four.

In addition, under certain conditions the buyer and seller must make certain notice filings with the Department of Justice and the Federal Trade Commission pursuant to the Hart-Scott-Rodino Antitrust Improvements Act of 1976, as amended (*e.g.*, the purchase price is more than $65.2 million and certain other thresholds concerning the size of the buyer and seller are met; see Chapter Three). Once the buyer and seller have received notification that the prescribed 30-day waiting period following the filing has been terminated or expired, the parties may proceed to closing.

It is now common practice for the buyer and seller to close without waiting for finality of the FCC grant. Where a lender is involved, the parties sometimes close prior to finality by placing into escrow the funds furnished by the lender and providing for the release of such funds to the seller (with any interest earned thereon) when the FCC grant of the assignment or transfer application becomes a Final Order. (Appendix J contains a sample Rescission or Unwind Agreement used by sellers and buyers who close the transaction prior to the time that the FCC grant becomes a Final Order.)

Long Lead Time Items

Plan ahead! Don't forget that it takes more time to complete some pre-closing preparations than others. While a corporate good standing certificate can be obtained in a day or two, a lien search may take three or four days, and a title search may take more than a week. You should expect that completion of a survey of real property or an environmental assessment may take as long as three to four weeks, depending on such variables as the kind of activities conducted on the property (*e.g.*, history of hazardous materials on the property or prior environmental damage), weather, size and location of real property parcel, and the like. You also need to allow sufficient time for the seller to obtain estoppel certificates from the contracting parties stating that the leases or other contracts

are in full force and effect, and that there are no modifications, riders, oral agreements or side agreements affecting the contract. Finally, keep in mind that obtaining the consent of third parties to an assignment of contracts to the buyer can take several days to several weeks or more. Some asset purchase agreements distinguish between material contracts that must be assigned as a condition of closing, and contracts in which the seller must exercise only its best efforts to achieve assignment to buyer.

Closing Documents

Documents that must be executed and delivered at the closing should be prepared and circulated well in advance. Stock acquisitions (and the delivery of stock as the purchase price) give rise to a specific set of required documents, while asset acquisitions require a different set of conveyance documents.

A. Common Documents

The acquisition agreement usually requires the buyer and seller to deliver to each other a certificate (often called a Closing Certificate) stating that the representations and warranties each made in the Agreement are true and correct in all material respects as of the closing. This is usually a simple certificate for the buyer; however, the seller must consider all of the representations and warranties it made in the Purchase Agreement (which were true and correct as of the date of the Purchase Agreement), especially those contained in the disclosure schedules. Seller must update or otherwise correct any outdated or inaccurate representations. For example, the assets may include four vehicles, but one was involved in an accident three days before closing and is now inoperable. This probably will require the seller to update its representation regarding the condition of the assets.

The buyer and seller typically deliver an Incumbency Certificate which identifies those persons authorized to execute closing documents on behalf of buyer, seller or in some cases, the selling stockholders. Each Incumbency Certificate may also have as an exhibit a good standing certificate from the Secretary of State's office and a copy of resolutions adopted by the Board of Directors of the buyer or the seller. Some agreements require the buyer and seller to render an opinion of counsel to the other covering such matters as the authority of the buyer (or the seller) to enter into the Agreement, that the Agreement is enforceable against the buyer (or seller) in accordance with its terms (with certain important exceptions) and other matters. Also, the seller's FCC counsel should expect to

deliver an opinion to the buyer regarding certain FCC matters related to the transaction. Most agreements require the adoption of resolutions of the seller and buyer authorizing the transaction.

Frequently, the seller and/or principal officers or stockholders of the seller must enter into non-competition agreements with the buyer which either call for a lump sum payment or payments over a period of time (say, five years). Additionally, some or all of the principal officers and/or stockholders of the seller may enter into consulting, employment, or employee non-solicitation agreements with the buyer or an affiliate of the buyer.

The buyer and seller may have to issue written instructions to an escrow agent regarding the release of a down payment or other funds to either buyer or seller (or some to both) in connection with the closing. In some transactions, the parties enter into an indemnity escrow agreement whereby a portion of the purchase price is held in escrow to fund certain post-closing obligations.

If the seller (in an asset acquisition) or the Company (in a stock acquisition) has any debt outstanding and if that debt is to be paid at the closing, it is not unusual for the seller to obtain "payoff" letters (and if necessary, lien releases) prior to the closing and for the buyer to pay off the creditor directly (usually with a wire transfer) at the closing and deduct such amount from that portion of the purchase price payable to the seller or the selling stockholders.

B. Stock Acquisition

The list of documents to be delivered in a stock acquisition is relatively short. It includes the stock certificates representing the shares to be acquired, properly endorsed for transfer (with or without a separate stock power). If there are many selling stockholders, the buyer may require that the signatures be "guaranteed" by a bank or broker. But, if the number of selling shareholders is small (and especially if all are present at the closing), a signature guarantee should not be required. The selling stockholders should deliver a document releasing the company from any claims the stockholders have or may have against the company arising out of activities occurring prior to the closing. As a corollary, the selling stockholders should also be required to pay any debts they owe the company.

C. Asset Acquisition

The closing on an asset acquisition requires more and quite different documents and instruments than a stock acquisition. Since one of the principal objectives of the closing

is to transfer title in the assets to the buyer, not surprisingly, different types of assets require different conveyance documents.

Most significantly, the seller will execute and deliver an "Assignment of FCC Licenses" to buyer. This is the document that evidences the fact the buyer is now the assignee of the various FCC authorizations associated with the station. The seller will deliver a Bill of Sale, which typically is used to transfer title to equipment, inventory, hardware, spare parts, furniture and similar tangible personal property. The seller will also deliver various Assignments of the Purchased Assets which typically assign to the buyer the seller's rights under or in accounts receivable (however, the buyer in many cases just acts as the agent for the seller and collects the accounts receivable on the seller's behalf), the intangibles, sales or advertising contracts, leases, security deposits or bonds, and all other (or just certain specified) contracts. Usually a separate Assignment and Assumption Agreement is executed to reflect the buyer's agreement to assume all or just certain contracts as specified in the Purchase Agreement.

The buyer and seller probably will each execute an Assumption Agreement, pursuant to which the buyer will assume certain specified liabilities of seller. Typically, these will include any obligations arising after the closing under contracts assumed by the buyer. The assumed liabilities might, but do not generally, also include accounts payable arising prior to the closing and incurred in the ordinary course of business to the extent not past due and reflected in the books and records of the seller at the closing. Frequently, the Assumption Agreement will recite that the buyer is not assuming any Excluded Liabilities (as such term is defined in the Purchase Agreement).

If applicable, the seller will deliver an Assignment of Intellectual Property (such as trademarks, copyrights, servicemarks, URLs, etc.). The transfer of ownership of a seller's web site will require a determination of where the domain name is registered and the completion and filing of transfer forms with the entity with which the seller's domain name is registered.

Some contracts, such as software license agreements and leases for real or personal property and network and syndication agreements, usually require the consent of the Licensor or Lessor to an assignment of the contract. Often a change of control of the Licensee or Lessee is treated as an assignment. It is in the interest of both the buyer and seller to cooperate in obtaining the consents. Certain contracts contain language that makes the agreements not assignable except

at the sole discretion of the other party. Consents under such contracts may take considerable time and negotiations to complete and, therefore, must be sought early in the process.

The title to motor vehicles usually is transferred by endorsing the relevant Certificate of Title issued by the appropriate state authority. These documents should be located early in the process of preparing for the closing; replacement or duplicate Certificates should be obtained for those missing. Endorsed Certificates of Title (with current odometer readings) should be delivered to the buyer.

D. Real Property

Title to real property is transferred by deed. The buyer will normally require the seller to execute and deliver at the closing a general warranty deed for each parcel of real property being transferred. Assuming that the buyer will obtain title insurance, it will order a title search and survey of the real property, and attorneys or representatives of the buyer and seller and a representative of the title company will negotiate and resolve any outstanding title issues (*e.g.*, encroachments, set-backs, etc.). The seller will execute various affidavits, and the buyer's representative will issue a letter of instructions to the title company. At the closing, the title company will receive funds from buyer and/or seller to cover pro-rated property taxes, recordation fees and title insurance premiums, while the deed will be delivered to the title company and usually will be recorded on that or the next business day.

E. Environmental Issues

If the buyer is acquiring real property in an asset acquisition, or the company owns real property and if the buyer is acquiring the stock of the company, the buyer (or in some transactions, the seller) probably will engage environmental consultants to inspect the property, including buildings or other improvements, to determine if there is any evidence of any environmental damage or hazard (*e.g.*, from an underground oil storage tank, or crumbling insulation containing asbestos) and if the operations comply with environmental laws (*e.g.*, all necessary permits are on hand). Some states require that filings and inspections be made prior to the transfer of certain real property. In general, such requirements are intended to insure that the buyer or seller corrects, or agrees to correct, any damage or hazardous conditions related to the property prior to transfer of title.

At the closing, if permitted by the applicable state law, the buyer and seller may enter into letter or side agreements relating to the same conditions, and the parties may agree that some portion of the purchase price will be deposited with an escrow agent to secure the seller's obligations to remediate any damage or hazardous condition. An escrow agreement among the buyer, seller and an escrow agent (perhaps a bank) will be prepared with specific instructions to the escrow agent governing the release of funds either to the seller (when the seller has completed the required remediation), to the buyer (to reimburse the buyer for all or a portion of its costs to remediate the damage or conditions), or both.

F. Financing Documents

If the buyer obtains financing for the purchase, whether it is take-back seller financing or traditional financing with a lender, then a separate family of financing-related documents must be prepared and coordinated. Many hands do not always make light work. For seller financing, these documents may include promissory notes, security agreement, a pledge agreement related to the acquired stock or some other stock owned by the buyer, UCC financing statements, a mortgage or deed of trust, and a guaranty of buyer's obligations perhaps by its parent or the principals.

The negotiation of subordination agreements between lenders and holders of the buyer's promissory note(s) is often time consuming and entails significant legal expense for the borrower. Traditional financing will include some or all of the foregoing documents as well as a credit agreement, various certificates relating to the financial condition of the buyer and opinions of the buyer's counsel. The closing room can get crowded quickly!

G. Purchase Price: The Mechanics

If the purchase price is paid in cash, it is usually delivered by wire transfer to a bank account designated by the seller. To ensure that wired funds are received by the seller on the closing date, the parties should send the wire instructions to the bank as early in the day as possible. The arrangements for the wire should be made several days before the closing so that on the day of closing, all the buyer has to do is release the wire.

If the purchase price is paid in stock or if the buyer is purchasing the licensee entity, rather than its assets, stock certificates should be delivered at the closing and counsel for the party issuing or selling should opine that the issuance or transfer of the stock is exempt from the registration requirements of federal and state securities laws.

Typically, the purchase price is adjusted to reflect prorations of real property taxes, utilities, deposits, and in the case of stock transactions, estimated working capital on hand, or accounts payable or receivable. In some cases, the seller deposits cash (or other consideration) in an escrow account as a contingency holdback (*e.g.*, to secure its post-closing obligations) for a specified time after closing.

In all cases, the seller or the selling stockholders (or a designee of the selling stockholders) should deliver a receipt for the purchase price to the buyer.

A Closing Word

Our purpose has been to provide the reader with a glimpse into the mechanics of preparing for and documenting a closing. Checklists will help but the heavy lifting usually takes the form of coordinating your actions and documents with those of others, spotting problems in advance, and developing, coordinating and implementing solutions to those problems. Also, consider holding a "pre-closing" at least one day prior to the closing so that documents may be revised prior to the scheduled date of the closing and the closing can consist only of wiring the money at the opening of business on the closing day. Since wiring sometimes takes longer than expected, the earlier the funds are wired, the better.

But the preparation and effort
are worth it. When the work is
complete, the buyer, the seller and
their counsel will have shepherded
the transaction to its intended
conclusion. As the poet Robert
Browning said, "God's in His
heaven; all's right with the world."

APPENDIX A

SAMPLE CONFIDENTIALITY AGREEMENT

[Date]

<u>CONFIDENTIAL</u>

[Name and Address of Prospective Buyer]

Dear _____:

In connection with your interest in a possible transaction involving _____, licensee of Station _____, _____, _____ (the "Company"), the Company is furnishing _____ ("you") with certain information which is confidential in nature. This information, supplied to you, your directors, officers, employees, agents or other representatives, including, without limitation, attorneys, accountants, consultants, investment bankers and financial advisors (collectively, "Representatives") and, in addition, the fact that discussions or negotiations are taking place regarding a possible transaction involving the Company, is hereinafter referred to as the "Information." In consideration of our furnishing you with the Information, you agree:

1. You will keep the Information confidential and will not disclose the Information to third parties, unless compelled by process of law or regulation. The Information shall not be used by you or your Representatives other than in connection with the possible transaction with the Company. You may reveal the Information to your affiliates, your Representatives and your affiliates' Representatives who need to know the Information for the purpose of evaluating such possible transaction and who are informed by you of the confidential nature of the Information. You shall be responsible for any breach of this Agreement

by your directors, officers, employees, agents or other representatives.

2. All copies of the Information in your possession will, upon the Company's written request, be destroyed.

3. The term Information shall not include such information which is or becomes generally available to the public other than as a result of a wrongful disclosure by you or your Representatives, or becomes available to you on a non-confidential basis from a source which is not to your knowledge prohibited from disclosing such information to you by a legal obligation to the Company.

4. In the event that you or anyone to whom you transmit the Information pursuant to this Agreement becomes legally compelled to disclose any of the Information, you will provide prompt notice to the Company so that, at its own expense, it may seek a protective order or other appropriate remedy and/or waive compliance with the provisions of this Agreement. In the event that such protective order or other remedy is not obtained, or that the Company waives compliance with the provisions of this Agreement, you will furnish only that portion of the Information which you are advised, by opinion of your counsel, is legally required, and you will exercise your best efforts to obtain reliable assurance that confidential treatment will be accorded the Information.

5. You agree that this Agreement shall be governed and construed in accordance with the laws of the State of _____ without regard to principles of conflicts of laws.

6. This Agreement and all of its terms shall terminate one year from the date hereof.

Accepted and Agreed to:

[NAME OF SELLER]   **[NAME OF PROSPECTIVE BUYER]**

By:_____   By:

_____

Title:_____   Title:

_____

Date:_____   Date:

_____

APPENDIX B

ILLUSTRATIVE LETTERS OF INTENT

The four letters of intent contained in this Appendix show different approaches that have been used by prospective buyers. Caveat: These letters should be regarded as a starting point to be tailored to meet your individual objectives and concerns. Two of the letters (B1-B6 and B14-B20) explicitly identify the terms that are binding and those that are not. The first three letters of intent are for the acquisition of assets and the fourth (B14-B20) for the purchase of stock. The first letter (B1-B6) is much more comprehensive than the second (B7-B9). The third letter (B10-B13) also contains a listing of documents needed for due diligence and sets forth the basic terms of a Local Marketing Agreement.

SAMPLE ONE

[Date]

CONFIDENTIAL

[Name and Address of Seller]

Dear _____:

The purpose of this letter of understanding (the "Letter of Understanding") is to outline the principal terms upon which _____ ("Buyer"), proposes to purchase from _____ ("Seller"), the Station Assets, as defined below, of Station [call letters, city of license] (collectively, "the Station" or "the Station Assets"). While Buyer and Seller recognize that the consummation of the transactions contemplated by this Letter of Understanding is conditioned upon the occurrence of a number of future events, including the inspection of the property of the Station, a review of Seller's books and records and the negotiation and execution of mutually agreeable definitive agreements of purchase (the "Definitive Agreements"), we intend this Letter of Understanding to set forth the fundamental points of agreement, and to express our mutual intent to proceed as expeditiously as possible to negotiate the transactions herein described.

1. **Description of Assets to be Delivered**. On the closing date, Seller will transfer to Buyer, free and clear of all liens, claims, and encumbrances of every kind, subject to the temporary escrow described below and to all of the terms and conditions of the Definitive Agreements, certain of the assets used in the conduct of the business and operations of the Station, including, but not limited to, the following (but excluding the assets specified in Section 3 hereof):

    (a) all of the licenses, permits, and other authorizations issued to Seller by any governmental authority and used in the operations of the Station, including all of the rights in and to the call letters of the Station;

    (b) the real property, together with all improvements thereon, currently used by Station, for its offices, studio and transmitter site.

    (c) the equipment, office furniture and fixtures, office materials and supplies, inventory, spare parts, and other tangible personal property of every kind and description, owned, leased, or held by Seller and used in the operations of the Station;

    (d) all programs, programming material, and music libraries of whatever form or nature owned by Seller and used or intended for use in the operations of the Station;

    (e) all of Seller's rights in and to the trademarks, tradenames, service marks, patents, URLs, any website content, franchises, copyrights, including registrations and applications for registration of any of them, call letters, jingles, logos, slogans, licenses, permits and privileges, trade secrets, and other similar intangible property rights and interests owned by it and used in the operations of the Station; and

    (f) all files, records, studies, data, lists, filings, general accounting records, books of account, computer programs and software and logs, of every kind, relating to the operations of the Station.

2. **Consideration to be Paid by Buyer**. The consideration for the sale of the Station Assets shall be _____ Dollars ($_____.00). [In addition, as consideration for the execution and delivery by Seller of the agreement not to compete with Buyer, as described in Section 6(b) below, Buyer shall pay to Seller the sum of _____ Dollars ($_____).] The Purchase Price will be payable as follows:

    (a)   _____ Dollars ($_____.00) in cash at closing, of which amount, Dollars ($_____), will be placed in escrow at the time of signing a formal contract;

    [(b)   _____ Dollars ($_____.00) in cash at closing as prepayment in full for Seller's agreement not to compete in the _____ media market for a period of ___ (_) years from the date of closing; and]

    [(c)   _____ Dollars ($_____.00), in the form of a Promissory Note of Buyer to Seller, payable at __% interest over a period of _____ (__) years with payment of interest only for _____ (__) years and principal at the end of _____ (__) years. Buyer and Seller recognize that this note shall be subordinate to Buyer's bank financing.]

3. **Excluded Assets**. Excluded from the assets to be sold to Buyer and from the definition of the terms "Station" and "Station Assets" as used herein, shall be: (a) Seller's corporate records; (b) all cash, cash equivalents or similar type investments of Seller; (c) all accounts receivable for services performed by Seller prior to the closing date; (d) the use of the name "_____" or "_____" or any confusingly similar derivation therefrom; (e) any and all contracts of insurance and insurance proceeds of settlement and insurance claims made by Seller relating to property or equipment repaired, replaced, or restored

by Seller prior to the closing date; and (f) all contracts used in the operation of the Station, unless specifically assumed or assigned by Buyer. In addition, Buyer shall not be obligated to continue the employment of any current employees of the Station and shall have no liabilities of any kind in connection therewith. All accounts receivable on the books at final closing are to be turned over to Buyer for collection only for a period of _____ (__) days. Buyer will remit all funds collected at the end of _____ (__) days, net of expenses of collection, and, at the end of this ___-day period, will provide a final accounting and return to Seller any accounts remaining uncollected at that time.

4. **Liabilities to be Assumed**. Subject to review, Buyer will assume whatever executory obligations exist on the closing date for the sale of air time and certain trade obligations under any contracts of Seller not in breach as of such date and such other obligations as may be mutually agreed to by the parties. Buyer shall assume no other liabilities or obligations of any kind and may require reasonable assurances that Seller will appropriately pay, discharge, and satisfy such liabilities and obligations from the proceeds of this transaction, or thereafter as and when they become due.

5. **Escrow; Closing**.

   (a) Upon the execution and delivery of the Definitive Agreements, Buyer will transfer to _____, as Escrow Agent, the sum of _____ Dollars ($_____.00).

   (b) Buyer and Seller shall agree to close immediately after the consent of the Federal Communications Commission ("FCC") to the assignment of the licenses granted under the authority of such agency shall have become a Final Order.

   (c) In connection with the closing, the parties agree either (i) to execute and enter into one or more agreements providing that a sum reasonably satisfactory to Buyer shall be held by an escrow agent in an interest bearing escrow account (the "Escrow Account") for a period of up to ___ (__) months, or (ii) to make other arrangements reasonably satisfactory to Buyer to satisfy any contingent liabilities of Seller related to the Station Assets.

6. **The Definitive Agreements**. In addition to the customary representations, warranties, and undertakings made by buyers and sellers in transactions of this type, the Definitive Agreements will contain the following provisions, among others.

   (a) **Conditions to Closing**. The Definitive Agreements will contain customary conditions that must be satisfied by both parties prior to the closing date, including specifically, but without limitation: (i) that Buyer is reasonably satisfied that the financial information set forth in the Station's financial statements for the year ending December 31, 200_ and the month ending _____ __, 20__ fairly and accurately present the financial performance and results of operations of the Station for the periods indicated; (ii) that prior to the execution and delivery of the Definitive Agreements (or a date certain after execution and delivery), it has (or will have) conducted such due diligence investigations, including such inquiries as it has determined necessary to verify the accuracy and adequacy of information furnished by Seller and as of the closing date, there have been no material adverse changes in the Station Assets; (iii) that any executory contracts or obligations to be assumed by Buyer will not be, singly or in the aggregate, materially disadvantageous to the business of the Station as proposed to be conducted by Buyer; (iv) that any necessary regulatory or contractual formalities have been complied within; and (v) that the sales and customer information given to the purchaser are accurate and complete.

   [(b) **Covenant Not to Compete**. For a period of ___ (__) years from the grant of the Final Order, neither Seller, nor any officer, director and stockholder of seller, shall directly or indirectly, own or operate a broadcasting business within the _____ media market.]

7. **Agreement to Negotiate in Good Faith**. Buyer and Seller agree to proceed diligently, expeditiously, and in good faith, to negotiate the Definitive Agreements relating to the sale of the Station Assets and the transactions contemplated thereby in accordance with the terms set forth in this Letter of Understanding. Buyer and Seller will each use its best reasonable efforts to negotiate the sale of the Station Assets and the transactions contemplated thereby on or before _____ __, 20__.

8. **FCC Fees and Expenses**. All filing and grant fees charged by the FCC in connection with this transaction, if any, will be paid equally by Buyer and Seller. Except as otherwise set forth in the Definitive Agreements, each party will be responsible for its own legal and other professional expenses.

9. **Seller's Representations, Warranties, and Covenants**. In order to induce Buyer to enter into this agreement, Seller represents, warrants, and covenants as follows:

   (a)   At Closing, Seller will convey to Buyer all of the assets to be sold hereunder, free and clear of all liens, charges, pledges, mortgages, and other encumbrances whatsoever.

   (b)   At Closing, the Station will be operated, in all material respects, in accordance with its FCC licenses, all underlying construction permits, and the rules and regulations of the FCC.

   (c)   All of the tangible personal property used or useful for Station operations is in good and acceptable operating condition and, subject to normal wear and tear, will be in the same condition at Closing.

   (d)   All statements made or information provided to Buyer by Seller or on its behalf by an authorized agent of Seller in connection with the negotiations concerning this transaction are complete and accurate in all material respects, and Seller is not aware of any pending or threatened claims or lawsuits which would result in a material adverse effect upon the Station or its business, operations, prospects, or conditions financial or otherwise.

(e) Until Closing, Seller will operate the Station in the ordinary course of business and substantially in the same manner as heretofore operated. There shall be no material adverse change in the operations and financial condition of the Station.

10. **Examination and Investigation**. It is understood that Buyer has not had an opportunity to conduct the kind of "due diligence" investigation of the Station and the Station Assets customarily performed with respect to a transaction of this nature. Seller shall give Buyer and its authorized representative access to the Station and the Station Assets and shall furnish all information relating thereto as they may request to enable Buyer to make such examinations and investigations thereof as Buyer shall deem necessary. Buyer will hold all information so obtained in confidence and if the transaction is not consummated, will return all confidential documents to Seller.

11. **Confidentiality**. Buyer and Seller each agree that it will use its best efforts to keep confidential (except for disclosure requirements of federal or state securities laws and securities markets along with such disclosure to attorneys, bankers, underwriters, investors, etc. as may be appropriate in the furtherance of this transaction) all information of a confidential nature obtained by it from the other (including the terms of this proposal and the identity of Buyer) in connection with the transactions contemplated by this letter, and in the event that such transactions are not consummated, will return to the other all documents and other materials obtained from the other in connection therewith.

12. **Publicity**. Buyer and Seller shall jointly prepare and determine the timing of, any press release, or other announcement to the public or the news media relating to

the execution of this letter. No party hereto will issue any press release or make any other public announcement relating to the transactions contemplated by this letter without the prior consent of each other party hereto, except that any party may make any disclosure required to be made by it under applicable law (including federal or state securities laws and the regulations of securities markets) if it determines in good faith that it is appropriate to do so and gives prior notice to each other party hereto.

13. **No Shop Agreement**. Seller agrees that until _____ __, 20__, or earlier if the parties mutually determine that they are unable to enter into the Definitive Agreements, it shall not offer or seek to offer, or entertain or discuss any offer, to sell the Station, nor shall it permit its officers, directors and management to offer, to seek to offer, or entertain or discuss any offer to sell, any interest in the Station to third parties.

14. **Binding Provisions**. Except for Paragraphs 7, 8, 9, 10, 11, 12, 13 and 14 which shall be legally binding in accordance with their respective terms, neither this letter nor the acceptance hereof is intended to, and nor shall it create a binding legal obligation, and the understanding set forth herein is subject to the execution of the Definitive Agreements.

The offer will expire _____ (__) days from the above date. If the foregoing is satisfactory, please so indicate by executing in the space provided below and returning the enclosed copy of this letter to the undersigned on or before _____ __, 20___.

Very truly yours,

[NAME OF BUYER]

By_____
[Name]
[Title]

AGREED AND ACCEPTED:

[NAME OF SELLER]

By: _____
                [Name]
                [Title]
Dated: _____

SAMPLE TWO

[Date]

CONFIDENTIAL

[Name and Address of Seller]

Dear _____:

_____ ("Buyer") hereby offers to purchase from _____ ("Seller") the Broadcasting Assets, as defined below, of Station _____, _____, _____, on the terms and subject to the conditions set forth herein.

1. **Purchase Price and Payment**. The purchase price for the Broadcasting Assets shall be _____ Dollars ($_____.00), of which _____ Dollars ($_____.00) shall be paid as earnest money upon the execution of a definitive agreement, and the balance of which shall be paid in cash at closing, subject to customary proration of all income and expenses.

2. **Assets to be Purchased**. The "Broadcasting Assets" shall include (a) all real property, together with all improvements thereon, used by the Station for its offices, studios and transmitter site; (b) all tangible personal property owned, leased or held by Seller and used or useful in the operation of the Station, including, without limitation, all equipment, office fixtures, office materials and supplies, inventory and spare parts; (c) all lease and operating contracts relating to the continuing operation of the Station unless otherwise specified in the Asset Purchase Agreement; (d) all licenses, permits and authorizations issued to Seller by any governmental authority and used in the operation of the Station, including all rights in and to the call letters of the Station; and (e) all other tangible and intangible assets owned, leased or held by Seller and used or useful by it in connection with the operation of the Station unless otherwise identified in the Asset Purchase Agreement as Excluded Assets (as defined below).

3. **Excluded Assets**. Excluded Assets shall include (a) all cash and cash equivalents, (b) all contracts and other rights and interests of Seller which relate to the operation of the Station but are identified as Excluded Assets in the Asset Purchase Agreement, (c) all accounts receivable with respect to the Station, and (d) such other assets as may be specified in the Asset Purchase Agreement.

4. **Liabilities**. Seller shall continue to be responsible for all, and Buyer shall not assume any of Seller's debts, liabilities and obligations with respect to the Station, except (a) those arising subsequent to the closing under the continuing contracts referred to in part (c) of Paragraph 2 above, (b) the accounts payable, and (c) other liabilities, if any, specified in the Purchase Agreement.

5. **No Financing Contingency**. Buyer has adequate financial resources, debt and equity, available to it to consummate the transactions contemplated by this letter. Thus, Buyer's obligations under the Asset Purchase Agreement will not be subject to its ability to provide financing.

6. **The Asset Purchase Agreement**. Upon execution by you of this letter of intent, Buyer's counsel will commence the drafting of the Asset Purchase Agreement for submission to you and your counsel for review. The Asset Purchase Agreement will contain provisions in accordance with this letter of intent, together with such representations, warranties and covenants as are usual and customary in such an agreement and as shall be mutually acceptable, including, without limitation:

   (a) representations as to good and marketable title to the Broadcasting Assets, the condition of the Broadcasting Assets, etc.; and

   (b) covenants as to the conduct of the Station prior to the closing; provided, however, that at all times prior to the closing Seller will remain in control of the Station.

Buyer may be willing to consider entering into a Local Marketing Agreement with Seller at the time the Asset

Purchase Agreement is executed. Seller agrees to negotiate in good faith the terms of the Asset Purchase Agreement during the "no shop" period specified in Paragraph 11.

7. **Examination and Investigation**. It is understood that Buyer has not had an opportunity to conduct the kind of due diligence investigation of the Station and the Broadcasting Assets customarily performed with respect to transactions of this nature. Seller shall give Buyer and its authorized representatives access to the Station and the Broadcasting Assets and shall furnish such information as Buyer may reasonably request. Buyer will endeavor to conduct such examinations and investigations in a manner that will protect the confidentiality of the transaction contemplated hereby and minimize disruptions to Seller's operation.

8. **Cost and Expenses**. Each of the parties shall bear all costs and expenses incurred by it in connection with the transactions contemplated hereby, including all legal and accounting fees, whether or not the transactions shall be consummated; provided, however, that the parties shall share equally all FCC filing and grant fees, if any.

9. **Broker Fees**. Each party represents that it has not used the services of, or incurred any obligation to, any broker or finder of any fee in connection with, the transactions contemplated hereby, other than _____, whose fee shall be paid by Seller. Each of the parties shall be responsible, and shall indemnify and hold harmless the other, for any fee, commission or charge of any broker, finder or consultant engaged by it in connection with the transactions contemplated hereby.

10. **Press Releases**. The parties will advise and consult with one another prior to the issuance of any public announcements pertaining to the transactions contemplated hereby, and no such announcement will be made by either party without the prior written consent of the other, except as otherwise required by law.

11. **Negotiations and Termination**. Effective on _____ ___, 20___, Seller will not conduct negotiations with any party other than Buyer with respect to the proposed sale of the Station, directly or indirectly, between _____ ___, 20___ and the earlier of (i) _____ ___, 20___, or (ii) the date on which Seller reasonably determines that Buyer has terminated negotiations under this letter.

This letter is expressly subject to agreement upon all the terms and conditions of the Asset Purchase Agreement and the execution and delivery thereof. This letter shall not create any rights in, or confer any benefits on, any third parties. Neither Buyer nor Seller shall have any obligation to the other until such time as the Purchase Agreement has been executed and delivered by Buyer and Seller.

This letter may be executed in two or more counterparts, each of which shall be an original, but all of which together shall constitute one instrument.

If the foregoing correctly sets forth the preliminary understanding of the parties, please so indicate by executing in the space provided below and returning to the undersigned the enclosed copy of this letter on or before _____ , 20__.

Very truly yours,

[NAME OF BUYER]

By_____
       [Name]
       [Title]

AGREED AND ACCEPTED:

[NAME OF SELLER]

By: _____
     [Name]
     [Title]

DATED: _____ __, 20__

SAMPLE THREE

[Date]

<u>CONFIDENTIAL</u>

[Name and Address of Seller]

Dear _____:

_____ ("Buyer"), wishes to purchase from _____ ("Seller"), all the assets associated with and used to operate the radio station _____ licensed to _____, _____ (the "Station"). This letter outlines the proposed procedure for entering into a Local Marketing Agreement (the "LMA") and a definitive asset purchase agreement (the "Asset Purchase Agreement") between Seller and Buyer.

This letter is subject to the following terms and conditions:

1. Buyer will purchase and Seller will sell and deliver to Buyer all of the tangible and intangible assets necessary or used in the operation of the Station, including but not limited to all of the following assets to the extent owned by Seller and assignable to Buyer: licenses and other authorizations of the Federal Communications Commission ("FCC"); all documents, files and records, including the local public file; the rights to use call letters and slogans, trade names, service marks, copyrights; all owned real estate, all towers and lease rights to tower sites, but excluding cash on hand and accounts receivable. The assets conveyed will include all replacements and additions thereto between the date of this letter and the closing date of the transaction. All assets shall be conveyed to Buyer free and clear of all liens, encumbrances and debts of any kind except to the extent explicitly assumed by Buyer. Seller will make representations and warranties as to the acquired assets and the Station as are customary in agreements of this type in the radio industry, including but not limited to accuracy of financial statements, the quality of and good title to the acquired assets, and the absence of certain liabilities. The Asset Purchase Agreement shall provide that the representations and warranties shall survive (1)

forever in the case of representations and warranties governing title to assets, authority, and the like; (2) for ___ days after expiration of the applicable statute of limitations with respect to claims asserted by third parties; and (3) for ____ years with respect to other claims. The Seller and its major shareholders will also enter into a noncompete agreement for a period of three years following the closing.

2. The total purchase price for the Station shall be _____ Dollars ($____.00). Upon the execution of the Asset Purchase Agreement, the Buyer will place in escrow an irrevocable Letter of Credit ("LOC") issued by _____, in an amount equal to ____ percent (___%) of the total purchase price. If the closing does not take place because the Buyer has not complied with all of Buyer's obligations under the Asset Purchase Agreement, the LOC shall be paid out to the Seller. If a closing does not take place because the Seller has not complied with all of Seller's obligations under the Asset Purchase Agreement, the LOC will be canceled.

3. Buyer and Seller agree to negotiate promptly and in good faith toward the preparation and execution of a definitive Asset Purchase Agreement and related documents within _____ (___) days of the Buyer's receipt of the information described in Paragraph 5 below. The Buyer will prepare the initial draft of the Asset Purchase Agreement.

4. Buyer and Seller agree to negotiate promptly and in good faith toward the LMA and all other documents and applications required for completing the transaction. Buyer and Seller agree to negotiate the LMA with the intent to execute the LMA simultaneous with the Asset Purchase Agreement with the following terms: (a) LMA shall cover the period beginning on the first Monday following the signing of the Asset Purchase Agreement until the asset purchase transaction closes; (b) at the commencement of the LMA, the employees of the Seller will be offered employment by the Buyer for the period of the LMA (employment following the closing will be subject to the provisions of the Asset Purchase Agreement); (c) during the LMA period the Buyer shall be responsible for all costs associated with the operation of the Station; and (d) during

the LMA period, Buyer shall receive all revenues from operation of the Station.

5. Within ___ (__) business days of the date hereof, Seller will deliver to Buyer one (1) copy of the following documents:

(i) Annual financial statements for the year 20__, monthly financial statements for _____, 20__, and interim monthly financials for _____ 20__;

(ii) Current budgets and the latest projections for _____ 20__ and _____ 20__, if available;

(iii) List of employees by position and compensation;

(iv) Real property descriptions;

(v) Summary of terms and conditions of any studio, office, tower or transmitter leases, with copies of the leases;

(vi) Any other information which the Seller believes is material to the value of the Assets and the future cash flows of the Station; and

(vii) Any contracts which the Seller expects the Buyer to assume.

Buyer will complete its review of the above information within the _____ (__) day period in Paragraph 3 above. Buyer and Seller agree that more complete information on the Station, contracts and other due diligence information will be reviewed by the Buyer after the execution of the Asset Purchase Agreement and the escrow deposit but prior to closing.

6. Within _____ (__) days after the execution of the Asset Purchase Agreement, Buyer and Seller will file an application with the FCC seeking consent for the proposed sale of the Station. Each party will bear its own expenses in connection with the preparation, filing and prosecution of such application. Each party will cooperate in taking actions reasonably necessary to complete this transaction.

7. The Buyer will collect Seller's accounts receivable, beginning with the commencement of the LMA, for a period of _____ (___) days with Buyer remitting amounts so collected at the end of the period. In addition, to the extent that Seller satisfies accounts payable related to the Station with cash payments following the effective date of the LMA, and provides Buyer with documentation of such accounts payable and cash payments, Buyer shall reimburse Seller for such expenses no later than the ____ day of the month following that in which the Seller makes the cash payments, and such amounts shall be deducted from the accounts receivable owed to Seller.

8. For the period from the date the Seller signs this letter through ____ _ ____, ____ (__) days after the date of receipt of information referred to in paragraph 5 above (the "No shop Period"), the Seller agrees not to sell, offer to sell, or solicit an offer to sell the assets of any interest in the Station to any person other than the Buyer. In the meantime, the Seller will suspend any discussions regarding any such offer or offers now outstanding; and will not provide any information to any party other than the Buyer regarding the possible sale or transfer of the Station. If at the end of ____ (__) day period, the Buyer and the Seller are still working to finalize the Asset Purchase Agreement, the No shop Period will be automatically extended for a further _____ (__) days.

9. Buyer and Seller acknowledge that the premature release of information about this transaction could be harmful to the interests of both the Buyer and the Seller who in recognition of this fact agree to maintain all information about this proposed transaction and the existence of this Letter of Intent in the strictest confidence advising no party except for employees and professional advisors as minimally needed to complete the transaction.

10. Buyer and Seller acknowledge that the proposed transaction will require further review of documentation and diligence, and further documentation, including the negotiation, preparation and execution of a formal agreement setting forth the transaction in greater detail. The Asset Purchase Agreement will contain a number

of conditions to closing, including but not limited to the Buyer's receipt of satisfactory title insurance commitments, surveys and Phase I environmental audit of all of Seller's real property. The Buyer and Seller will share the cost of such items on a 50-50 basis.

11. Except as otherwise provided herein and in the Asset Purchase Agreement, Buyer and Seller agree that they will pay their respective fees and expenses incurred in connection with this Letter of Intent, the Asset Purchase Agreement and any other agreements or documents contemplated hereby. The Buyer will pay any and all fees which may be due to _____.

12. The Buyer and Seller shall use their best efforts to close the anticipated purchase transaction within _____ (_) months from the signing of this letter.

13. This offer will expire at _:00 PM ___, _____ __, 20___.

We hope you will find these terms acceptable. If so, please indicate your acceptance by executing and returning a copy of this letter to me. We look forward to working with you in the months and years ahead.

Very truly yours,

[NAME OF BUYER]

By_____
       [Name]
       [Title]

ACCEPTED AND AGREED:

[NAME OF SELLER]

By: _____
    [Name]

_____
  [Title]

DATED: _____ __, 20__

[Date]

<u>CONFIDENTIAL</u>

[Name and Address of Seller]

Re: **Letter of Intent to Purchase Capital Stock and Equity Interests**

Dear _____:

This letter is intended to summarize the principal terms of a proposal being considered by _____ (the "Buyer") regarding its possible acquisition of all of the outstanding capital stock and equity interests in _____ (the "Company"), the licensee of Station _____, _____, _____ (the "Station"). At present, all of such capital stock and equity interests are owned by (1) _____, (2) _____, (3) _____ and (4) _____, and such persons are sometimes referred to herein, collectively, as the "Sellers". In this letter, (i) the Buyer and the Company are sometimes called the "Parties," and (ii) the Buyer's possible acquisition of all of the capital stock and other equity interests in the Company is sometimes called the "Possible Acquisition."

PART ONE

The Parties wish to commence negotiating a definitive written acquisition agreement providing for the Possible Acquisition (a "Definitive Agreement"). The Parties contemplate that the Possible Acquisition may be structured as a merger between the Company and a subsidiary of the Buyer, in which the Company will be the surviving entity, or as a share exchange, in either case in accordance with the Corporation Act of the State of _____. To facilitate the negotiation of a Definitive Agreement, the Parties request that the Buyer's counsel prepare an initial draft. The execution of any such Definitive Agreement would be subject to: (1) the satisfactory completion of the Buyer's ongoing investigation of the

Company's business; and (2) approval by the Buyer's Board of Directors.

Based on the information currently known to the Buyer, it is proposed that the Definitive Agreement include the following terms:

1. BASIC TRANSACTION

The Possible Acquisition would be implemented through a plan of merger or share exchange (the "Plan"). The Company anticipates that the Plan will provide for the Sellers to sell all of their capital stock and other equity interests in the Company to the Buyer at the price (the "Purchase Price") set forth in Paragraph 2 below. The closing of this transaction (the "Closing") would occur no later than _____ __, 20__, and is subject to the prior approval of the Federal Communications Commission (the "FCC").

2. PURCHASE PRICE

The Purchase Price (subject to adjustment as described below) for all of the capital stock and other equity interests in the Company would be _____ Dollars ($_____.00). In accordance with the Plan, the Purchase Price would be payable in the following manner:

A portion of the Purchase Price in the amount of _____ Dollars ($_____.00) would be paid at Closing. As set forth in the Plan, such payment would be applied as follows: (a) to retire the Company's outstanding debt (including principal and accrued interest); (b) to terminate the interests of the holders of the outstanding shares of Preferred Stock in the Company; (c) to terminate the interests of the holders of options (whether vested or unvested) to purchase common shares in the Company; and (d) to the holders of outstanding shares of common stock in the Company.

The Plan will provide for the remaining balance of the Purchase Price to be payable solely to the holders of the outstanding shares of common stock as of the Closing, in three scheduled installments. The projected amount of each installment and the date paid would be as follows: (a) _____

Dollars ($_____.00) on _____ __, 20__; (b) _____
Dollars ($_____.00) on _____ __, 20__ and (c) _____
Dollars ($_____.00) on _____ __, 20__. However,
the actual amount paid in respect to each such installment
would equal ___ percent (____%) of the pre-tax profit of the
Company before corporate allocations, including a _____
percent (___%) asset charge (including such charge, the
"PBA") for the period from Closing (or the most recent
scheduled installment date, as applicable) through the date of
determination for such installment.

The Purchase Price assumes that the Company will have
stockholders' equity as of the Closing at least equal to the
stockholders' equity as of ____ , 20__. The Purchase Price
would also be adjusted (increased or decreased) based on
changes in the Company's stockholders' equity as of the
Closing, on a dollar-for-dollar basis. The Definitive Agreement
would specify when such adjustment to the Purchase Price is
finally determined and paid.

In determining the stockholders' equity as of the Closing, all
assets shall be valued in accordance with historic practices
of the Company, including, without limitation, inventory being
valued at cost, receivables being reported at face value with
the appropriate allowance for doubtful accounts using the
Company's current method for establishing such reserves and
computing depreciation in accordance with past practices.

3. EMPLOYMENT AND NONCOMPETITION AGREEMENTS

At the Closing:

(a) the Buyer (or the Company) and _____ will
enter into a ____-year employment agreement under which
the Buyer would agree to compensate _____ at an
agreed upon rate to serve as President of the Company; and

(b) each of the Sellers will, if requested by the Buyer, execute
a ____-year non-competition agreement in favor of the Buyer
and the Company.

4. OTHER TERMS

In the Definitive Agreement, the Company will make comprehensive representations and warranties (which, other than those with respect to ownership, taxes, employee benefits and environmental matters, shall survive for _____ (__) months after the Closing) to the Buyer, and will provide comprehensive covenants, indemnities and other protections for the benefit of the Buyer. Each of the Sellers will make customary representations to the Company or the Buyer, as applicable, regarding ownership of its capital stock and/or other equity interests in the Company. The Definitive Agreement would address the liability of any one or more of the Sellers for any breach of any representation or warranty by the Company. The consummation of the contemplated transactions by the Buyer will be subject to the satisfaction of various conditions, including but not limited to, (a) the absence of any material adverse change in the business, assets, condition or prospects of the Company since the date of the most recent financial statements furnished to the Buyer, (b) the Buyer's satisfaction in its sole discretion with the results of its due diligence review of the Company, (c) the approval of the Buyer's Board of Directors, (d) obtaining all third party or governmental consents and approvals necessary or desirable to facilitate consummation of the transaction, (e) the Buyer's execution of a _____-year employment contract with _____ (an employee of ____) at a mutually agreeable level of compensation, and (f) the prior consent of the FCC to the transfer in control of the Company.

PART TWO

The following paragraphs of this letter (the "Binding Provisions") are the legally binding and enforceable agreements of _____, the Buyer and the Company.

1. ACCESS

During the period from the date this letter is signed by _____ and the Company (the "Signing Date") until the date on which either Party provides the other Party with written notice that negotiations toward a Definitive Agreement are terminated (the "Termination Date"), the Company will afford the Buyer full and free access to the Company, its personnel, properties, contracts, books and records, and all other documents and data.

2. EXCLUSIVE DEALING

Until _____ __, 20__, neither the Company nor _____ will, directly or indirectly, through any representative or otherwise, solicit or entertain offers from, negotiate with, or in any manner encourage, discuss, accept, or consider any proposal of any other person relating to the acquisition of the shares of capital stock or other equity interest in the Company, or in its assets or business, in whole or in part, whether directly or indirectly, through purchase, merger, consolidation, or otherwise (other than sales of inventory in the ordinary course).

3. CONDUCT OF BUSINESS

During the period from the signing of this Letter of Intent up until _____ __, 20__, the Company shall operate its business in the ordinary course and refrain from any extraordinary transactions.

4. CONFIDENTIALITY

Except as and to the extent required by law, the Buyer will not disclose or use, and will direct its representatives not to disclose or use to the detriment of any Seller or the Company, any Confidential Information (as defined below) furnished by the Sellers, the Company, or their respective representatives to the Buyer or its representatives at any time or in any manner other than in connection with its evaluation of the transaction proposed in this letter. For purposes of this paragraph, "Confidential Information" means any information about the Company stamped "confidential" or identified in writing as such to the Buyer by the Company or any Seller promptly following its disclosure, unless (i) such information is already known to the Buyer or its representatives or to others not bound by a duty of confidentiality or such information becomes publicly available through no fault of the Buyer or its representatives, (b) the use of such information is necessary or appropriate in making any filing or obtaining any consent or approval required for the consummation of the Possible

Acquisition, or (c) the furnishing or use of such information is required by or necessary or appropriate in connection with legal proceedings. Upon the written request of the Company, the Buyer will promptly return to the Company or destroy any Confidential Information in its possession and certify in writing to the Company that it has done so.

5. DISCLOSURE

Either the Buyer or the Company may make directly or indirectly any public comments, statements, or communications with respect to, or otherwise disclose or permit the disclosure of, the execution of this letter or the existence of discussions regarding a possible transaction between the Parties; provided, that neither _____ nor either Party shall disclose any of the financial terms of the transaction proposed in this letter. If _____ or a Party is required by law to make any such disclosure, it must first provide to the other Party(ies) the content of the proposed disclosure, the reasons that such disclosure is required by law, and the time and place that the disclosure will be made.

6. COSTS

Each of _____, the Buyer and the Company will be responsible for and bear all of his or its own costs and expenses (including any broker's or finder's fees and the expenses of its representatives) incurred at any time in connection with pursuing or consummating the Possible Acquisition.

7. ENTIRE AGREEMENT

The Binding Provisions constitute the entire agreement among _____ and the Parties, and supersede all prior oral or written agreements, understandings, representations and warranties, and courses of conduct and dealing between or among them on the subject matter hereof. Except as otherwise provided herein, the Binding Provisions may be amended or modified only by a writing executed by _____ and the Parties.

8. GOVERNING LAW

The Binding Provisions will be governed by and construed under the laws of the State of _____ without regard to conflicts of laws principles.

9. JURISDICTION; SERVICE OF PROCESS

Any action or proceeding seeking to enforce any provision of, or based on any right arising out of, this letter may be brought against _____ or either of the Parties in either the courts of the State of _____, County of _____ or the courts of the State of _____, County of _____, or, if it has or can acquire jurisdiction, in the United States District Court for the _____ District of _____ or the _____ District of _____, and _____ and each of the Parties consents to the jurisdiction of such courts (and of the appropriate appellate courts) in any such action or proceeding and waives any objection to venue laid therein. Process in any action or proceeding referred to in the preceding sentence may be served on _____ or either Party anywhere in the world.

10. TERMINATION

The Binding Provisions will automatically terminate on _____ __, 20__ and may be terminated earlier upon written notice by either Party to the other Party unilaterally, for any reason or no reason, with or without cause, at any time; provided, however, that the termination of the Binding Provisions will not affect the liability of a Party for breach of any of the Binding Provisions prior to the termination. Upon termination of the Binding Provisions, _____ and the Parties will have no further obligations hereunder, except as stated in Paragraphs 2, 4, 6, 7, 8, 9, 10, 11, and 12 of this Part Two, which will survive any such termination.

11. COUNTERPARTS

This letter may be executed in one or more counterparts, each of which will be deemed to be an original copy of this letter and all of which, when taken together, will be deemed to constitute one and the same agreement.

12. NO LIABILITY

The paragraphs and provisions of Part One of this letter do not constitute and will not give rise to any legally binding obligation on the part of either of the Parties or _____. Moreover, except as expressly provided in the Binding Provisions (or as expressly provided in any binding written agreement that the Parties and _____ may enter into in the future), no past or future action, course of conduct, or failure to act relating to the Possible Acquisition, or relating to the negotiation of the terms of the Possible Acquisition or any Definitive Agreement, will give rise to or serve as a basis for any obligation or other liability on the part of the Parties or _____.

*   *   *   *   *   *

[Signatures on next page]

If you are in agreement with the foregoing, please sign and return one copy of this letter agreement, which thereupon will constitute our agreement with respect to its subject matter.

Very truly yours,

[NAME OF BUYER]

By: _____
[Name]
[Title]

Duly executed and agreed on _____ __, 20__.

[NAME OF COMPANY]

By: _____
[Name]
[Title]

Duly executed and agreed on _____ __, 20__.

SELLING STOCKHOLDER(S)

_____
[Name]

_____
[Name]

_____
[Name]

Duly executed and agreed on _____ __, 20__.

APPENDIX C

SAMPLE CONSULTING AGREEMENT

THIS CONSULTING AGREEMENT is dated as of _____ __, 20___, by and between _____ ("Licensee"), and _____("Consultant").

WITNESSETH:

WHEREAS, Licensee owns and is the licensee of Station_____, _____ (the "Station");

WHEREAS, Licensee and Consultant have entered into an Asset Purchase Agreement of even date whereby Licensee proposes to sell certain assets of the Station subject to the prior approval of the Federal Communications Commission;

WHEREAS, Consultant is familiar with and has expertise in the sale of advertising time by radio broadcast stations; and

WHEREAS, Licensee desires that Consultant provide to Licensee certain consulting services, and Consultant desires to provide such services, on the terms and conditions set forth in this Agreement.

NOW, THEREFORE, in consideration of the mutual promises herein made, Licensee and Consultant hereby agree as follows:

Section 1. Consulting Services to be Provided. Consultant shall, beginning on _____ __, 20___, and continuing until the closing or termination of the Asset Purchase Agreement (the "Consulting Period"), provide Licensee with the following consulting services (the "Services"):

(a)   consultation on improving the sales of the Station;

(b)   consultation on the hiring and training of sales representatives for the Station; and

(c)   such other consulting services as may be mutually agreed upon between the parties in writing.

Section 2. Payment for Consulting Services. As compensation for consulting services upon and subject to the terms and conditions of this Consulting Agreement, Licensee agrees to pay Consultant a fee of _____ Dollars ($ _____.00) per month.

Section 3. Providing of Services. The Services to be furnished hereunder by Consultant will be rendered as Licensee may from time to time reasonably request. All out-of-pocket expenses incurred by Consultant in providing consulting services hereunder, including charges for transportation, meals and long-distance telephone usage, shall be reimbursed by Licensee to Consultant.

Section 4. Place of Work. Consultant may perform the Services at any location he deems appropriate. Licensee agrees to provide Consultant and the staff of Consultant with the use and occupancy of its studio office.

Section 5. Consultant's Right of Control. Consultant will perform the Services in a manner satisfactory to Licensee. Licensee shall have the right to be advised and to evaluate Consultant's work in the performance of this Agreement. Consultant shall have the right to hire sales representatives for the Station subject to the approval of Licensee. Consultant reserves the right to control and direct the method and means by which the Services are to be performed.

Section 6. Licensee's Right of Control. Nothing in this Agreement shall be construed to prevent or hinder the Licensee from retaining and exercising full and complete control over the Station, including, but not limited to, control of its finances, personnel and programming.

Section 7. Cooperation. Licensee and Consultant mutually acknowledge their interest in maximizing the sale of advertising time on the Station. Consultant shall provide Licensee with recommendations on the hiring of sales representatives for the Station and the purchase of promotional materials to enhance the sales of the Station.

Licensee shall provide funding for implementing the recommendations of Consultant in accordance with the budget set forth in Attachment A. Licensee and Consultant shall cooperate with one another to fulfill the purposes of this Agreement, including, but not limited to, the provision of adequate funding by Licensee to implement the recommendations of Consultant.

Section 8. Confidentiality. Consultant agrees to hold in strictest confidence all information concerning Licensee furnished to or obtained by Consultant in the course of providing the services contemplated hereby (except to the extent that such information has been (i) in the public domain through no fault of Consultant or (ii) lawfully acquired by Consultant from sources other than Licensee, and Consultant shall not disclose or release any such confidential information to any person, unless such disclosure or release is compelled by judicial or administrative process.

Section 9. Default. If either party believes the other to be in default hereunder, the former party shall provide the other with written notice specifying in reasonable detail the nature of such default. If the default is not curable or has not been cured within ___ (__) days after delivery of that notice, then the party giving such notice may terminate this Agreement, subject to the right of the party to contest such action through appropriate proceedings.

Section 10. Assignment. This Consulting Agreement and the rights and duties of the parties hereunder shall not be assignable or transferable by either party without the prior written consent of the other party hereto.

Section 11. Governing Law. This Consulting Agreement shall be governed by and construed in accordance with the laws of the State of _____, without regard to the principles of conflict of laws thereof.

Section 12. Notice. All notices and other communications hereunder shall be in writing and shall be delivered by hand, facsimile transmission or mailed by registered or certified mail, return receipt requested, to the parties at the following addresses (or to such other address as either party may have furnished to the other in writing in accordance herewith), and shall be deemed effective on the date on which such notice is received:

If to Consultant: _____
_____
_____
_____

If to Licensee: _____
_____
_____
_____

Section 13. Amendments. This Consulting Agreement may not be modified or amended except by an agreement in writing signed by the parties.

Section 14. Waivers. The failure of either party at any time to require strict performance by the other party of any provision hereof shall not waive or diminish such party's right to demand strict performance thereafter of that or any other provision hereof.

Section 15. Relationship of Parties. Nothing contained herein shall be deemed to constitute the appointment of either party as the agent of the other. Consultant enters into this Agreement as an independent contractor.

IN WITNESS WHEREOF, the parties have caused this Consulting Agreement to be duly executed as of the day and year first above written.

[LICENSEE]

By: _____
[Name]
[Title]

[CONSULTANT]

By: _____
[Name]

APPENDIX D

ABCs OF LMAs
AND
TIME BROKERAGE CHECKLIST FOR
THE LICENSEE

ABCs OF LMAs: A SHORT
COURSE ON FCC POLICIES

THE LAW IN A NUTSHELL

Here's a two-sentence summary of the law governing Local Marketing Agreements (LMAs):** (1) the licensee must retain control over all aspects of station operation, especially the areas of finances, personnel and programming and (2) licensee's time brokerage of any other broadcast station in the same market for more than 15 percent of the brokered station's weekly broadcast hours results in counting the brokered station toward the brokering licensee's ownership limits.

The determination concerning compliance with the FCC's radio ownership rules should be made prior to entering into an LMA.

CONTRACT PROVISIONS

Do's:
>   Include provisions which make clear that:

- Licensee retains the right, <u>without</u> <u>limitation</u>, to suspend, cancel or reject any programs or commercials.

- Licensee retains the right to preempt any program for another program deemed to be of greater national, regional, or local interest or importance; in case of an emergency; or to comply with federal, state, or local laws.

- Licensee shall be solely responsible for maintaining

---

*   * The phrase LMA does not adequately describe the many differing arrangements whereby a licensee sells a block of programming time and/or commercial avails to a third party. These arrangements have also been referred to as time brokerage agreements, local market agreements, bulk time sales agreements, joint ventures, local management agreements, local network agreements, sales representative agreements, joint sales agreements and leasing agreements (a term viewed with disfavor by the FCC).

the station logs and political and public inspection files, filing Biennial Ownership Reports and other reports and applications, receiving and responding to telephone inquiries related to station operations, complying with the political broadcasting rules and broadcasting proper station identification announcements.

- Licensee shall be responsible for the salaries, taxes, insurance, and related costs of its own employees and station operation.

- Licensee shall be responsible for complying with the FCC's technical requirements and for payment of costs associated with operating the transmitter and antennas.

- Licensee shall oversee, and take ultimate responsibility for, the broker's advertising and program practices with respect to the provision of equal opportunities, lowest unit charge and reasonable access, and other requirements contained in the FCC's political rules.

Don'ts:

Don't omit any of the above provisions.

Avoid provisions which provide that:

- Licensee shall pay an excessive amount of money as liquidated damages in the event it terminates the agreement.

- Broker shall be responsible for purchasing new equipment and making repairs to the existing equipment.

- Broker shall be responsible for expenses related to the Licensee's studio and broadcast transmitter (*e.g.*, tower and studio rent, utilities, telephone, property taxes).

- Broker has the right to terminate the agreement but Licensee has no reciprocal right.

- The term of the agreement exceeds the expiration of the station's license or eight years.

POST-CONTRACT SUGGESTIONS FOR THE LICENSEE

- Maintain a "meaningful management and staff" presence during regular business hours at the station (defined by the FCC as at least one management employee and one staff employee).

- Make sure the station complies with all of the FCC's political broadcasting rules (equal opportunities, reasonable access, lowest unit charge, sponsorship identification).

- Prepare the quarterly issues/programs reports.

- Maintain the public inspection file in good order.

- Make sure the station's programming responds to the needs of its community of license (it is recommended that the licensee take responsibility for producing and airing some issue-responsive public affairs programming and public service announcements).

- Document efforts to oversee station operations and retain written records of when programming of the broker has been rejected or preempted.

- Continue to maintain control over station finances (*e.g.*, payment of salaries, insurance, taxes, etc.) and to supervise station employees.

- File reports (*e.g.*, Biannual Ownership Report, Broadcast Mid-Term Report) and pay FCC Regulatory Fees.

- Establish procedures (*e.g.*, regular meetings and review sessions) to make sure the broker complies with provisions of the agreement pertaining to licensee control.

POTHOLES AND PITFALLS

- Complaints by competitor stations alleging anticompetitive conduct and violation of state and/ or federal antitrust laws.

- Complaints filed with the FCC alleging an unauthorized transfer of control (lead to potential imposition of forfeitures and institution of license revocation proceedings).

- Post-termination problems (*e.g.*, rebuilding of programming and sales staffs, valuation issues for prospective purchasers).

- Stay alert for any new "rules of the road" adopted by the FCC and/or Congress.

TIME BROKERAGE AGREEMENT CHECKLIST FOR THE LICENSEE

The following checklist summarizes the terms of the Time Brokerage Agreement between _____ ("Licensee") and _____ ("Programmer") and provides recommendations on complying with the letter and the spirit of the Agreement. Although Programmer has contracted for the right to use the broadcast transmission facilities of Station _____, the essential ingredient of the Agreement is that Licensee continues to be ultimately responsible for programming, personnel and finances. Accordingly, the Licensee is still in charge and has the absolute right to reject any program or commercial furnished by Programmer which it deems is not in the public interest.

☐ **Overall Operation of Station.** Licensee shall retain ultimate control and authority over the policies, programming and operations of the Station, including, without limitation, the right to decide whether to accept or reject any programming or advertisements, the right to refuse any programming or part of programming deemed by Licensee to not be in the public interest or to not meet Licensee's programming standards, the right to interrupt or preempt any programming at any time in order to broadcast programming deemed by Licensee to be of significant national, regional or local interest, and the right to take any other actions necessary for compliance with federal, state and local laws, the Communications Act and the rules, regulations and policies of the Commission (including the prohibition on unauthorized transfers of control) and the rules, regulations and policies of other federal government entities, including the Federal Trade Commission and the Department of Justice. Licensee has reserved up to two hours per week of programming time on Sunday between the hours of 6:00 a.m. and 12 Noon during which it may broadcast programming of its choice.

Recommended Actions:

1. Schedule periodic meetings with Programmer's staff (the meetings should be conducted by Licensee's General Manager).

2. Monitor Programmer's programming to make sure that it complies with FCC rules and policies, including, but not limited to, obscene and indecent programming and sponsorship identification.

3. Maintain written records of meetings with Programmer's staff and of instances where the programming of Programmer has been preempted.

4. Establish a mutually-acceptable method of dealing with the press and members of the public with the goal of dispelling any perception that Programmer, as opposed to the Licensee, owns and operates the Station.

☐ **Responsibility for Employees and Related Expenses.** Licensee will provide and be responsible for the Station's personnel necessary for the broadcast transmission of Programmer's programs (including, without limitation, the General Manager of the Station and another full-time employee). Licensee shall maintain insurance reasonably satisfactory to Programmer covering the Station's facilities. Whenever on the Station's premises, all personnel shall be subject to the overall supervision of Licensee's General Manager.

Recommended Actions:

1. Continue to employ a General Manager and another full-time employee.

2. Continue to pay in a timely fashion the salaries, taxes, insurance and related costs for the above personnel, lease payments, utilities, taxes, etc. and provide Programmer with a schedule of such timely payments (including invoices) within 30 days following the end of each month.

3. Make sure that Programmer pays for the salaries, commissions, taxes, insurance and all other related costs for all personnel employed by it.

☐ **Political Advertising.** Any qualified political candidate will have access to the Station at the rates prescribed by the Station pursuant to the Communications Act and the rules, regulations and policies of the Commission. All requests for the purchase of political advertising time must be approved by the General Manager.

Recommended Actions:

1. Advise candidates for public office that all orders for the purchase of time must be approved by the General Manager.

2. Advise Programmer's sales personnel that any questions concerning the Station's political broadcasting policies (*e.g.*, lowest unit charges, equal opportunities, reasonable access to the Station's facilities) should be directed to the General Manager.

3. Be familiar with the FCC's political broadcasting rules (*e.g.*, the need to provide each candidate with a written statement disclosing the Station's political advertising policies)

☐ **Responsibility of Licensee's Employees.** The General Manager and other full-time employee or employees shall report to and be accountable solely to the Licensee. The General Manager shall direct the day-to-day operation of the Station. Whenever on the Station's premises, Programmer's personnel shall be subject to the supervision and the direction of Licensee's General Manager and other full-time employee or employees.

Recommended Actions:

1. Don't allow Programmer's employees to assume managerial functions at the Station.

2. Make sure that a management-level person employed by the Licensee is either at the Station or reachable by telephone during normal business hours.

☐ **Compliance with Governmental Requirements.** Licensee shall at all times be solely responsible for meeting all of the Commission's requirements with respect to public service programming and for maintaining the political and public inspection files and the Station's logs. Licensee shall also retain the right to break into Programmer's programming in case of an emergency. Licensee will be responsible for the proper broadcast of station identification announcements.

Recommended Actions:

1. Monitor the Station's programming to make sure that appropriate station identification announcements are broadcast (station identification announcements containing the call letters followed by the name of the city of license must be broadcast at the beginning and ending of each day of operation, and hourly, as close to the hour as feasible at a natural break in programming).

2. Make sure that the Station's local public inspection file is in order. (The Time Brokerage Agreement should be placed in the local file.)

☐ **Issues/Programs List.** Licensee shall, on a regular basis, assess the needs of its community, address those needs in connection with the preparation of its public affairs programming, and document such needs and programming in a quarterly report (the "issues/ programs list"). Licensee shall also record those needs and place the issues/programs list in the public inspection file. Further, Licensee shall receive written information from Programmer with respect to such of Programmer's programs which are responsive to public needs and interests as to assist Licensee in the preparation of required programming in the satisfaction of his community service needs and in preparation of the issues/programs list. At Licensee's request, Programmer shall submit to Licensee in writing monthly reports in a form reasonably satisfactory to Licensee and Programmer, which reports will cover programs and commercials delivered by Programmer and broadcast by the Station.

Recommended Actions:

1. Prior to the beginning of each quarter, the General Manager should advise Programmer of the community needs and issues of greatest importance which should be treated by the Programmer during the forthcoming quarter and shall confer with Programmer as to the scheduling and broadcast of programs which will be responsive to those community needs and interests.

2. Immediately after the end of each quarter, Programmer shall furnish the General Manager with a list of issue-responsive programs and public service announcements (PSAs) (including a brief description of the program or PSA, the length

of the program or announcement, and the date and time on which it was broadcast). The General Manager shall include this material in preparing the issues/programs list for the Station.

☐ **Filing of Reports with FCC.** Licensee shall file with the FCC the Biennial Ownership Report (FCC Form 323) and Mid-Term EEO Report (FCC Form 397) for the Station. All reports and applications required to be filed with the Commission (including ownership reports and renewal applications) or any other government entity, department or body in respect of the Station, will be filed in a timely manner and will be true and complete and accurately present the information contained and required thereby. All such reports and documents, to the extent required to be kept in the public inspection files of the Station, will be kept in such files.

☐ **Sponsorship Identification and Payola/Plugola.** On an annual basis, or more frequently if requested by the licensee, Programmer agrees to execute and provide Licensee with Anti Payola/Plugola Affidavits.**

Recommended Action:

Make sure that you receive from Programmer copies of Anti Payola/Plugola Affidavits signed by employees of Programmer who are involved in the selection of programming.

---

*   * An example of an Anti Payola/Plugola Affidavit appears as Attachment A to Appendix E.

APPENDIX E

ILLUSTRATIVE TIME BROKERAGE AGREEMENTS

The two sample Time Brokerage Agreements contained in this Appendix E are virtually identical in many respects. Most of the common provisions are designed to comply with FCC rules and policies governing Time Brokerage and Local Marketing Agreements. The second Agreement (E12-E21) covers a situation where the "Broker" has entered into an Asset Purchase Agreement with the "Licensee."

SAMPLE ONE

TIME BROKERAGE AGREEMENT

This Time Brokerage Agreement ("Agreement") dated as of _____, 20__, by and between _____, the licensee of Radio Station _____ ("Licensee") and _____ ("Broker").

WHEREAS, Licensee owns and operates Station _____, _____, _____ ("Station");

WHEREAS, Licensee has available for sale broadcast time on the Station; and

WHEREAS, Broker desires to purchase time on Licensee's Station for the broadcast of certain of the programming of the Station, and to sell advertising time for inclusion in said programming;

NOW, THEREFORE, for and in consideration of the mutual covenants herein contained, the parties hereto, intending to be legally bound, have agreed and do agree as follows:

W I T N E S S E T H :

1. **Facilities**. Licensee agrees to make broadcasting transmission facilities available to Broker and to broadcast on the Station, or cause to be broadcast, Broker's programs which may originate either from Broker's own studios or from Licensee's studios.

2. **Payments**. Broker hereby agrees to pay Licensee for the broadcast of the programs hereunder _____ Dollars ($_____.00) ("Monthly Broker Fee"). The Monthly Broker Fee is due and payable in full _____ (___) days following the end of the preceding broadcast month. The failure of Licensee to demand or insist upon prompt payment in accordance herewith shall not constitute a waiver of its right to do so.

3. **Term**. The term of this Agreement shall be for a period of ____ (_) years from the effective date of this Agreement. Broker shall have the right to extend the Agreement for a renewal term of an additional ___ (_) years upon written notice to the Licensee at least _____ (__) days prior to the conclusion of the term of this Agreement.

4. **Programs**. Broker shall furnish or cause to be furnished the artistic personnel and materials for the programs which shall be in good taste and in accordance with the rules, regulations and policies of the Federal Communications Commission ("Commission" and/or "FCC") and the Communications Act of 1934, as amended ("Act"). Broker shall make available to Licensee its programming during a sufficient number of hours to enable the Station to meet the minimum hours of operation required under the Commission's Rules. All advertising messages and promotional material or announcements shall comply with all applicable federal, state and local laws, regulations and policies.

5. **Station Facilities**.

    A. **Operation of Station**. The Station operates in accordance with the authorizations issued to it by the Commission. Throughout the term of this Agreement, Licensee shall make available to

Broker the maximum authorized facilities of the Station for up to one hundred sixty-eight (168) hours per week, Sunday through Saturday, except for downtime occasioned by routine maintenance. Any maintenance work affecting the operation of the Station at full power shall be scheduled with the approval of Broker, which shall not be unreasonably withheld, upon at least _____ (__) hours prior notice to Broker.

B. **Interruption of Normal Operations**. If the Station suffers any loss or damage of any nature to its transmission facilities which results in the interruption of service or the inability of the Station to operate with its maximum authorized facilities, Licensee shall immediately notify Broker and shall undertake such repairs as are necessary to restore full-time operation of the Station with its maximum authorized facilities within _____ (_) days from the occurrence of any such loss or damage. If such repairs are not completed within the allotted period, Broker may give notice to Licensee of Broker's intention to terminate this Agreement, in which event this Agreement shall terminate on the _____ (____) day following such notice, any other provision of this Agreement notwithstanding.

C. **Studio Location**. Licensee shall maintain a main studio in accordance with Commission rules and policies.

6. **Handling of Mail**. Except as required to comply with Commission Rules and policies, including those regarding the maintenance of the public inspection file (which shall at all times remain the responsibility of the Licensee), Licensee shall not be required to receive or handle mail, emails, or overnight carrier deliveries in connection with programs broadcast hereunder unless Licensee, at the request of Broker, has agreed in writing to do so.

7. **Programming and Operations Standards**. Broker agrees to cooperate with Licensee in the broadcast of programs of the highest possible standards of excellence.

Broker further agrees that if, in the sole judgment of Licensee, Broker does not comply with said standards, Licensee may suspend or cancel any programs not in compliance.

8A. **Staffing Requirements**. Both Licensee and Broker will be in full compliance with the main studio staffing requirements as specified by the Commission. Licensee and Broker hereby agree that Licensee's personnel may be involved in the sale of advertising time on the programs delivered by Broker.

8B. **Responsibility for Employees and Expense**. Broker shall employ and be responsible for the salaries, commissions, taxes, insurance and all other related costs of all personnel involved in the production and broadcast of its programming (including air personalities, engineering personnel, salespersons, traffic personnel, board operators and other programming staff members). Broker may establish, staff and maintain a remote control point for the Station, subject to the control and oversight of the Licensee. Licensee will provide and be responsible for the Station personnel necessary for the broadcast transmission of Broker's programs (including, without limitation, the Station General Manager and Engineer), and will be responsible for the salaries, taxes, insurance and related costs for all the Station personnel involved in the broadcast transmission of Broker's programs. Whenever on the Station's premises, Broker's personnel shall be subject to the supervision and the direction of Licensee's General Manager and/or Engineer. Broker shall pay for all telephone calls associated with program production and listener responses, for the fees to ASCAP, BMI, SESAC and Sound Exchange, and for any other copyright fees attributable to its programming broadcast on the Station pursuant to this Agreement.

9. **Advertising Revenues**. Broker shall retain all revenues from the sale of advertising time on the programs it delivers to the Station. Broker may sell advertising in combination for Station _____, _____, _____, and Station, or any other broadcasting stations of its choosing. Licensee shall retain the revenue from the

sale of any advertising on the Station on programs not produced or delivered to it by Broker. Any qualified political candidate will have access to the Station under this Agreement at the rates prescribed by the Station pursuant to the Act and the rules, regulations and policies of the Commission.

10. **Operation of Station**. Notwithstanding anything to the contrary in this Agreement, Licensee shall have full authority and power over the operation of the Station during the period of this Agreement. Licensee shall be responsible for the payment of the salary of the Station's General Manager and Engineer, both of whom shall report solely to and be accountable solely to the Licensee. Station's General Manager shall direct the day-to-day operation of the Station. Licensee shall retain control (said control to be reasonably exercised) over the policies, programming and operations of the Station, including, without limitation, the right to decide whether to accept or reject any programming or advertisements, the right to preempt any programs not in the public interest or in order to broadcast a program deemed by Licensee to be of greater national, regional or local interest, and the right to take any other actions necessary for compliance with federal, state and local laws, the Act and the rules, regulations and policies of the Commission (including the prohibition on unauthorized transfers of control) and the rules, regulations and policies of other federal government entities, including the Federal Trade Commission and the Department of Justice. Licensee shall at all times be solely responsible for meeting all of the Commission's requirements with respect to public service programming, for maintaining the political and public inspection files and the Station's logs, and for the preparation of issues/ programs lists. Licensee shall also retain the right to interrupt Broker's programming in case of an emergency. Licensee shall, on a regular basis, assess the needs of its community and address those needs in connection with the preparation of its public affairs programming. Licensee shall also record those needs and place the issues/ programs list in the public inspection file. Further, Licensee shall receive information from Broker with respect to such of Broker's programs which are responsive to public needs

and interests so as to assist Licensee in the preparation of required programming in the satisfaction of its community service needs. Broker shall also provide upon request such other information necessary to enable Licensee to prepare other records and reports required by the Commission or other local, state or federal government entities.

11. **Station Identification**. Licensee will be responsible for the proper broadcast of station identification announcements.

12. **Special Events**. Licensee reserves the right, in its discretion, to preempt any of the broadcasts of the programs referred to herein for the broadcast of special programs of importance. In all such cases, Licensee will use its best efforts to give Broker reasonable notice of its intention to preempt Broker's programs, and, in the event of such preemption, Broker shall receive a pro rata payment credit for the programs preempted.

13. **Force Majeure**. Any failure or impairment of facilities or any delay or interruption in the broadcast of programs, or failure at any time to furnish facilities, in whole or in part, for broadcast, due to causes beyond the control of Licensee, shall not constitute a breach of this Agreement.

14. **Right to Use the Programs**. The right to use the programs and to authorize their use in any manner and in any media whatsoever shall be, and remain, vested in Broker.

15. **Payola/Plugola**. Broker agrees that it will not accept any consideration, compensation or gift or gratuity of any kind whatsoever, regardless of its value or form, including, but not limited to, a commission, discount, bonus, material, supplies or other merchandise, services or labor (collectively "Consideration"), whether or not pursuant to written contracts or agreements between Broker and merchants or advertiser, unless the payer is identified in the program for which Consideration was provided as having paid for or furnished such Consideration, in accordance with the Act and FCC requirements. Broker agrees to annually, or more frequently at the request of

the Licensee, execute and provide Licensee with an Anti Payola/Plugola Affidavit, substantially in the form attached hereto as Attachment A.

16. **Compliance With Law**. Broker agrees that, throughout the term of this Agreement, Broker will comply with all laws, rules, regulations and policies applicable to the conduct of Licensee's business and Broker acknowledges that Licensee has not urged, counseled or advised the use of any unfair business practice.

17. **Indemnification Warranty**. Broker will indemnify and hold Licensee harmless against all liability for libel, slander, unfair competition or trade practices, infringement of trade marks, trade names or program titles, violation of rights of privacy and infringement of copyrights and proprietary rights resulting from the broadcast of programming furnished by Broker. Further, Broker warrants that the broadcasting of its programs will not violate any rights of others and Broker agrees to hold Licensee, the Station and its employees harmless from any and all damages, liabilities, costs and expenses, including reasonable attorney's fees, arising from the broadcast of such programs. Broker's obligation to hold Licensee harmless against the liabilities specified above shall survive any termination of this Agreement and shall be in effect until the expiration of all applicable statutes of limitation.

18. **Events of Default; Cure Periods and Remedies**. The following shall, after the expiration of the applicable cure periods, constitute Events of Default:

   A.   **Non-Payment**. Broker's failure to timely pay the consideration provided for in Paragraph 2, hereof.

   B.   **Default in Covenants or Adverse Legal Action**. The default by either party hereto in the material observance or performance of any material covenant, condition or agreement contained herein, or if either party (i) shall make general assignment for the benefit of creditors, (ii) files or has filed against it a petition for bankruptcy, reorganization or an arrangement for the benefit of creditors, or for the appointment of a receiver, trustee or creditor representative for the property or assets of such party under any federal or state insolvency law, which, if filed against such party, has not been dismissed or discharged within _____ (__) days thereof.

C.   **Breach of Representation**. If any material representation or warranty herein made by either party hereto, or in any certificate or document furnished by either party to the other pursuant to the provisions hereof, shall prove to have been false or misleading in any material respect as of the time made or furnished.

D.   **Cure Periods**. An Event of Default shall not be deemed to have occurred until _____ (__) business days after the nondefaulting party has provided the defaulting party with written notice specifying the event or events that if not cured would constitute an Event of Default and specifying the action necessary to cure the Default within such period. This period may be extended for a reasonable period of time, if the defaulting party is acting in good faith to cure the default and such default is not material adverse to the other party. Non-payment shall be deemed to be an Event of Default on the day after timely payment is due, and no notice of default is required, nor is any cure period provided.

E.   **Termination Upon Default**. Upon the occurrence of an Event of Default, the nondefaulting party may terminate this Agreement provided that it is not also in material default hereunder. If Broker has defaulted in the performance of its obligations, Licensee shall be under no further obligation to make available to Broker any further broadcast time or broadcast transmission facilities and all amounts accrued or payable to Licensee up to the date of termination which have not been paid shall immediately become due and payable. If Licensee has defaulted in the performance of its obligations hereunder, Broker may terminate this Agreement.

F. **Liabilities Upon Termination**. Broker shall be responsible for all liabilities, debts and obligations of Broker based upon the purchase of air time and use of Licensee's transmission facilities including, without limitation, accounts payable, barter agreements and unaired advertisements, but not for Licensee's federal, state and local income and business franchise tax liabilities or taxes levied upon Licensee's real estate or personal property.

19. **Broker Termination Options**. Broker shall have the right, at its option, to terminate this Agreement at the end of the first year after the effective date hereunder. Broker may also elect to terminate this Agreement at any time during the term hereof in the event that Licensee preempts or substitutes other programming for that supplied by the Broker during _____ percent (__%) or more of the total hours of operation of the Station during any calendar month. In the event Broker elects to terminate this Agreement pursuant to this provision, it shall give Licensee notice of such election at least _____ (__) days prior to the termination date. Upon termination, all sums owing the Licensee shall be paid and neither party shall have any further liability to the other except as may be provided by Paragraph 17, above.

20. **Licensee Termination Option**. Licensee shall have the right, at its option, to terminate the Agreement. In the event the Licensee elects to terminate the Agreement, it shall give Broker notice of such election at least _____ (__) days prior to the termination date. Upon termination, all sums owing to Licensee shall be paid and neither party shall have any further liability to the other except as may be provided by Paragraph 17, of the Agreement.

21. **Sale of Station**. In the event Licensee decides to sell the Station to a third party during the term of this Agreement, Licensee shall give Broker notice of its intent to sell at least _____ (__) days prior to entering into any agreement providing for such sale and, in the event any

such sale is completed during the term of this Agreement, Licensee shall pay Broker _____ Dollars ($_____.00) to compensate Broker for the loss of its business opportunity, unless the third party agrees to assume the duties and obligations of Licensee as set forth in this Agreement pursuant to an appropriate assignment and Broker approves the assignment as provided for in Paragraph 28, below.

22. **Termination Upon Order of Governmental Authority**. In the event that a federal, state or local government authority designates a hearing with respect to the continuation or renewal of any authorization held by Licensee for the operation of the Station or orders the termination of this Agreement and/or the curtailment in any manner material to the relationship between the parties hereto of the provision of programming by Broker hereunder, at its option, Broker may seek administrative or judicial relief from such order(s) (in which event Licensee shall cooperate with Broker, provided that Broker shall be responsible for legal fees and costs incurred in such proceedings) or Broker shall notify Licensee that it will terminate this Agreement in accordance with such order(s). If the Commission designates the renewal application of the Station for a hearing as a consequence of this Agreement or for any other reason, or initiates any revocation or other proceeding with respect to the authorizations issued to the Licensee for the operation of the Station, and Licensee elects to contest the action, then Licensee shall be responsible for its expenses incurred as a consequence of the Commission proceeding; provided, however, that Broker shall at its own expense cooperate and comply with any reasonable request of Licensee to assemble and provide to the Commission information relating to Broker's performance under this Agreement. In the event of termination upon any government order(s), Broker shall pay to Licensee any fees due but unpaid as of the date of termination as may be permitted by such order(s), and Licensee shall cooperate reasonably with Broker to the extent permitted to enable Broker to fulfill advertising or other programming contracts then outstanding, in which event Licensee shall receive as compensation for the carriage of such programming

that which otherwise would have been paid to Broker hereunder. Thereafter, neither party shall have any liability to the other except as may be provided pursuant to Paragraph 17, above.

23. **Representations and Warranties**.

A. **Mutual Representations and Warranties**. Both Licensee and Broker represent that they are legally qualified, empowered and able to enter into this Agreement, and that the execution, delivery and performance hereof shall not constitute a breach or violation of any agreement, contract or other obligation to which either party is subject or by which it is bound.

B. **Licensee's Representations, Warranties and Covenants**. Licensee makes the following further representations, warranties and covenants:

i. **Authorizations**. Licensee owns and holds all licenses and other permits and authorizations necessary for the operation of the Station as presently conducted (including Licenses, permits and authorizations issued by the Commission), and such Licenses, permits and authorizations will be in full force and effect for the entire term hereof, unimpaired by any acts or omissions of Licensee, its principals, employees or agents. There is not now pending or, to Licensee's best knowledge, threatened, any action by the Commission or other party to revoke, cancel, suspend, refuse to renew or modify adversely any of such Licenses, permits or authorizations and, to Licensee's best knowledge, no event has occurred which allows or, after notice or lapse of time or both, would allow, the revocation or termination of such Licenses, permits or authorizations or the imposition of any restrictions thereon of such a nature that may limit the operation of the Station as presently conducted. Licensee has no reason to believe that any such License, permit or authorization will not be renewed during the term of the Agreement in its ordinary course. Licensee is not in any material violation of any statute, ordinance, rule, regulation, policy, order or decree of any federal, state, local or foreign government entity, court or authority having jurisdiction over it or over any part of its operations or assets, which default or violation would have an adverse effect on Licensee or its assets or on its ability to perform this Agreement.

C.   **Filings**. All reports and applications required to be filed with the Commission (including ownership reports, broadcast mid-term reports, and renewal applications) or any other government entity, department or body in respect of the Station have been, and in the future will be, filed in a timely manner and are and will be true and complete and accurately present the information contained and required thereby. All such reports and documents, to the extent required to be kept in the public inspection files of the Station, are and will be kept in such files.

D.   **Facilities**. The Station's facilities will be maintained at the expense of Licensee and comply in all material respects with the maximum facilities permitted by the Commission's authorizations and will be operated in all material respects in accordance with good engineering standards necessary to deliver a high quality technical signal to the area served by the Station and with all applicable laws and regulations (including the requirements of the Act and the rules, regulations, policies and procedures of the Commission promulgated thereunder). All capital expenditures reasonably required to maintain the quality of the Station's signal shall be made promptly at the expense of Licensee. Further, Licensee will take whatever actions are necessary to improve the technical facilities of the Station, including, but not limited to, increasing the Station's power or tower height, subject to FCC approval where necessary.

E. **Title to Properties**. Licensee has, and will throughout the term hereof, maintain good and marketable title to all of the assets and properties used in the operation of the Station, free and clear of any liens, claims, claims or security interests. Licensee will not dispose of, transfer, assign or pledge any such asset, except with the prior written consent of Broker, if such action would affect adversely Licensee's performance hereunder or the business and operation of Broker permitted hereby.

F. **Insurance**. Licensee will maintain in full force and effect throughout the term of this Agreement insurance with responsible and reputable insurance companies or associations covering such risks (including fire and other risks insured against by extended coverage, public liability insurance, insurance for claims against personal injury or death or property damage and such other insurance as may be required by law) and in such amounts and on such terms as is conventionally carried by broadcasters operating radio stations with facilities comparable to those of the Station. Any insurance proceeds received by Licensee in respect of damaged property will be used to repair or replace such property so that the operation of the Station conforms with this Agreement.

24. **Notices**. All necessary notices, demands and requests permitted or required under this Agreement shall be in writing and shall be deemed given _____ (_) days after being mailed by certified mail, return receipt requested, postage prepaid, addressed as follows:

If to Broker: _____

_____

_____

If to Licensee: _____

_____

_____

.25.　Modification and Waiver. No modification of any provision of this Agreement shall in any event be effective unless the same shall be in writing and then such modification shall be effective only in the specific instance and for the purpose for which given.

26. Construction. This Agreement shall be construed in accordance with the laws of the State of _____ and the obligations of the parties hereof are subject to all federal, state and local laws and regulations now or hereafter in force and to the rules, regulations and policies of the Commission and all other government entities or authorities presently or hereafter to be constituted.

27. **Headings**. The headings contained in this Agreement are included for convenience only and no such heading shall in any way alter the meaning of any provision.

28. **Assignment**. This Agreement may not be assigned by Broker without the approval of Licensee.

29. **Counterpart Signature**. This Agreement may be signed in one or more counterparts, each of which shall be deemed a duplicate original, binding on the parties hereto notwithstanding that the parties are not signatory to the original or the same counterpart. This Agreement shall be effective as of the date first above written.

30. **Entire Agreement**. This Agreement embodies the entire agreement between the parties and there are no other agreements, representations, warranties or understanding, oral or written, between them with respect to the subject matter hereof. No alteration, modification or change of this Agreement shall be valid unless by like written instrument executed by an authorized principal.

31. **No Partnership or Joint Venture Created**. Nothing in this Agreement shall be construed to make Licensee and

Broker partners or joint ventures or to afford any rights to any third party other than as expressly provided herein.

32. **Severability**. Subject to the provisions of Paragraph 22 hereof, in the event any provision contained in this Agreement is held to be invalid, illegal or unenforceable, such holding shall not affect any other provision hereof and this Agreement shall be construed as if such invalid, illegal or unenforceable provision had not be contained herein.

IN WITNESS WHEREOF, the parties executed this Agreement to be effective as of the date first above written.

[NAME OF LICENSEE]

By _____
                [Name]
                [Title]

[NAME OF BROKER]

By _____
                [Name]
                [Title]

ATTACHMENT A

City of _____)

County of _____)   SS:

State of _____)

ANTI PAYOLA/PLUGOLA AFFIDAVIT

_____, being first duly sworn, deposes and says as follows:

1. He/she is _____ (position) for _____ [name of licensee].

2. He/she has acted in the above capacity since _____.

3. No matter has been broadcast by Station _____ for which any service, money or other valuable consideration has been directly or indirectly paid, or promised to, or charged, or accepted, by him/her from any person, which matter at the time so broadcast has not been announced or otherwise indicated as paid for or furnished by such person.

4. So far as he/she is aware, no matter has been broadcast by Station _____ for which any service, money, or other valuable consideration has been directly or indirectly paid, or promised to, or charged, or accepted by Station _____ or by any independent contractor engaged by Station _____ in furnishing programs, from any person, which matter at the time so broadcast has not been announced or otherwise indicated as paid for or furnished by such person.

5. In the future, he/she will not pay, promise to pay, request, or receive any service, money, or any other valuable consideration, direct or indirect, from a third party, in exchange for the influencing of, or the attempt to influence, the preparation or presentation of broadcast matter on Station _____.

6. Nothing contained herein is intended to, or shall prohibit receipt or acceptance of, anything with the expressed knowledge and approval of my employer, but henceforth any such approval must be given in writing by someone expressly authorized to give such approval.

7. He/she, his/her spouse and his/her immediate family do__ do not__ have any present direct or indirect ownership interest in (other than an investment in a corporation whose stock is publicly held), serve as an officer or director of, whether with or without compensation, or serve as an employee of, any person, firm or corporation engaged in:

   1. The publishing of music;

   2. The production, distribution (including wholesale and retail sales outlets), manufacture or exploitation of music, tapes, recordings or electrical transcriptions of any program material intended for broadcast use;

   3. The exploitation, promotion, or management of persons rendering artistic, production and/or other services in the entertainment field;

   4. The ownership or operation of one or more radio or radio stations;

   5. The wholesale or retail sale of records intended for public purchase;

   6. Advertising on Station _____, or any other station owned by its licensee (excluding nominal stockholdings in publicly owned companies).

8. The facts and circumstances relating to such interest are none__ as follows__:

   _____

   _____

   _____

                                                    Affiant

Subscribed and sworn to before me
this ___ day of _____, 20___.

_____

Notary Public
My commission expires: _____

SAMPLE TWO

TIME BROKERAGE AGREEMENT

THIS TIME BROKERAGE AGREEMENT ("Agreement") dated as of_____ _, 20__, by and between _____, the licensee of Radio Station _____, _____, _____ ("Licensee"), and _____ ("Broker").

WHEREAS, Licensee owns and operates Station _____ ("Station") pursuant to licenses issued by the Federal Communications Commission ("Commission" and/or "FCC");

WHEREAS, Broker is experienced in radio station ownership and operation;

WHEREAS, Licensee wishes to retain Broker to provide programming for the Station that is in conformity with Station policies and procedures, FCC policies for time brokerage arrangements, and the provisions hereof;

WHEREAS, Broker agrees to use the Station exclusively to broadcast such programming of its selection that is in conformity with all rules, regulations and policies of the FCC and subject to Licensee's full authority to control the operation of the Station;

WHEREAS, Broker and Licensee agree to cooperate to make this Time Brokerage Agreement work to the benefit of the public and both parties and as contemplated in this Agreement; and

WHEREAS, the parties have entered into an Asset Purchase Agreement whereby Broker has agreed to purchase the Station in accordance with the terms and conditions thereof;

NOW, THEREFORE, for and in consideration of the mutual covenants herein contained, the parties, intending to be legally bound, agree as follows:

WITNESSETH:

1. **Payments.** Broker hereby agrees to reimburse Licensee for the payment of certain expenses of the Station specified in Schedule 2.

2. **Effective Date and Term**.

   Effective Date. This Agreement shall be effective on the date selected by Broker which shall be no later than _____(__) business days after the date of this Agreement the "Effective Date").

   Term. This Agreement shall commence on the Effective Date and unless earlier terminated pursuant to Section 11, 12, 13, and 14 of this Agreement, shall expire (a) on the consummation of the Asset Purchase Agreement (b) the termination of the Asset Purchase Agreement, or (c) _____ (__) months from the Effective Date, whichever is earlier.

   Programs. Broker shall furnish or cause to be furnished the artistic personnel and materials for the programs which shall be in good taste and in accordance with the rules, regulations and policies of the FCC and the Communications Act of 1934, as amended (the "Act"). Broker shall make available to Licensee its programming during a sufficient number of hours to enable the Station to meet the minimum hours of operation required under the Commission's Rules. All advertising messages and promotional material or announcements shall comply with all applicable federal, state and local laws, regulations and policies.

3. **Station Facilities.**

   Facilities. Licensee agrees to make broadcasting transmission facilities available to Broker and to broadcast or cause to be broadcast on the Station, Broker's programming.

Operation of Station. Licensee shall be responsible for assuring that the Station will be operated in accordance with the authorizations issued to it by the Commission. Throughout the term of this Agreement, Licensee shall make available to Broker the maximum authorized facilities of the Station for up to one-hundred sixty-eight (168) hours per week, Sunday through Saturday, except for downtime occasioned by routine maintenance. Any maintenance work affecting the operation of the Station at full power shall be scheduled with the approval of Broker, which shall not be unreasonably withheld, upon at least _____ (__) hours prior notice to Broker. Licensee reserves for its own use _____ (__) hours per week of programming time (the "Reserved Time"). All such time used by Licensee shall be broadcast consecutively, in blocks of at least one-half hour in length. The programming of Licensee shall be broadcast between the hours of 6 a.m. and 12 noon on Sunday morning, at hours mutually agreed to by the parties. Licensee shall give Broker at least _____ (__) days' notice of its intent to use any of the Reserved Time.

Interruption of Normal Operations. The failure of either party hereto to comply with its obligations under this Agreement due to acts of God, strikes or threats thereof or force majeure, or due to causes beyond such party's control, such as brief interruptions in service due to technical failures, will not constitute an Event of Default under Section 11 of this Agreement and neither party will be liable to the other party therefor. Broker and Licensee each agree to exercise its best efforts to remedy any conditions adversely affecting its own facilities as soon as practicable.

4.   **Expenses, Revenues and Accounts Receivable**.

Expenses. Broker will be responsible (i) for the salaries, taxes, insurance and related costs for all personnel used in the production of the Programs supplied to Licensee, (ii) for the costs of delivering the programs to Licensee (or Licensee's transmission facilities), (iii) for ASCAP, BMI, SESAC and Sound Exchange license fees for all programming provided by Broker, and (iv) for the costs of telephones used by Broker at Licensee's facilities. Broker will use its own production facilities or Station's facilities to create the programs and will be responsible for all costs associated with preparing or delivering the programs from those facilities to Licensee at Licensee's transmitting facility. Licensee will pay for those operating costs required to be paid to maintain Station's broadcast operations in accordance with FCC rules and policies and applicable law. Licensee will also pay for all utilities to its transmitter site. Licensee will employ the minimum number (*i.e.*, two (2)) and type of personnel required by the policies and rules of the FCC to be employed by Licensee for the Station (both of whom shall report to and be accountable solely to Licensee) and will be responsible for the salaries, taxes, insurance and related costs for all such personnel. Subject to the provision for reimbursement specified in Schedule 1, Licensee shall be responsible for maintenance of its facilities, the transmitting equipment, and for all capital costs (such as replacement of transmitting equipment) necessary to carry out the intent of this Agreement.

Advertising, Programming Revenues and Contracts. Broker will be entitled to all revenue from the sale of commercial advertising or program time on the Station during the hours of airtime purchased by Broker pursuant to this Agreement. All contracts for such advertising or program time which may be entered into by Broker shall terminate upon the termination of this Agreement.

Broker's Accounts Receivable. Broker will be responsible for the collection of its own accounts receivable arising from its sale of advertising for the hours during which it is responsible for programming the Station. Broker agrees to cooperate fully with Licensee with respect to clients owing both Licensee and Broker. Broker will not make any solicitations for the payment of receivables in any manner which would indicate that Broker controls Licensee, or owns the Station, or controls the operation of the Station. Licensee will not make any solicitations for the payment of receivables in any manner which would indicate that Licensee controls Broker.

Licensee's Accounts Receivable. Licensee shall retain and collect all accounts receivable due the Licensee as a result of its operation of Station prior to the Effective Date of this Agreement. Licensee agrees to maintain, to the best of its ability, the good will and relationships with the advertisers of the Station whose receivables are retained by Licensee under the terms of this paragraph.

5. **Operation of Station**. Notwithstanding anything to the contrary in this Agreement, Licensee shall have full authority and power over the operation of the Station during the period of this Agreement. Licensee's Station Manager shall direct the day-to-day operation of the Station. Licensee shall retain control (said control to be reasonably exercised) over the policies, programming and operations of the Station, including, without limitation, the right to decide whether to accept or reject any programming or advertisements, the right to preempt any programs not in the public interest or in order to broadcast a program deemed by Licensee to be of greater national, regional or local interest, and the right to take any other actions necessary for compliance with federal, state and local laws, the Act and the rules, regulations and policies of the

Commission (including the prohibition on unauthorized transfers of control) and the rules, regulations and policies of other federal government entities, including the Federal Trade Commission and the Department of Justice. Although both parties shall cooperate in the broadcast of emergency information over the Station, Licensee shall also retain the right to interrupt Broker's programming in case of an emergency or for programming, which, in the good faith judgment of Licensee, is of greater local or national importance. In all such cases, Licensee will use its best efforts to give Broker reasonable notice of its intent to preempt Broker's programs and in the event of such preemption, Broker shall receive a pro rata payment credit for any advertisements preempted which cannot be rescheduled.

6. **Additional FCC Obligations**. Licensee shall (i) maintain and staff a main studio, as that term is defined by the FCC, (ii) prepare and place in the Station's public inspection file in a timely manner all material required by Section 73.3526 of the Commission's rules, including without limitation the Station's quarterly issues and programs list, and (iii) prepare and file with the FCC in a timely manner all reports, applications and other documents required under FCC rules, including but not limited to applications for renewal of license, Annual EEO Reports, and Biennial Ownership Reports. Licensee shall coordinate with Broker the Station's hourly station identification and any other announcements required to be aired by FCC rules. Licensee shall oversee and take ultimate responsibility for complying with the FCC's rules and requirements governing uses of the Station's facilities by legally qualified candidates for public office. Broker shall cooperate with Licensee in ensuring such compliance and shall provide Licensee with copies of any information that may be necessary to comply with the recording

and lowest unit charge requirements of political law. Broker agrees that it will not accept any consideration, compensation or gift or gratuity of any kind whatsoever, regardless of its value or form, including, but not limited to, a commission, discount, bonus, material, supplies or other merchandise, services or labor (collectively "Consideration"), whether or not pursuant to written contracts or agreements between Broker and merchants or advertiser, unless the payer is identified in the program for which Consideration was provided as having paid for or furnished such Consideration, in accordance with the Act and FCC requirements.

7.   **Indemnification Warranty**

Broker's Indemnification. Broker shall indemnify and hold harmless Licensee from and against any and all claims, losses, costs, liabilities, damages, expenses (including reasonable legal fees and other expenses incidental thereto) of every kind, nature and description, including but not limited to, slander or defamation or otherwise arising out of Broker's broadcasts and sale of advertising under this Agreement to the extent permitted by law.

Licensee's Indemnification. Licensee shall indemnify and hold harmless Broker from any and against any and all claims losses, costs, liabilities, damages, expenses (including reasonable legal fees and other expenses incidental thereto) of every kind, nature and description, arising out of broadcasts originated by Licensee pursuant to the Agreement to the extent permitted by law.

Procedure. Neither Licensee nor Broker shall be entitled to indemnification pursuant to this section unless such claim for indemnification is asserted in writing, delivered to the other party, together with a statement as to the factual basis for the claim and the amount of the claim. The party making the claim (the "Claimant") shall make available to the other party (the "Indemnitor") the information relied upon by the Claimant to substantiate the claim. With respect to any claim by a third party as to which the Claimant is entitled to seek indemnification hereunder, the Indemnitor shall have the right at its own expense to participate in or assume control of the defense of the claim, and the Claimant shall cooperate fully with the Indemnitor, subject to reimbursement for actual out-of-pocket expenses incurred by the Claimant at the request of the Indemnitor. If the Indemnitor does not elect to assume control or participate in the defense of any third party claim, it shall be bound by the results obtained by the Claimant with respect to the claim.

8. **Assignment of Certain Agreements and Rights.** Licensee shall promptly pay and satisfy all obligations owing to third parties during the term of this Agreement or with respect to the operation of the Station prior to the Effective Date. Broker shall not obligate Licensee to any third parties after the termination of this Agreement. Following termination of this Agreement, Broker shall promptly pay and satisfy all obligations owing to third parties with respect to its operation of the Station under this Agreement.

9. **Events of Default; Cure Periods and Remedies**. The following shall, after the expiration of the applicable cure periods, constitute Events of Default:

   a. **Non-Payment**. Broker's failure to pay when due the consideration provided for in Paragraph 2 hereof;

   b. **Default in Covenants or Adverse Legal Action**. The default by either party hereto in the material observance or performance of any material covenant, condition or agreement contained herein, or if either party (i) shall make general assignment for the benefit of creditors, (ii) files or has filed against it a petition for bankruptcy, reorganization or an arrangement for the benefit of creditors, or for the appointment of a receiver, trustee or creditor representative for the property or assets of such party under any federal or state insolvency law, which, if filed against such party, has not been dismissed or discharged within _____(__) days thereof; or

c. **Breach of Representation**. If any material representation or warranty herein made by either party hereto, or in any certificate or document furnished by either party to the other pursuant to the provisions hereof, shall prove to have been false or misleading in any material respect as of the time made or furnished.

Cure Periods. An Event of Default shall not be deemed to have occurred until _____ (__) business days after the nondefaulting party has provided the defaulting party with written notice specifying the event or events that if not cured would constitute an Event of Default and specifying the action necessary to cure the Default within such period. This period may be extended for a reasonable period of time, if the defaulting party is acting in good faith to cure the default and such default is not materially adverse to the other party. Non-payment shall be deemed to be an Event of Default on the day after timely payment is due, and no notice of default is required, nor is any cure period provided.

Termination Upon Default. Upon the occurrence of an Event of Default, the nondefaulting party may terminate this agreement provided that it is not also in material default hereunder. If Broker has defaulted in the performance of its obligations, Licensee shall be under no further obligation to make available to Broker any further broadcast time or broadcast transmission facilities and all amounts accrued or payable to

Licensee up to the date of termination which have not been paid shall immediately become due and payable. If Licensee has defaulted in the performance of its obligations hereunder, Broker may terminate this Agreement. In addition to these remedies, either party has the right to collect monetary damages for failure to perform the obligations under this Agreement, including any balance due by Broker under this Agreement.

Liabilities Upon Termination. Following termination, Broker shall be responsible for all liabilities, debts and obligations of Broker based upon the purchase of air time and use of Licensee's transmission facilities including, without limitation, accounts payable, barter agreements and unaired advertisements, but not for Licensee's federal, state and local income and business franchise tax liabilities or taxes levied upon Licensee's real estate or personal property after termination; in addition, Licensee shall acquire the transmitting equipment purchased by Broker for the Station during the Agreement.

Specific Performance. In addition to either party's right of termination hereunder (and in addition to any other remedies available to that party), in the event of an uncured Event of Default, either party may seek specific performance of this Agreement, in which case the other party shall waive the defense in any such suit that the other party has an adequate remedy at law and shall interpose no opposition, legal or otherwise, as to the propriety of specific performance as a remedy hereunder.

10. **Broker Termination Options**. Broker may elect to terminate this Agreement at any time during the term hereof in the event that Licensee preempts or substitutes other programming for that supplied by

the Broker during _____ percent (___%) or more of the total hours of operation of the Station during any calendar week. In the event Broker elects to terminate this Agreement pursuant to this provision, it shall give Licensee notice of such election at least _____ (__) days prior to the termination date. Upon termination, all sums owing the Licensee shall be paid and neither party shall have any further liability to the other except as may be provided by Paragraphs 8 and 24 of this Agreement.

11. **Licensee Termination Option**. Licensee shall have the right, at its option, to terminate the Agreement if it provides Broker with at least _____ (__) days' written notice. Upon termination, all sums owing to Licensee shall be paid and neither party shall have any further liability to the other except as may be provided by Paragraphs 8 and 24 of this Agreement.

Termination Upon Order of Governmental Authority. In the event that a federal, state or local government authority designates a hearing with respect to the continuation or renewal of any authorization held by Licensee for the operation of the Station or orders the termination of this Agreement and/or the curtailment in any manner material to the relationship between the parties hereto of the provision of programming by Broker hereunder, Broker, at its option, may seek administrative or judicial relief from such order(s) (in which event Licensee shall cooperate with Broker, provided that Broker shall be responsible for the legal fees and costs incurred in such proceedings) or Broker shall notify Licensee that it will terminate this Agreement in accordance with such order(s). If the Commission designates the renewal application of the Station for a hearing as a consequence of this Agreement or for any other reason, or initiates any revocation or other proceeding with respect to the authorizations issued to the Licensee for the operation of the Station, and Licensee elects to contest the action, then Licensee and Broker shall each be responsible for one half (1/2) of the expenses incurred as a consequence of the Commission proceeding; provided, however, that Broker shall at its own expense cooperate and comply with any reasonable request of Licensee to assemble and provide to the Commission information relating to Broker's performance under this Agreement. In the event of termination upon any government order(s), Broker shall pay to Licensee any fees due but unpaid as of the date of termination as may be permitted by such order(s), and Licensee shall cooperate reasonably with Broker to the extent permitted to enable Broker to fulfill advertising or other programming contracts then outstanding, in which event Licensee shall receive as compensation for the carriage of such programming that which otherwise would have been paid to Broker hereunder. Thereafter, neither party shall have any liability to the other except as may be provided pursuant to Paragraphs 8 and 27 of this Agreement.

12. **Representations and Warranties.**

Mutual Representations and Warranties. Both Licensee and Broker represent that they are legally qualified, empowered and able to enter into this Agreement, and that the execution, delivery and performance hereof shall not constitute a breach or violation of any agreement, contract or other obligation to which either party is subject or by which it is bound. The signatures appearing for Broker and Licensee at the end of this Agreement have been affirmed pursuant to such specific authority as, under applicable law, is required to bind them.

Licensee's Representations, Warranties and Covenants. Licensee makes the following further representations, warranties and covenants:

Authorizations. Licensee owns and holds all licenses and other permits and authorizations necessary for the operation of the Station, and such licenses, permits and authorizations will be in full force and effect for the entire term hereof. There is not now pending or, to Licensee's best knowledge, threatened, any action by the Commission or other party to revoke, cancel, suspend, refuse to renew or modify adversely any of such licenses, permits or authorizations and, to Licensee's best knowledge, no event has occurred which allows or, after notice or lapse of time or both, would allow, the revocation or termination of such licenses, permits or authorizations or the imposition of any restrictions thereon of such a nature that may limit the operation of the Station as authorized by the Station's outstanding FCC authorizations. Licensee has no reason to believe that any such license, permit or authorization will not be renewed during the term of the Agreement in its ordinary course. Licensee is not in any material violation of any statute, ordinance, rule, regulation, policy, order or decree of any federal, state, local or foreign government entity, court or authority having jurisdiction over it or over any part of its operations or assets, which default or violation would have an adverse effect on Licensee or its assets or on its ability to perform this Agreement.

Filings. All reports and applications required to be filed with the Commission (including ownership reports and renewal applications) or any other government entity, department or body in respect of the Station have been, and in the future will be, filed in a timely manner and are and will be true and complete and accurately present the information contained and required thereby. All such reports and documents, to the extent required to be kept in the station public inspection, are and will be kept in such files, and if required to be posted on the station's website, will be posted.

Facilities. Subject to the reimbursement of expenses provided in Paragraph 5.1, the Station's facilities will be maintained at the expense of Licensee and comply in all material respects with the maximum technical facilities permitted by the Commission's authorizations and will be operated in all material respects in accordance with good engineering standards necessary to deliver a high quality technical signal to the area served by the Station and with all applicable laws and regulations (including the requirements of the Act and the rules, regulations, policies and procedures of the Commission promulgated thereunder). All capital expenditures reasonably required to maintain the quality of the Station's signal and facilities shall be made promptly at the expense of the Licensee, subject to immediate reimbursement by the Broker.

Title to Properties. Licensee has, and will throughout the term hereof, maintain good and marketable title to all of the assets and properties used in the operation of the Station, free and clear of any liens, claims or security interests. Licensee will not dispose of, transfer, assign or pledge any such asset, except with the prior written consent of Broker, which the Broker will not unreasonably withhold, if such action would affect adversely Licensee's performance hereunder or the business and operation of Broker permitted hereby.

Insurance. Licensee will maintain in full force and effect throughout the term of this Agreement insurance with responsible and reputable insurance companies or associations covering such risks (including fire and other risks insured against by extended coverage, public liability insurance, insurance for claims against personal injury or death or property damage and such other insurance as may be required by law) and in such amounts and on such terms as is conventionally carried by broadcasters operating radio stations with facilities comparable to those of the Station. Any insurance proceeds received by Licensee in respect of damaged property will be used to repair or replace such property so that the operation of the Station conforms with this Agreement.

13. **Notices**. All necessary notices, demands and requests permitted or required under this Agreement shall be in writing and shall be deemed given (i) when delivered personally, or (ii) transmitted by facsimile with hard copy confirmation by hand delivery, certified mail, return receipt requested, or (iii) overnight courier, postage prepaid, with return receipt requested and addressed as follows:

If to Licensee:

_____
_____
_____
_____

With a copy (which shall not constitute notice) to:

_____
_____
_____
_____

If to Broker:

_____

_____

_____

_____

With a copy (which shall not constitute notice) to:

_____

_____

_____

_____

14. **Modification and Waiver**. No modification of any provision of this Agreement shall in any event be effective unless the same shall be in writing and then such modification shall be effective only in the specific instance and for the purpose for which given.

15. **Construction**. This Agreement shall be construed in accordance with the laws of the State of _____ without regard to the laws of such State relating to conflicts of law, and the obligations of the parties hereof are subject to all federal, state and local laws and regulations now or hereafter in force and to the rules, regulations and policies of the Commission and all other government entities or authorities presently or hereafter to be constituted.

16. **Headings**. The headings contained in this Agreement are included for convenience only and no such heading shall in any way alter the meaning of any provision.

17. **Assignability; No Third Party Rights**. Neither this Agreement nor any of the rights, interests or obligations of either party hereunder shall be assigned, encumbered, hypothecated or otherwise transferred without the prior written consent of the

other party. The covenants, conditions and provisions hereof are and shall be for the exclusive benefit of the parties hereto and their permitted assigns, and nothing herein, express or implied, is intended or shall be construed to confer upon or to give any person or entity other than the parties hereto and their permitted assigns any right, remedy or claim, legal or equitable, under or by reasons of this Agreement.

18. **Counterpart Signature**. This Agreement may be signed in one or more counterparts, each of which shall be deemed a duplicate original, binding on the parties hereto notwithstanding that the parties are not signatory to the original or the same counterpart.

19. **Entire Agreement**. This Agreement embodies the entire agreement between the parties and there are no other agreements, representations, warranties or understanding, oral or written, between them with respect to the subject matter hereof. No alteration, modification or change of this Agreement shall be valid unless by like written instrument executed by an authorized principal.

20. **No Partnership or Joint Venture Created**. Nothing in this Agreement shall be construed to make Licensee and Broker partners or joint ventures or to afford any rights to any third party other than as expressly provided herein.

21. **Invalidity**. If any provision of this Agreement or the application thereof to any person or circumstances shall be held invalid or unenforceable to any extent, the parties shall negotiate in good faith and attempt to agree on an amendment to this Agreement that will provide the parties with substantially the same rights and obligations, to the greatest extent possible, as the original Agreement in valid, binding and enforceable form.

22. **Severability**. In the event any provision contained in this Agreement is held to be invalid, illegal or unenforceable, such holding shall not affect any other provision hereof and this Agreement shall be construed as if such invalid, illegal or unenforceable provision had not be contained herein.

23. **Certification — FCC Rules**. Pursuant to Section 73.3555(a)(3)(ii) of the FCC's rules, the parties certify as follows:

    (i) Licensee certifies that it shall at all times maintain ultimate control of the Station's facilities, including specifically control over station finances, personnel and programming.

    (ii) Broker certifies that this Agreement complies with the provisions of Section 73.3555(a)(1) of the FCC's rules.

24. **Confidentiality**. Neither party shall disclose the terms of this Agreement to any third party, except when such disclosure is required by law.

25. **Attorney's Fees and Expenses**. In the event of any dispute arising under this Agreement, the prevailing party shall be entitled to its reasonable attorney's fees incurred in connection therewith and all related costs and expenses.

IN WITNESS WHEREOF, the parties executed this Agreement as of the date first above written.

[NAME OF LICENSEE]

By _____

[Name]
[Title]

[NAME OF BROKER]

By _____

      [Name]
      [Title]

SCHEDULE 1

Broker hereby agrees to pay Licensee for the broadcast of the programs hereunder _____ Dollars ($_____.00) per month ("Monthly Broker Fee"). The Monthly Fee is due and payable in full on the _____ (___) day following the end of the preceding broadcast calendar month. The failure of Licensee to demand or insist upon prompt payment in accordance herewith shall not constitute a waiver of its right to do so. The Monthly Broker Fee amount relating to a month in which this Agreement is in effect for only part of the month shall be prorated.

Broker shall reimburse Licensee on a monthly basis for all operating costs of the Station incurred by Licensee on the _____ (___) day of the subsequent broadcast month, provided, that Licensee shall submit an invoice to Broker on the last day of each broadcast month which includes reasonable supporting documentation for all items identified on such invoice, which may include, but are not limited to (i) costs relating to the maintenance of the Station's transmission equipment and facilities, including the antenna, transmitter and transmission line; (ii) all repairs as are necessary to maintain full-time operation of the Station with its maximum authorized facilities; (iii) salaries, taxes, insurance, 401K contributions, other benefit costs, and any other related costs for Licensee's personnel employed pursuant to Section 5 hereof; (iv) costs relating to the maintenance of the Station's transmission equipment and facilities, including the antenna, transmitter and transmission line; (v) all lease payments for the main studio and tower site and all taxes and other costs incident thereto; (vi) all FCC regulatory fees; (vii) real estate and personal property taxes; and (viii) utility costs (telephone, electricity, etc.) relating to the transmitting site, transmitter and antenna.

APPENDIX F
LICENSE/EXPIRATION AND RENEWAL
APPLICATION FILING DEADLINE DATES

STATES	AM/FM EXPIRA-TION DATES	AM/FM FILING DATES	STATES	AM/FM EXPIRATION DATES	AM/FM FILING DATES
ALABAMA	APR 1 , 2012	DEC 1, 2011	NE-BRASKA	JUN 1, 2013	FEB 1, 2013
ALASKA	FEB 1, 2014	OCT 1, 2013	NEVADA	OCT 1, 2013	JUNE 1, 2013
AMER. SAMOA	FEB 1, 2014	OCT 1, 2013	NEW HAMP-SHIRE	APR 1, 2014	DEC 1, 2013
ARIZONA	OCT 1, 2013	JUNE 1, 2013	NEW JERSEY	JUN 1, 2014	FEB 1, 2014
ARKANSAS	JUN 1, 2012	FEB 1, 2012	NEW MEXICO	OCT 1, 2013	JUNE 1, 2013
CALIFOR-NIA	DEC 1, 2013	AUG 1 , 2013	NEW YORK	JUN 1, 2014	FEB 1, 2014
COLO-RADO	APR 1, 2013	DEC 1, 2012	N. CAR-OLINA	DEC 1, 2011	AUG 1, 2011
CONNECTI-CUT	APR 1, 2014	DEC 1, 2013	NORTH DAKOTA	APR 1, 2013	DEC 1, 2012
DELAWARE	AUG 1, 2014	APR 1, 2014	OHIO	OCT 1, 2012	JUN 1, 2012
DIS. CO-LUMBIA	OCT 1, 2011	JUN 1, 2011	OKLA-HOMA	JUN 1, 2013	FEB 1, 2013
FLORIDA	FEB 1, 2012	OCT 1, 2011	OREGON	FEB 1, 2014	OCT 1, 2013

STATES	AM/FM EXPIRATION DATES	AM/FM FILING DATES	STATES	AM/FM EXPIRATION DATES	AM/FM FILING DATES
GEORGIA	APR 1, 2012	DEC 1, 2011	PENN-SYLVA-NIA	AUG 1, 2014	APR 1, 2014
GUAM	FEB 1, 2014	OCT 1, 2013	PUERTO RICO	FEB 1, 2012	OCT 1, 2011
HAWAII	FEB 1, 2014	OCT 1, 2013	RHODE ISLAND	APR 1, 2014	DEC 1, 2013
IDAHO	OCT 1, 2013	JUNE 1, 2013	S. CARO-LINA	DEC 1, 2011	AUG 1, 2011
ILLINOIS	DEC 1, 2012	AUG 1, 2012	SOUTH DAKOTA	APR 1, 2013	DEC 1, 2012
INDIANA	AUG 1, 2012	APR 1, 2012	TENNES-SEE	AUG 1, 2012	APR 1, 2012
IOWA	FEB 1, 2013	OCT 1, 2012	TEXAS	AUG 1, 2013	APR 1, 2013
KANSAS	JUN 1, 2013	FEB 1, 2013	UTAH	OCT 1, 2013	JUNE 1, 2013
KEN-TUCKY	AUG 1, 2012	APR 1, 2012	VER-MONT	APR 1, 2014	DEC 1, 2013
LOUISIANA	JUN 1, 2012	FEB 1, 2012	VIRGIN IS-LANDS	FEB 1, 2012	OCT 1, 2011
MAINE	APR 1, 2014	DEC 1, 2013	VIR-GINIA	OCT 1, 2011	JUN 1, 2011
MARIANA ISLANDS	FEB 1, 2014	OCT 1, 2013	WASH-INGTON	FEB 1, 2014	OCT 1, 2013
MARY-LAND	OCT 1, 2011	JUN 1, 2011	WEST VIR-GINIA	OCT 1, 2011	JUN 1, 2011

STATES	AM/FM EXPIRA-TION DATES	AM/FM FILING DATES	STATES	AM/FM EXPIRATION DATES	AM/FM FILING DATES
MASSA-CHUSETTS	APR 1, 2014	DEC 1, 2013	WIS-CONSIN	DEC 1, 2012	AUG 1, 2012
MICHIGAN	OCT 1, 2012	JUN 1, 2012	WYO-MING	OCT 1, 2013	JUNE 1, 2013
MINNE-SOTA	APR 1, 2013	DEC 1, 2012			
MISSIS-SIPPI	JUN 1, 2012	FEB 1, 2012			
MISSOURI	FEB 1, 2013	OCT 1, 2012			
MONTANA	APR 1, 2013	DEC 1, 2012			

APPENDIX G

SAMPLE DUE DILIGENCE REQUESTS FOR INFORMATION

The user should tailor these three requests to reflect the details of the specific transaction (*e.g.*, asset or stock acquisition, debt to be assumed, etc.)

SAMPLE ONE

MEMORANDUM
Confidential

RE: Acquisition of Station _____
**   Preliminary Legal Due Diligence-Review**

DATE: _____ _, 20__

Set forth below is a preliminary list of the documents and information requested in connection with the proposed acquisition of _____, _____, _____ (the "Station"). As our review proceeds, we may request additional items:

As used in this memorandum, the term "Company" should be understood to mean and include the corporation which owns the Station.

1. **Corporate Records**

   1.1   The Company's charter (certificate of incorporation, partnership agreement or limited liability company agreement), together with all amendments to date.

   1.2   The bylaws of the Company (or similar partnership or LLC documentation) as currently in effect.

   1.3   The Company's minute book, including minutes of meetings and consents of the Board of Directors,

Executive Committee and any other Committee of the Board of Directors and shareholders of the Company. [This provision and the following section 1.4 are necessary for a stock purchase but not for an asset purchase.]

1.4 A list of the Company's shareholders and a copy of any shareholders' agreement or other agreement imposing restrictions on transfer of shares or payment of dividends.

1.5 A list of all jurisdictions in which the Company is qualified to do business and in which the Company has officers or personnel or otherwise conducts business.

1.6 A list of Station employees (including officers) including each person's position, salary and benefits.

2. **Governmental Regulations and Filings**

2.1 List all federal, state and other regulatory authorities that have, or during the past three years have had, regulatory jurisdiction over the Company and its business. Describe the Company's compliance history with each such authority during the past three years, including the filing of required reports and statements.

2.2 Reports, applications, requests and pleadings filed by or on behalf of the Company and significant correspondence relating to the Company with or from the FCC during the past three years.

2.3 List and attach existing FCC and all other governmental permits, licenses, etc. of the Company necessary for the conduct of the Company's business.

2.4 List and attach all documents pertaining to administrative proceedings or governmental investigations or inquiries, pending or threatened, affecting the Company, during the past three years.

3. **Loans and Other Financings**

    3.1   All documents and agreements evidencing borrowings, whether secured or unsecured, by the Company, including loan and credit agreements, promissory notes and other evidences of indebtedness.

    3.2   Bank letters or agreements confirming lines of credit of the Company. [Applicable in stock acquisitions or where the buyer will be assuming debt.]

    3.3   All documents and agreements evidencing other financing arrangements of the Company including sale and leaseback arrangements, installment purchase, etc. and any related indentures, pledge agreements, security agreements, waivers and consents.

    3.4   Correspondence with lenders (including entities committed to lend) for the last three years including all compliance reports submitted by the Company or its independent public accountants.

    3.5   Computations demonstrating the Company's compliance with covenants in existing financing documents, if relevant.

4. **Financial Materials**

    4.1   A schedule listing all relevant information pertaining to the Company's bank accounts.

    4.2   Financial and operating statements of the Company for the past three years and the current year.

    4.3   Budgets and cash flow projections for the same periods as the financial statements.

    4.4   A listing of barter balances as of the end of the last month (this should agree with the balance in the financial statement.

4.5 An aged listing of accounts receivable outstanding at the end of the last month (this should agree with the financial statement).

4.6 A list of current uncollectible or doubtful accounts as well as the station's bad debt history for the past three years.

4.7 A listing of accounts payable at the end of the last month (this should agree with the financial statement).

4.8 Federal, state and local tax returns, revenue agents' reports and administrative appeals relating to the Company for all open years and any agreements extending statute of limitations or a period for review by federal, state and local tax authorities.

4.9 All letters from the Company's independent public accountants to the Company in the past three years regarding the Company's control systems, methods of accounting, adequacy of reserves, etc.

5. **Agreements**

5.1 All agreements, contracts or commitments relating to the employment of any person by the Company, or any bonus, deferred compensation, pension, profit sharing, stock option, employee stock purchase, change-in-control, severance, retirement, collective bargaining or qualified or non-qualified employee benefit plan or arrangement for the Company's employees. Describe all vacation, holiday, overtime, sick leave, expense reimbursement, automobile and perquisite policies. List the number of employees as of the end of the last three fiscal years and turnover and absentee data for such years. Describe any labor disputes, requests for arbitrations or grievance proceedings during the past three years.

5.2 Describe, and attach copies of, all contracts (including purchase orders) to which the Company is a party that involve an aggregate amount in excess of _____ Dollars ($____.00) or a term of one year or more. Please indicate which, it any, of these would require the consent of any party in order to consummate the proposed transaction.

5.3   List and attach all loan agreements or documentation relating to loans or advances by the Company to, or investments by the Company in, any other person or entity, or any agreements, contracts or commitments relating to the making of any such loan, advance or investment.

5.4   List and attach all guarantees given by the Company in respect of any indebtedness or obligation of any other person or entity.

5.5   List and attach all management, joint sales, time brokerage, service, consulting or similar contracts involving the Company.

5.6   List and attach all agreements, contracts or commitments, limiting the freedom of the Company to engage in any line of business or to compete with any other person or other non-competition agreements or covenants with any other party that benefit the Company.

5.7   List and attach all agreements, contracts or commitments involving the Company which are not cancellable without penalty within thirty (30) days.

5.8   List any debts (whether or not evidenced in writing) to stockholders, directors, officers or employees and debts of stockholders, directors, officers or employees to the Company.

5.9   List and attach all insurance policies of the company or for which the Company is a named insured or loss payee and describe the insurance claim history of the company during the past three years.

5.10 List and attach all contracts or agreements with or pertaining to the Company and to which any of the shareholders, directors or officers of the company are parties.

5.11 List and attach all confidentiality and nondisclosure agreements with employees and former employees that are still in effect.

6. **Assets**

6.1 List and describe all material tangible personal property owned or used by the company in connection with its business, and attach copies of any financing statements affecting such property.

6.2 Provide a legal description, title report and survey of any real property owned by the Company or used in the Company's business.

6.3 List and attach all leases of real property or personal property to which the Company is a party, either as lessor or lessee.

6.4 List and attach a copy of the Station's detailed depreciation and amortization schedules.

6.5 List and attach all appraisals of the Company's assets performed within the last three years.

6.6 List and attach all engineering studies covering the towers and equipment owned by the Company.

7. **Environmental Matters**

7.1 Describe the Company's activities as they involve environmental matters and attach all documents relating to any environmental permits, investigations, orders, etc. pertaining to the real estate owned by the Company.

7.2 List any underground or other storage tanks located on the company's property, the substances stored therein No. 2 heating oil, kerosene, etc.), and the respective capacity and date of installation of each.

Provide copies of any registration reports filed with respect to each such tank.

7.3   List all environmental permits held by the Company, and provide expiration date and type of permit for each.

7.4   Describe the Company's environmental compliance history for the past five years, and the existence and status of any violations. Include a listing and copy of any request for information, notice of claim, demand letter, or other notification in connection with, or relating or pertaining to the company during the past five years.

7.5   Describe any pending or threatened litigation, or any litigation that was pending or threatened in the past five years, against the Company with respect to any environmental matter.

7.6   Describe any investigations, orders, etc., pertaining to the Company or any real property owned or used by the Company and attach documents relating thereto and any notices to or from the company respecting violations or enforcement of environmental laws.

7.7   List and attach any contracts entered into by the Company for waste removal, management or storage.

7.8   List all environmental consultants of the Company and attach any reports or site assessments received from them within the past three years with respect to the business or facilities of the Company.

8. **Miscellaneous**

8.1   List and attach all letters from the Company's attorneys to the Company's independent public accountants in the past three years regarding litigation in which the Company is or may be involved.

8.2 Describe all litigation to which the Company is a party, or that may be pending or threatened against the Company, and all litigation to which the Company was a party within the last five years. Include in this description a statement of the nature of the litigation; the identity of the parties; the identity, address and telephone number of the Company's counsel; and whether any liability to the Company may be covered by insurance.

8.3 List and attach all consent decrees, judgments, other decrees or orders, settlement agreements and other agreements to which the Company is a party or is bound, requiring or prohibiting any future activities.

8.4 Recent analyses of the Company or its business prepared by investment bankers, engineers, management consultants, accountants or others, including marketing studies, credit reports and other types of reports, financial or otherwise.

8.5 Schedule of major advertisers for the past three .fiscal years, giving annual dollar amounts purchased.

8.6 List and attach all engineering reports, proofs of performance and interference studies prepared by or on behalf of the Station or the Company.

8.7 Copy of sick pay policy or description and estimate of the amount paid for sick pay benefits in 20__ and accruals for 20__ and 20__.

8.8 Copy of vacation policy and schedules of accrued vacation liability as of _____ __, ____ .

8.9 Contour map showing the strength of the Station's signal over its service area.

8.10 Employee benefits handbook or similar literature given to employees.

8.11 List of former employees eligible for benefits under the Consolidated Omnibus Reconciliation Act (COBRA).

SAMPLE TWO

Confidential

INFORMATION REQUEST

Re: Proposed Acquisition of Station _____

Date: _____

1. ## Company Records

    1.1   The company charter (certificate or articles of incorporation) and by-laws (or similar partnership or LLC documentation) for Seller.

    1.2   List of any person or entity whose consent to the proposed sale will be required and copies of relevant documents.

    1.3   Any stockholder, buy-sell or similar agreements which may relate, directly or indirectly, to the proposed transaction.

    1.4   List of shareholders (or partners or other equity holders), officers, and directors.

2. ## General

    2.1   Any partnership, joint venture, distributorship, franchise, licensing or similar agreements or contracts to which Seller is a party; and any other agreements which prohibit or restrict (i) Seller's ability to compete in any business anywhere in any geographic area or (ii) the customers with which Seller may do business or (iii) the prices Seller may charge for its services.

    2.2   List of ten largest advertisers of Seller and copies of any material agreements with any such advertisers.

    2.3   List of all trade, barter and advertising agreements that will survive closing, including annual dollar amounts sold in recent years and estimates for current year.

2.4 Any form agreements or contracts used in connection with Seller's business.

2.5 Any other agreements or contracts used in connection with Seller's business that will survive closing.

2.6 All contracts with officers, directors, shareholders or partners (or their affiliates).

3. <u>Legal/Financial</u>

3.1 Copies of current budgets (and capital expenditure budgets) and long range and/or operation plans for Seller.

3.2 Letters of credit outstanding (amounts, terms) if any.

3.2 All documents purporting to create liens, mortgages, security agreements, pledges, charges or other encumbrances on the stock of Seller, on any real or personal property of Seller or in favor of Seller. Indicate whether Seller has been in continual compliance with the financial covenants contained in these agreements. All Uniform Commercial Code (UCC) searches and financing statements filed with respect to the above.

3.4 List of aged account receivables by customer.

3.5 Historical financial statements for 20___, 20___ and 20__ (on an annual basis) and for 20__ and 20__ (on a monthly basis), and projections for _____ (on a monthly basis), including supporting assumptions. Copies of any reports to management from the auditors over the past three years. Include summary of significant accounting policies used by Seller and provide details of any off-balance sheet financing. List all year-end non-recurring adjustments made as of the end of the latest fiscal year, including special reserves.

3.6 Schedule of tax and/or book bases of assets by asset category. Schedule of tax liabilities or benefits that are not reflected on Seller's balance sheet.

3.7 Copies of any and all tax sharing or tax allocation agreements relating, in wholeor in part, to Seller.

3.8 Listing of all contingent liabilities not reflected in most current balance sheet.

3.9 List of all outstanding indebtedness and financing agreements of the Seller including promissory notes, term loan agreements, revolving loan agreements, lines of credit, escrow agreements, letters of credit and capitalized leases with a description of respective outstanding balances, maturity dates, payout schedules, name of payees and guarantors.

3.10 List of all guaranties and comfort letters issued by the Seller.

3.11 Listing of items identified as other assets on Seller's balance sheet.

4. **Property**

4.1 List of real property (owned or leased) used in the Seller's business, including   size, location, use (*i.e.*, studio, transmitter, etc.) and legal description of each parcel. For leased properties, include copy of lease. Copies of property tax data for all such real property.

4.2 All leases, subleases, options, deeds, mortgages, construction contracts and other commitments and title insurance policies relating to real property owned or leased in connection with the Seller's business.

4.3 Any appraisals obtained within the past three years of Seller's real or personal property.

4.4　Inventory of personal property owned or leased (including studio and transmitter equipment), and copies of all contracts (including supplier, ASCAP, BMI, SESAC, Arbitron or other rating service), leases (including, without limitation, automobile, computer and other equipment leases) and security agreements, etc. relating to material equipment or personal property or licenses regarding equipment usage. Provide list of scheduled repairs to, replacement of, and description of physical condition of such personal property and copies of service or maintenance contracts, if applicable.

4.5　Schedule of trademarks, trade names, service marks, copyrights or patents owned by, licensed to or applied for by or on behalf of Seller and correspondence files relating thereto, including dates of registration with state or   federal agencies along with identifying registration numbers, if any. Copy of all licenses, assignments, royalty agreements and other contracts and instruments relating to the foregoing. Name of contact person who handles patent, trademark or copyright matters for Seller with whom we may discuss issues.

4.6　Description of policies to protect intellectual property rights owned by Seller or otherwise used in Seller's business. Documents relating to any claims of infringement of intellectual property rights owned by Seller or related to its business either (a) by Seller or any of its stockholders against the rights of other or (b) by others against the rights of Seller or its stockholders.

4.7　Schedule of items in production library.

5. **Programming**

5.1　Provide a copy of all network affiliation, syndication and other programming agreements.

5.2　Existing line-up on the stations by day-part.

5.3 List of on-air talent. Copies of employment agreements with on-air talent if available, or summary of terms of employment including severance or termination provisions and non-compete provisions. Indicate day-part and time that they are on the air, tenure with the station and current salary.

5.4 Provide the name of the Program Director(s), a copy of the employment contract, if available, or summary of terms of employment.

5.5 Indicate if station(s) uses a programming consultant and provide a copy or description of the Programming Consulting agreement.

5.6 Indicate if the station undertakes any type of viewer research, indicate type of research and provide copy or description of agreements, if any.

5.7 Description of the targeting strategy of the station in the opinion of the PD (target demographics; competitive positioning; music, talent and promotional direction, etc.)

5.8 Copy of most recent Arbitron book showing ratings and trends. Copies of any other market analyses or research reports.

6. **Management/Employees**

6.1 All corporate policy manuals covering hiring, regulatory compliance, internal controls, etc. Include number of employees by department or other relevant classification. Affirmative action plans and current EEO-1 and EEO Public File Reports.

6.2 Copies of employment contracts, confidentiality agreements, noncompetition agreements, management and consulting contracts, union contracts, collective bargaining agreements, employee manuals, benefit plan summaries, etc.

6.3 Documents representing all profit sharing and savings plans, pension or retirement plans, deferred compensation plans, medical, dental or other health and welfare plans and any bonus, incentive, performance or similar plans or arrangements and related agreements; and the latest applicable trust accounting, actuarial reports and other applicable financial statements. Summary plan descriptions for each of the foregoing to the extent available.

For each qualified plan, provide a copy of the most recent IRS favorable determination letter (including a copy of the request for such determination) with respect to such plan. In addition, for each plan for which Form 6600 is required to be filed, please provide copies of the three most recently filed Form 6600 with the schedules attached. Calculation of estimated retiree medical liability (if any) and cash flow impact over next several years. Schedule of pension liabilities and assets (if any).

6.4 Copies of any other management compensation plans or programs.

6.5 National sales representative, consultant or similar agreements currently in   effect.

6.6 Commission agreements with non-employee salespersons, buyers, or other agents.

6.7 All contracts or agreements with or pertaining to Seller to which any officer, director or stockholder (or family member of any of the foregoing) of Seller is or will be bound.

6.8 Description of any threatened or pending labor disputes, work stoppages, work slowdowns, walkouts, lockouts or union organizing activities since inception, indicating disposition   thereof. Copies of NLRB or Department of Labor filings, if any.

6.9 Schedule of all compensation paid during the last fiscal year to employees showing separately salaries, commissions, bonuses and non-cash compensation, including bonuses paid or accrued, direct or indirect benefits or perequisites, and all benefits paid or accrued under all employee benefit plans.

6.10 Chart describing employee organization.

6.11 Description of structure of any sales commission policy currently in effect.

7. Litigation

7.1 Current list of all litigation, administrative or regulatory proceedings, notices, investigations or governmental actions involving Seller or its business with brief description of basis for each such matter. Include name of court or agency in which the litigation proceeding is pending, date instituted, docket number (if available) and the principal parties thereto.

7.2 Description of currently threatened litigation, legal claims or other actions or proceedings, including regulatory actions.

7.3 Any currently effective consent decrees, judgments, other decrees or orders, settlement agreements and other similar agreements to which Seller is a party or by which Seller or any of its assets is bound (or to which any stockholder or partner of Seller is a party or by which any such stockholder or partner or any of its assets is bound and which relates, directly or indirectly, to Seller).

8. Insurance

8.1 A schedule of all policies or binders of insurance or self-insurance arrangements, including medical, workers compensation, disability, automobile, general liability, fire and casualty, products liability, professional liability, officers and directors' liability and key-man life insurance, with deductibles, coverage limits and other significant terms. Please indicate the name and address of all insurance agents, brokers and companies.

8.2 Premium and loss histories for the past five (5) year period for the above-referenced insurance.

9. **FCC/Regulatory Filings**

9.1 Reports and significant correspondence to and from any state or federal regulatory agencies (including, without limitation, the FCC, EPA and state level environmental regulators, OSHA and EEOC).

9.2 A schedule of all material governmental permits, fees, licenses, etc. of Seller, including, without limitation, FCC licenses, CPs, environmental permits, exemptions or proceedings.

9.3 Description of any inquiries, inspections or known noncompliance with any laws or regulations (including FCC, OSHA, EPA, EEOC, etc.) for the past five years and the disposition and status thereof.

9.4 Any FCC filings and submissions and all material correspondence relating thereto and all notices relative to signal, interference or antennae.

9.5 Any documents in the FCC public inspection file.

10. **Miscellaneous**

10.1 Copies of any broker's fee or bonus compensation arrangements regarding the proposed transaction.

10.2 All correspondence and documents relating to contingent liabilities exceeding $5,000, not otherwise duplicative with responses to items listed above.

10.3 Any other documents, information or data which are significant with respect to the business of Seller or which should be considered and reviewed in making disclosures regarding the business and financial condition of Seller to prospective investors.

Unless otherwise indicated, documents should be made available for all periods subsequent to _____ __, ____ and should include all amendments, supplements or other ancillary documents related to the documents requested. Please provide for each predecessor and subsidiary of Seller, all of the documents requested above.

SAMPLE THREE

DUE DILIGENCE INFORMATION REQUEST

1. Historic (preferably audited or reviewed) annual Financial Statements for the past five (5) years including Income Statements, Balance Sheets, and Cash Flow Statements. Also interim financial statements for the current year-to-date.

   If possible, Income Statements should include year-to-year comparisons, and be broken out in the following detail:

   a) Gross Revenue

      Local Direct
      Local Agency
      National/Regional
      Other (please specify)
      Trade

   b) Direct Cost of Sales (adjustments such as bad debt, agency and rep commissions)

   c) Net Revenue

   d) Operating Expenses:

      Technical
      Programming
      Advertising and Promotion
      Sales
      General and Administrative

   e) Total Operating Expenses

   f) Total Income from Operations

   g) Other Expenses:

      Depreciation
      Amortization

Interest Expense
Other (please be specific)

h) Trade Expenses

2. A schedule of capital expenses incurred during the past five (5) years with a brief description of the purchase price and the property, plant, equipment, etc. purchased.

3. A month-to-month operating budget for the current year broken down into the same general accounts as the Income Statements.

4. Any financial forecasts that have been prepared by management for the next five (5) years. The format should break down figures in the same manner as the Income Statements.

5. A summary sales projection report which details, by month, the amounts of any pre-sold advertising contracts entered into by the Company through the end of the current year.

6. A schedule setting out the Company's anticipated annual capital expenditures over the next _____ (____) years.

7. A schedule projecting annual depreciation and amortization expenses for the next five years.

8. A schedule with the details of the Company's existing or anticipated principal and interest obligations (if any) on all outstanding debt (if any) over the next _____ (___) years,

9. The Federal and State tax rates applicable to the station's pre-tax income.

10. A payroll register identifying all of the station's employees, their positions and respective salaries.

11. A schedule/summary of all favorable contractual agreements, such as personal service contracts, music publishing licenses, studio, office, and tower space leases, reciprocal barter agreements, long term contracts with advertisers, network affiliation agreements, program

service agreements, syndication agreements, vendor service contracts, ratings service licenses, etc. which might carry value in a sale transaction (with amounts and expiration dates).

12. An inventory of all current RF and broadcast equipment (including make, model number, year purchased, and replacement value), an inventory of the Company's office equipment, furniture and fixtures, and a copy of the depreciation schedule associated with these assets.

13. A copy of any real estate appraisals performed on Company-owned property and copies of last year's real estate tax bills.

14. Copies of any reports on total market revenue which may be available from independent sources such as Price-Waterhouse, Miller-Kaplan or Hungerford, etc. for 20__, 20__, 20__, 20__, 20__ (year-end), and 20___ (year-to-date).

15. A copy of the station's audience share figures (where available in rated markets), specifically:

>Market Map
>Market Profile Section
>Station Facilities Page
>12-plus Audience Share Trends Pages (full week)
>Metro Cume Duplication Page

16. A copy of the most recent accounts receivable, including:

a) total amounts and % of total receivables at 30 +, 60 +, 90 +, and 120 + days; and

b) bad debt provision (%) and year-to-date write-offs by month.

17. A summary of all payables which are ninety (90) or more days outstanding.

18. A schedule of all pending judgments or legal actions which may result in a future financial obligation for the Company.

19. Any and all documents not included in the above list, which are viewed by management to be material to the Company's operations and should be disclosed to _____ relative to its effort to conduct its due diligence in connection with the evaluation of the estimated fair market value of the station.

APPENDIX H

SAMPLE RESCISSION OR UNWIND AGREEMENT

RESCISSION AGREEMENT

THIS RESCISSION AGREEMENT ("Agreement") dated as of _____ ____, 20__, by and between _____ ("Seller") and _____ ("Buyer").

WHEREAS, Seller and Buyer have entered into an Asset Purchase Agreement dated as of _____ ___, 20__ (the "Agreement") providing for the purchase by Buyer of Station _____, _____, _____ (the "Station");

WHEREAS, consummation of the Agreement is subject to the approval of the Federal Communications Commission (the "FCC");

WHEREAS, the FCC has approved the sale and assignment of the licenses of the Station from Seller to Buyer but such approval has not yet become "final";

WHEREAS, the sale of the Station to Buyer is being consummated, simultaneously with the execution of this Rescission Agreement; and

WHEREAS, in the unlikely event that such approval of the sale and assignment of the licenses of the Station does not become final and the FCC and/or any court of competent jurisdiction requires the parties, in effect, to rescind the sale of the Station to Buyer, the parties wish to set forth the basis on which such rescission shall occur.

NOW, THEREFORE, in consideration of the mutual covenants contained herein, Seller and Buyer hereby agree as follows:

1. **Terms of Rescission**. If the FCC or a court of competent jurisdiction, in an order or decree not subject to any

administrative or judicial stay, shall either disapprove the sale and assignment of the licenses of the Station from Seller to Buyer and shall order a rescission of the sale of the Station to Buyer, then Seller and Buyer agree to use their respective best efforts to restore the parties, with respect to the Station, to the status quo existing prior to consummation of the Agreement, and agree to cooperate one with the other to bring about the fair and equitable restoration of each such party to its position prevailing prior to consummation of the sale. In that event, and to that end:

(a) Rescission. Seller and Buyer agree that they will rescind the transactions previously carried out pursuant to the Agreement.

(b) Return of Monies. Seller and Buyer agree that Seller will return to Buyer all monies paid to it by Buyer pursuant to the Agreement.

(c) Return of Assets. Seller and Buyer agree that, subject to any necessary FCC consent, Buyer will convey to Seller all tangible and intangible assets (including FCC licenses) previously conveyed to Buyer pursuant to the Agreement (except for assets disposed of by Buyer in the ordinary course of business of the Station), together with any additions, improvements, replacements and alterations thereto and proceeds thereof made between the date hereof and the date of such reconveyance, free and clear of all liens, security interests and encumbrances except for those to which such assets were subject immediately prior to the sale of the Station to Buyer. Such assets shall be in substantially the same condition as on the date hereof, reasonable wear and tear in ordinary usage excepted.

(d) Assignment of Contracts. Buyer agrees that it shall assign to Seller, and Seller agrees to assume, all contracts assigned to and assumed by Buyer pursuant to the Agreement, together with all contracts entered into in the ordinary course of business of the Station between the date hereof and the date of such reassignment.

(e) <u>FCC Filings</u>. Buyer and Seller agree that they shall prepare and execute any and all applications, documents and instruments for filing with the FCC that may be required by law or by the applicable requirements of the FCC or court rescission order.

2. **Other Documents**. Each party shall, at its expense, execute and deliver to the other party such other documents, and do such other acts or things, as are reasonably necessary for the implementation and consummation of the transactions contemplated by this Rescission Agreement.

3. **Control and Supervision**. Nothing contained in this Rescission Agreement shall give to Seller directly or indirectly any right to control or supervise the programming or operations of the Station prior to the consummation of the rescission of the Agreement, and Buyer shall exercise complete control and supervision of the programming and operations of the Station prior thereto.

4. **Consummation of Agreement**. Each party agrees to use its best efforts to perform and fulfill all conditions and obligations on its part to be performed and fulfilled under this Rescission Agreement, to the end that the transactions contemplated by this Rescission Agreement shall be fully carried out.

5. **Asset Agreement**. Nothing in this Rescission Agreement shall affect or limit the rights, obligations or liabilities of the parties under the Agreement.

6. **Interim Operation of Station**. Buyer covenants and agrees with Seller that, between the date hereof and (i) the date on which the FCC Orders shall have become Final Actions or (ii) consummation of rescission of the Agreement, Buyer shall:

(a) Carry on the business of the Station in the ordinary course of business. Without limiting the generality of the foregoing, Buyer shall in all material respects, operate the Station in accordance with the terms of its FCC Licenses and in compliance with all applicable laws and FCC rules and regulations. Buyer will promptly file any necessary applications for renewal of the FCC Licenses.

(b) Maintain in full force and effect property damage and liability insurance in commercially reasonable amounts with respect to the assets of the Station.

(c) Conduct the business of the Station in good faith and with reasonable diligence, including the timely payment of all obligations of the Station and maintain the assets of the Station in normal operating condition and repair, wear and tear in ordinary usage excepted.

(d) Buyer shall be entitled to retain all revenues and profits earned in the operation of the Station (and all operating expenses and losses shall be for the account of Buyer) during the interim period prior to the Rescission Date.

7. **Certain Claims**. Buyer shall be and remain solely responsible for, and shall indemnify Seller from an against all liabilities, obligations, actions, suits, proceedings or claims of any kind (including, without limitation, reasonable attorneys' fees and other legal costs and expenses) occasioned by, arising out of or resulting from the operation of the Station during the period from and after the Closing under the Agreement and ending upon closing of the rescission hereunder, and without regard to whether any such action, suit, proceeding or claim is pending, threatened or asserted before, on or after the date of such rescission.

IN WITNESS WHEREOF, the parties hereto have caused these presents to be executed by the duly authorized officers on the day and year first above written.

SELLER:

[NAME OF SELLER]

By _____
      [Name]
      [Title]

BUYER:

[NAME OF BUYER]

By _____
      [Name]
      [Title]

ABOUT THE AUTHORS

 **ERWIN G. KRASNOW** has been described as "a dean of the Washington communications bar" by Legal Times, as a "super lawyer of communications" by American Film magazine, as "the guru of communications law" by the Broadcast Cable Financial Journal, and as a "Super Lawyer" in the 2007, 2008 and 2009 editions of Washington, D.C. Super Lawyers magazine. He served as Senior Vice President and General Counsel of the National Association of Broadcasters.

Mr. Krasnow is co-author of 15 books, including Broadcast Towers: A Step-by-Step Guide to Making Money on Vertical Real Estate, The Politics of Broadcast Regulation, 100 Ways to Cut Legal Fees and Manage Your Lawyer, An Insider's Guide to Radio Station Acquisition Contracts, Radio Deals: A Step by Step Guide, and FCC Lobbying: A Handbook of Insider Tips and Practical Advice, and has written over 280 articles and monographs on communications law and FCC decision making.

Described by Paul Kagan Associates as "one of the broadcast industry's leading dealmakers," Mr. Krasnow has represented sellers and buyers of broadcasting, tower, cable and telecommunications properties in transactions totaling in excess of $21 billion. He is the Founding Director of Broadcast Capital Inc., a minority broadcast investment fund; Director and Vice Chair of the Minority Media and Telecommunications Council; and Washington counsel to the Media Financial Management Association.

Mr. Krasnow was selected by the Office of Communication, United Church of Christ, to receive the Donald H. McGannon Award for his "special contribution in advancing the role of women and people of color in the media." He also received the Distinguished Education Service Award, an honor bestowed for "a significant and lasting contribution to the American system of broadcasting," by the Broadcast Education Association. *COMM/ENT Law Journal*, Hastings College of Law, selected him for the Roscoe Barrow Award for "outstanding achievement in the field of communications." He was inducted into the Minority Media and Telecommunications Council's Hall of Fame for "extraordinary service to the cause of diversity and inclusion in the media and telecommunications industries."

ekrasnow@gsblaw.com TEL (202) 965-7880 x2161

JOHN M. PELKEY - Ever since his teenage years when he would fabricate antennas from broom handles and aluminum wire for operation on the then exotic 144 MHz band, John Pelkey has had a continuing interest in communications matters. After graduating from the Georgetown University School of Foreign Service and the Georgetown University Law Center, where he was Managing Editor of the American Criminal Law Review, John spent two years clerking for the District of Columbia Court of Appeals. Upon conclusion of his clerkship in 1977, he joined the legacy communications law firm of Haley, Bader & Potts, where one of his first assignments was to draft MCI's successful brief to the United States Supreme Court in the Execunet case that opened up the nation's phone system to competition. He successfully argued before the FCC and the federal court the case that led to the issuance of the nation's first cellular authorization awarded through comparative hearing. He was co-counsel in the successful federal court proceeding that struck down the Fairness Doctrine.

During his nearly 30 years of practice before the FCC, John Pelkey has represented broadcasters in virtually all types of proceedings within the FCC's jurisdiction, including hearings, transactions, rulemakings, and applications. During that time, he has represented sellers or buyers in numerous broadcast transactions involving hundreds of broadcast stations, including sales of individual stations, sales of stations emerging from insolvency, and transactions involving entire station groups with station clusters in multiple markets.

Included among the licensees that he has represented are group owners who, due to the complexity of the licensees' financing arrangements and the need to ensure compliance with the FCC's ownership rules and policies, have required the creation of complex ownership structures involving the establishment of numerous subsidiaries and affiliates. He is proficient at coordinating with lenders and venture capital groups to bring multifaceted transactions to closure.

jpelkey@gsblaw.com TEL (202) 965-7880 x 2 5 2 8

JOHN WELLS KING - John King's experience in the field of broadcasting began on the "live" side of the microphone, as a precinct reporter for NBC News during the 1968 presidential election. Upon his graduation from law school, Mr. King associated with the Washington, D.C. communications law firm of Haley Bader & Potts. The firm affiliated with Garvey Schubert Barer in March 2000.

Mr. King is a past Editor-In-Chief of the *Federal Communications Bar Journal,* and past Co-Editor of the *FCBA News,* the newsletter of the Federal Communications Bar Association. He is a frequent contributor to communications industry trade publications including *The Financial Manager* and *Radio World.* Mr. King is Washington, D.C. counsel to *Radio Ink,* where his articles on FCC-related topics appear regularly. He is an associate member of the Association of Federal Communications Consulting Engineers.

Mr. King is a frequent speaker before such national industry meetings as BCFM and the NAB, as well as state broadcast association meetings. He has participated in the NAB's license renewal "road show" seminars, and was a panelist on BCFM Distance Learning Seminars on FCC EEO regulations and on political broadcasting.

Mr. King counsels clients in traditional broadcast matters, in new technologies, and in related areas such as trademark, copyright, licensing, and associated intellectual property issues. He also concentrates on transactional matters for radio and television stations, cable operators, internet service providers, and related entities.

Mr. King has served as Briefs Judge for the National Telecommunications Moot Court Competition of the Columbus School of Law at the Catholic University of America in Washington, D.C. He holds a Juris Doctor degree, with distinction, from the University of Nebraska. Mr. King is admitted to practice in the District of Columbia, Virginia, and Nebraska, and is a member of the Bar of the Supreme Court of the United States.

An accomplished campanologist, Mr. King is a past President of the North American Guild of Change Ringers, and former Ringing Master of the Washington Ringing Society, which performs on the bells of Washington National Cathedral. He is a member of the Ancient Society of College Youths, the oldest British bell ringing society.

jking@gsblaw.com (202) 965-7880 x 2 5 2 0

LaVergne, TN USA
. 11 January 2010
169670LV00003B/152/P